Armenian Allegations
The Truth Must be Told

An Autobiography
by
Edward Tashji

Published
by
Rose International Publishing House

USA

ISBN: 193057435-5

Printed in the United States of America
1st Printing: July, 2004
2nd Printing: August, 2004
3rd Printing: April, 2005
Rose International Publishing House

"... We aim to bridge the gaps Mankind is wont to create... From Keltia to Anatolia, *Do Not Let the Light Go Out!*"

Dedication

In their lives together as husband and wife, they achieved no wealth, no fame, and no significant effect upon the events of human history at large. Yet, they each possessed a rare quality of human compassion, which this writer in this his first literary effort, proudly proclaims to be his lifelong inspiration in his search for brotherhood among peoples sharing a mutual history and culture. With eternal love and profound respect for my beloved parents, George and Isabel Tashji, the pages herein are dedicated to their sacred memory in gratitude for their gift of love.

Dearest mother and father, in your name I offer the reader a true living story of my lifelong efforts in an area which not one person of my ethnicity has had the courage or the desire to dwell. In your wisdom you have instilled in the hearts of your two sons the philosophy that love must prevail over hatred. For your monumental gift to us to be free of animosity, I pledge to you to continue your mission of cultural harmony, and therefore, I dedicate this work, before the world, to you both in your beloved memory.

Your loving son, Edward

Acknowledgements

In the preparation of this autobiography there was no interview with or material obtained from any historian, government official, or university academician. There are people to whom I remain eternally grateful for their guidance, their moral support, their encouragement, and above all, their love not only for me but for all humanity. As the pages which follow will describe, the significant contributions made by the people below, are presented here with the deep love, profound respect, and undying appreciation:

My beloved late parents, George and Izabel Tashji; my beloved wife of forty-two years, Mary; Mr. Tarik Bulut, the late Dr. Selâhattin Büyükünal, Dr. Oktay Cumhur Akkent, Mr. Ergün Kirlikovali, His Grace Bishop Vsevolod of Scoples, the Primate of the Ukrainian Orthodox Church; the Archbishop, Metropolitan and clergy of the Syrian Orthodox (in Turkish, Sűryani) Church; and Dr. Ata Erim. I pray God bless each of them for their wisdom, compassion and humanity.

As the names listed above, will be included in this book, additional information in this section would be repetitious. However, I must in all good conscience, extend proper recognition to a gentleman who is beyond praise, and certainly beyond my ability to honor him with expressions of respect, love, and profound gratitude. For years, Dr. Ata Erim had urged, pleaded, at times with frustration and a hint of anger in his voice, demanded that this book be written. Without his friendship, his patient guidance, and support, this compilation of historical events and years of experiences, this biography would not have been brought to print.

I remain in your eternal debt, dear friend, my mentor, my beloved brother!

Foreword

The American College dictionary defines the word autobiography as "an account of a person's life written by him/her."

It is obvious that my edition was printed at a time prior to our "political correctness" era, for certainly the definition should also include: "… by *herself.*"

Now we may correctly proceed. Bookshelves are filled with published materials pertaining to every facet of human existence, of civilization, religion, science, nature, history, politics, and as an example of our "advanced" civilization, we may include even books about pornography. Name the subject, to be sure someone somewhere has written a book about it: Historic events, famous people, art, discoveries, inventions, cookbooks, ad infinitum; yes each has been researched and written about by authors worldwide since the inception of the printed word. So does the world need another biography? Probably not, especially since the author in his lifetime has not, and most likely will never be recognized for any appreciable achievement or success. Now that we have concluded with our humility, permit me to describe the sincere feelings of many people who would challenge even the suggestion that this writer has not achieved success and fame during his lifetime. It should be understood that neither has been my objective in my lifelong efforts pertaining to Turkish-Armenian history and relations. As a result we have been manifestly condemned by one community and praised by another.

The first time a suggestion was made to me that I should write a book took place in 1968; the significance of that year will be described in a later chapter. Since then, till the present time many people, even those not personally involved in the subject matter, have repeated to me this idea, not merely to be complimentary, but because they truly believed that there was a need for our story to be told. After a long and deeply personal consideration, agreeing that this biography indeed had to be a story unlike any other, I decided to go ahead. Most assuredly, there would never be a similar true life experience as will be described in these pages.

But written by whom?

Certainly not me! I was born of humble background, suffered poor health during my youth, was shy, lacking the scholarly credentials of even a novice author, and as if these were not challenging enough, I had never considered myself capable of influencing the intellect or the emotions of anyone beyond the age of six. So, no, not me, certainly not to pen an *autobiography.*

"But who knows better the events of your life, than you?" I've been asked, "How can you deny to people of good will, irrespective of their national origin, your efforts on behalf of harmony and brotherhood among peoples?"

Now at the final stage of my life, dispelling earlier negativity, I have begun the humble attempt to describe here the events in the life of this writer. As extremely helpful have been the individuals revealed in my acknowledgments, especially Dr. Ata Erim, I have come to recognize that ours is a living story which conveys a message to all peoples. By any measure, we can not observe our country and nations worldwide, without the realization that Mankind is at the threshold of self-destruction. Hatred, racism, political confrontation, famine, poverty, pollution, crime and immorality. Sounds very depressing, does it not?

This book does not suggest that the solutions for the problems which plague the earth are to be found in these pages. But it does offer the reader a factual account of one average American's lifelong dedication to the reduction, if not the total elimination, of the worst of our world's ills – that being hatred. In fact, as a result of our humble efforts we have proven that indeed goodness and compassion can eliminate hate and vengeance. Success might be achieved with a college degree, it might be baking a cake, and it could conceivably even be transforming hatred into love.

Is this what we have done? As you read these lines, are you asking if this author claims to have uncovered a mysterious formula to an unattainable equation? The answers are debatable, which means some have said that I have *not* succeeded – in fact committed grievous and unforgivable sins against my people. While at the same time and with equal emphasis, others have said quite the contrary, that our tireless efforts and immeasurable successes are worthy of the highest praise, as they serve as an endeavor which should be emulated by all peoples of this faltering earth. The reader of this book will hopefully decide, opting for a condemnation or commendation. For me, unequivocally, I'd hope it would be the latter – but then you expected this sentiment, yes?

The lifelong effort, the fervent wish, coupled with the fusion of emotion, frustration, sadness, and joy, has prompted this continuation of the ancestral brotherhood between the Turkish and the Armenian peoples. Well, that is just fine; but if you are not of either background, why should you be interested enough to read this book?

Firstly, you have paid the price of this book and it would be a waste to discard it while you are reading the Foreword. Secondly, and far more importantly, if you are a loving parent, if you are closely affiliated with any religious or educational institution, if you are concerned about the historical accuracy of a loyal and staunch ally of the United States, and finally if you believe that goodness must prevail over evil, then this is a story worth reading. My main challenge in this work is to maintain the interest of the reader, especially if the reader is outside of the Turkish and Armenian communities. But the offering of this text promises to be factually informative and accurate, while hoping to be philosophically stimulating. Whether I succeed in this endeavor, at this time remains uncertain; however, the accuracy of the following pages and the honesty of my motivation in preparing this autobiography is totally irrefutable. The reader will find no pseudonyms, no mythical places or events, in this work; there will be authentic names, places, dates (where possible) or events, from which has evolved an American "Friend of the Turks."

And now, the controversy, the inexplicable dilemma which this writer has faced most of this life. As the pages herein will reveal, there has been, for well over eighty years, a manifestation of bitter hatred within the Armenian community (outside of the Republic of Turkey), toward the Turkish nation and her people. If the reader has even a minimum knowledge of the history of these peoples, it is a certainty that the Armenian version of the events which had taken place in Ottoman Turkey during the early years of this century, have been read over and over again. In the United States of America and in many other countries, the Armenian perspective of the most tragic period of Turkish-Armenian history has been accepted as *historical fact.* As a result, a relentless and highly financed movement – fully active to this day – remained unchallenged, and numerous non-Armenian authors have written books on the subject of a mythical genocide inflicted upon the

Armenian population of Turkey. During this monumental onslaught upon the history and honor of the Turkish people, what was the response of Turkey and in particular, the Turkish-American community?

Defying all comprehension, there was no response, no effective action to correct the historical fabrications of extremist political groups functioning to this day, in the United States.

Then one day there appeared an individual born of an Armenian mother, who publicly declared his strong opposition to the Armenian position, and there you have my inexplicable dilemma: Do I follow the popular and espoused position of my own people, or do I remain faithful to my own fundamental principles, and attempt to give voice to countless facts which must be considered if there is to be a rational and unbiased review of this most contentious subject? The latter has been my choice!

The writer has referred briefly to his parents and their two sons, of which he is the younger. As this autobiography will describe actual names and events, a more specific identification of my family and that of myself, I believe, would assist the reader in being more aware of the background of one who has become to be known as a "Turk Dostu" in Turkish, or: *Friend of the Turks.*

My mother, whom I have identified as being born of Armenian ancestry, was born in the city of Balikesir (Ottoman) Turkey. My father was the only child of Syrian Orthodox parents born in Urfa (Ottoman era) Turkey, known today as Şanliurfa. This community known as *Sűryaniler* in Turkish, had (and still does), prospered in culture and religion for centuries, as did all the ethnic and religious groups, within the Ottoman Empire. The Ottoman *millet* system was instituted to differentiate the many segments of its population such as: Greek, Arab, Jewish, Kurdish, Armenian, Muslim Turkish, Syrian Orthodox, among others. A land of multiple faiths, languages, and ethnic origins, flourishing in harmony, long before these freedoms came to the *new world.* Because my father was not an ethnic Armenian, the suffix *ian* or *yan,* does not appear at the end of our surname.

My wife's parents were both of Armenian birth, also born in Ottoman Turkey. Her father, who died in Massachusetts, USA, when she was three years of age, had been born in Adiyaman, and her mother had been born in Harput. In her home Armenian and English were spoken, whereas in ours my parents spoke to my bother, Terrence, in Turkish and to me in Armenian. We were raised with the culture, the foods, music, and the history of our parents and people as described by them, totally void of all animosity, for the land, the nation, and the people of The Republic of Turkey. This was their legacy to their sons.

May they rest in peace.

Table of Contents:

Author's Note

There is no conceivable way in which the author can prove the statements, opinions, descriptions of a life in Ottoman Turkey as revealed to me in our home, during the lifetime of my beloved parents. Within the front chapters of this book, where the influences of my parents had manifested itself in our home, are specifically described as I remember them. Their factual experiences are presented here with no exaggerations or personal interpretations on my part. If I were to enter in these pages untruthful statements or experiences of my parents, I might deceive the reader; but one day, maybe very soon, I will have to answer to my God for any deliberate deception. In order to make or prove a point, I have not resorted to fraud of any kind, this I solemnly swear to you, the reader.

In like manner, where the author lacks specific knowledge of names, dates, places, and events, it will be so stated. I am now living the final phase of my life and the purpose for this autobiography is not self aggrandizement or financial gain. This authentic compilation of events and experiences strives to emphasize a philosophy of love and compassion being far more desirable and constructive than hatred and the corruption of young minds. Before my God, this is my legacy, not only to the Turkish and Armenian peoples, but to all Mankind. Accept this therefore as my humble effort to continue the love and the wisdom of my beloved parents to a degree far beyond their expectations, and certainly beyond my scope to fully comprehend my destiny of becoming a most unique *Friend of the Turks*.

Edward Tashji

I. It began in Ottoman Turkey.

This most unique story began in Ottoman Turkey, many years before the birth of the author. How then, it may be asked, could an autobiography begin before the author was born? As the reader will discover, this authentic description of the life of one "average" American, is filled with many inexplicable events which had confounded peoples of different backgrounds, as well as the author himself. It is the events which took place in a country about which most Americans had little knowledge during the Ottoman period, which are most pertinent to this factual story as it brings together a young man and a young woman who had very little in common, but shared the total upheaval and human suffering caused by a World War conflagration which had destroyed their way of life in their homeland. As far as knowledge or recognition is concerned, I feel many of my fellow-Americans would have difficulty in locating a staunch ally of the United States, a nation of almost seventy million people, on the world map.

Mother Izabel Tashji was born as Zabel Tashjian, in Balikesir, Turkey, to Armenian parents in a family of six children. Father George Tashji was born as the only child of Sűryani (Syrian Orthodox) parents, in the town of Urfa, Turkey. His name had been Circi (pronounced Jirgi) Monofar, Tashji, and much of his life in Urfa (today known as Şanliurfa), remains unknown to this writer due to the fact my interest in our family history had not developed during the lifetime of my beloved father. I do know my paternal grandfather had been crippled by severe arthritis, which to a lesser degree has been passed on to me. My paternal grandmother had devoted her life caring for her invalid husband; and each of them had aspired their son would become a doctor. Though his youth was uneventful, my father became educated and had been fluent in Arabic, French, Armenian, Ottoman Turkish, and English. He spoke and wrote these languages, and as fate would have it, his linguistic accomplishments were to be most beneficial to him toward the conclusion of the First World War.

During my formative years listening to the stories of my beloved parents, I do not recall a single comment from my father pertaining to any social or political conflicts among the numerous ethnic and religious entities living in harmony in his town and the neighboring cities of Southeastern Turkey, near the Syrian border. But in the case of my mother, where her birth place, Balikesir, was on the western region of the country, near the Aegean coast, conditions were drastically different and eventually most volatile. As it had been in Urfa, and in other regions of the empire, Balikesir had numerous ethnic districts where Greek, Armenian, Turkish and other communities would reside in mutual harmony and peace. In all districts each community enjoyed property ownership, many with farmlands, trade and business ventures, their respective press (limited to the development of that time), their schools, churches, and civil matters, were all conducted in freedom without interference from the central Ottoman government. The central commercial area of Balikesir would bring all ethnic groups together, where trade would take place, the baths would be visited and coffee houses would be filled with the aroma of Turkish coffee and delicious food and pastries.

By the standards of our communities in the modern age, we would find life in Balikesir mundane and void of pleasures. Travel to regions near and far was common and available to anyone who desired to visit other cities. My mother would mention towns (then) which are cities now, such as: Manisa, Tekirdagh, Yalova, and the major cities of Izmir, Bursa, and Istanbul, as destinations where family members used to visit.

The centuries of mutual harmony among the indigenous peoples, including the Christian and Muslim communities, entered an ominous period toward the late 1800s. Political strife and communal suspicions began to destroy a historical and cultural brotherhood. Who did what against whom, and when, depends on who describes the ruination of the essential character of the coexistence of many segments of Ottoman society. The dark clouds of hatred and revolution preceded the convulsion of a nation, and the reverberations of a World War created a human calamity of immeasurable proportions. Historians to this day differ on their interpretation of events which took place in Ottoman Turkey before and during the period of the First World War.

The position of the author pertaining to the conflict between the Turkish and Armenian peoples of Ottoman Turkey has been described to the extent that I remain emphatically opposed to the Armenian allegation that the Ottoman leaders had carried out an organized *genocide* upon the Armenians of Turkey, starting in 1915. With that said, what remains to be added? A great deal I dare say. Rather than enter here the Turkish perspectives, let us review Armenian sources: Certainly my brethren would not fault me for such a fair gesture. By their (Armenian) own published statements, we learn that in 1885 the Armenakan Political Party was established in Ottoman Turkey with the intent of causing civil unrest and revolution against the Ottoman authority and the country where for six centuries Turks, Armenians, and other minorities had lived in total harmony.

If the avowed position of the author is pro-Turkish – as it certainly is – why then not present in this work, the position of the Turkish Government and its historians based upon its own research of its own resources?

To do so would surely invite the wrath of the anti-Turkish elements by denouncing my offerings as merely pro-Turkish propaganda. But what would they say to my presenting here the irrefutable comments of *Armenian* sources?

In the ongoing debate, at this writing spanning more than eighty five years, an impartial reader need not examine Turkish sources in search of historical accuracy. Study, if you will, the Armenian perspective and there you will discover the truth.

If the American media and most of its political leaders accept the Armenian version of its history in Ottoman Turkey, then rather than chastise this writer, he should be applauded for revealing here what is presented *by* Armenian writers themselves. Does not this posture on my part, *display my total lack of bias in either direction?*

Let us observe, briefly, the Armenakan Party strictly from an *Armenian* writer's viewpoint. In 1963, a book was published, *titled: The Armenian Revolutionary Movement,* authored by Ms. Louise Nalbandian. In her 220-page book, on page 90, we find the following introduction: "The Armenakan Party was the first Armenian political party in the 19th Century to engage in revolutionary activities. It was organized at Van (an Ottoman-Turkish city), in 1885 by the students of one of Armenia's foremost educators, Mekertitch Portugalian."

This mentor, this creator of disaster, was born in Istanbul (Constantinople then), in 1848, his father a wealthy banker. Interesting, to say the least, to this day the Armenian scenario refers to the persecution and subjugation of the Armenians by Turks. So, here we have *the son of a wealthy Armenian banker* in the (then) capital of Ottoman Turkey. This contradiction, this Armenian fraud will be described by further examples in a later chapter.

In Nalbandian's book, on page 97, she presents: *The Program of the Armenakan Party,* and within its seven sections, part II, describes its *Methods,* in part, as follows: "... by inculcating in the people the spirit of self-defense, training them in the use of arms and military discipline, supplying them with arms and money, and organizing guerilla forces...".

This example of Armenian loyalty is exemplified by yet another entity known as the Hunchakian Revolutionary Party.

The Hunchakian Revolutionary Party was formed by seven Russian-Armenians and it was the first Socialist party in the homeland. These young Marxists were from wealthy bourgeois families in Russia who had financially supported their "creative" sons in establishing in 1887, in Geneva, Switzerland, this other example of Armenian treason for the purpose of furthering revolutionary activity in Ottoman Turkey. Nalbandian on page 110 offers the reader, in part, the following: "... The Hunchaks said that the existing social organization in Turkish Armenia (?), could be changed by violence against the Turkish Government, and described the following methods: Propaganda, Agitation, Terror, Organization, and Peasant and Worker Activities." Under the heading Terror, we find this interesting entry: "...Terror was to be used as a method of protecting the people and winning their confidence in the Hunchak program. The party aimed at terrorizing the Ottoman Government, thus contributing toward lowering the prestige of that regime and working toward its complete disintegration. The government itself was not to be the only focus of terrorist tactics. The Hunchaks wanted to annihilate the most dangerous of the Armenians and Turkish individuals who were then working for the government, as well as to destroy all spies and informers. To assist them in carrying out all of these terrorist acts, the party was to organize an exclusive branch, specifically devoted to performing acts of terrorism…."

My autobiography has not been distracted, I just felt it would be useful to describe briefly, here at the beginning of my book, the events taking place in Ottoman Turkey PRIOR to the tragic events of the First World War.

Before we return to Balikesir, let me introduce the most infamous of the Armenian revolutionary organizations: in Armenian this maniacal band of miscreants is called: *Dashnaktsuthiun;* in Turkish: *Dashnaksagan;* and better known in English: The Armenian Revolutionary Federation. It seems the words 'Armenian' and 'Revolutionary' are inseparable.

I have mentioned three, but there is a fourth group in this family of revolutionaries, and they are called *Ramgavar.* The latter group is the shadow of the other Armenian "hate merchants," whose philosophy of hate continues to this day.

A brief introduction of the Dashnak (another spelling) group would also be useful to the reader, if it is to understand the Armenian obsession with hatred.

The Dashnak party came into existence in Russia, in the year 1890, intended to be a merger of various Armenian political groups, and the following is taken from their printed pamphlet: "…the Armenian Revolutionary Federation (ARF), known as Dashnaksoutioun (yes, another spelling), carried on this struggle with all available means: Political action, propaganda, and, at times, armed struggle…"

The extent of their fanaticism in Ottoman-Turkey was translated here in the United States, as described by the following two examples of terrorism: in 1933 during Christmas Mass in an Armenian Church in New York City, the Armenian Bishop Tourian was knifed to death by Dashnak members because of some internal problem. During the 1970s and the 1980s, their A.S.A.L.A group murdered of nearly sixty Turkish diplomats and innocent American civilians in their campaign of terror against Turkish officials and Turkish social and business centers.

Armenian terrorism in the United States raised its ugly head for the first time in the city of Santa Barbara, California, in 1973, when a 73-year-old man, named Yanikyan, murdered the Turkish Consul General and his Vice Consul.

For two decades the world became aware of what the Turks had known for ninety years, namely that acts of Armenian terror against Turks would continue, and not only during the Ottoman period, but throughout the world, even almost *sixty years* after the end of the First World War. American and European media for the first time were filled with "Armenian Terrorism," the term used by the headlines for the barbarous attacks. Never before had the editorials portrayed an anti-Armenian position, and as it had happened in Ottoman Turkey, Armenian fanaticism eventually destroyed itself. In the end, almost all of those innocent Turkish and non-Turkish citizens who were murdered in numerous countries, by maniacal Armenian extremists, *were not even born during the conflict in Ottoman Turkey.*

Eventually the Armenian hate merchants put aside their bombs and automatic weapons and commenced a new attack against the Turkish people in a different arena – the school classroom. This endeavor which continues to this day will be discussed later in this book; however let us now return to Balikesir and the events around the 1915 period, the year Armenians claim as the beginning of the "genocide."

During her youth, my mother Izabel would on many occasions describe to me her memories of the political organizations which I have briefly introduced above. "In their meetings there would always be physical confrontations and much spilling of blood in our town of Balikesir," would be one of her statements.

I would ask: "Were the fights between the Armenians and the Turks?"

Her response would be an emphatic: "No!"

When I would enquire, "Then between *whom* did the confrontations take place?"

She'd respond, "It was always among one Armenian political group against another group." Then she'd continue, "I remember conversations in our home; the Dashnak would attack the Hunchaks, the Hunchaks would beat up the Ramgavar, the mutual hate and fighting would never stop!"

Yes indeed, these had been the statements of my mother, and there was more, much more: "This continual and violent unrest became known to the authorities, and our (Armenian) church leaders were warned many times to terminate this destructive behavior, as it would result in harmful reaction toward the entire Armenian community."

The warnings of the Ottoman authority remained unheeded, and with the result that Armenian political groups had for *25 years* engaged in revolutionary activities against the Ottoman state, the plight of all Armenians throughout the country was brought to the threshold of catastrophic events.

To compound the calamity of the disintegration of the Ottoman Empire, she entered the First World War within a global conflict. The Russians, the British, and the French were more than eager to secure Armenian military support in their war against Ottoman Turkey, and they aided the Armenians in their rebellion against the land which had preserved their Armenian culture, religion, and language for over *six centuries.*

The Ottoman era was slowly and painfully coming to a close and in sheer desperation, the government chose to relocate the Armenian population to the Eastern regions of its empire in a final attempt to maintain its control and sovereignty of its homeland. All Armenians were forced to leave Balikesir and other areas, as harmony and brotherhood were replaced by hatred and intolerable human suffering.

In the countless number of books written by historians, politicians, reporters, and writers, irrespective of their position concerned with the peoples and the period to which this book refers, the graphic descriptions of human suffering, deprivation and massacres, have been excessively exhibited with heart-wrenching detail.

Such a narrative will not be found in these pages even though my mother's stories did indeed include the suffering she endured as a girl of about seventeen years of age. I will however, relate one of her terrible moments, after the following observation: During the period of enmity and warfare between Armenians and Turks which no one will disagree happened, brutal killings took place, perpetrated by each side against each other.

Innocents on both sides perished by the thousands.

My mother was the sole survivor of a family of ten, she had no logical reason to reveal to me what she remembered, what she had seen. The intent of this book is not to describe the extent of the suffering of my people – for that you must look elsewhere. It was a war, what else needs to be said? Everyone endured that horrible period in history. In spite of the suffering of the Armenian people, I am convinced IT WAS NOT as the result of an organized 'genocide.' Look at the map of Turkey, then and today, my mother's nightmarish journey began in her town of Balikesir and ended in the town known as Kilis, in Southeastern Turkey; part of which was made on foot.

The next chapter will present a totally unexpected development. But first, the following will describe one of her painful memories.

During many long conversations with my beloved mother about her experiences, I had often asked, "Mom, you lost your entire family, please think carefully, do you remember ever seeing a family member, or even a stranger, killed by a Turkish person?"

Her response to me was just as I am recording it here: "I don't remember the location or the date, but one day I witnessed a man on horse, attack a defenseless man on the ground."

"Mom," I pressed on, "please *think* carefully about the person on the horse: Was he a soldier, did he wear a uniform?"

"No, it was not a soldier."

"Do you remember words spoken in Turkish or Arabic?"

"No, I remember it was neither of these languages, nor was it either Greek or Armenian; but it was a language that I could not recognize."

"Could it have been Kurdish?"

After a long pause, my mother replied, "It could have been." Then, as tears slowly filled her eyes, "I wish we had never seen those days."

By this exchange the horrendous effects of war upon all the ethnic peoples, certainly was not decreased, but it does reveal that many Armenians and Turks lost their lives to the Kurdish brigands, who had been without allegiance to *any government.* As a homeless young refugee, my mother's destiny brought to her circumstances which she could not have foreseen or dreamed of.

II. In the midst of War and Anguish, a Love Story, ca. 1916.

It had taken six agonizing months for my mother to arrive in the town of Kilis, and though much of the events in Kilis, are unknown to the author, what is known is that my mother, as a refugee and with no family, had become acquainted with an Armenian family who had invited her to stay at their home.

This totally unexpected development occurred a few days after her arrival in Kilis. The Armenian Church assisted the relocated Armenians in obtaining shelter, resettlement, and work. It appears to me that Zabel's odyssey had been predetermined by God, because the first of many coincidences took place while she was being taken to the Armenian Church by a stranger in horse-drawn carriage. It was there that an Armenian family aware of my mother's plight, offered her assistance. Being homeless, young, with no family, and certainly in desperate need of nourishment, the only decision she could make became quite obvious. My mother accepted this magnificent gesture by people of her own ethnic and religious background, and the family's son and daughter being of the same age as my mother, enabled the family to accept her as one of their own. Two items of major significance are included in the chance meeting between an Armenian family and my mother:

The humanitarian gesture of this family had an ulterior motive which became evident a few months after Mother joined her new 'family.' The family's son was of marrying age, and my mother's warm personality and beauty, appealed to the entire family, hence their hope that my mother, Zabel, would marry their son. The second, and far more historically significant aspect, is the fact that to this day, the Armenians continue to accuse the Turks of committing the heinous crime of 'genocide,' *during* the hostilities around the year of 1915, in the town of Kilis, an Armenian family was *living in their own home!*

Therefore can we not assume there were other Armenian and Sűryani families also residing in Kilis? As my mother had lived there for about three years, the 'genocide' is proven groundless!

One warm and sunny afternoon, my mother was seated next to the family's daughter (I have no names and none will be invented), on a bench in their family's garden, adjacent to a walkway. Zabel had been very distressed because she had received a letter from her brother Minas, sent to her from Balikesir. The following will explain how Minas knew where to locate my mother: The Armenian churches had kept records of its members, and their location and status would be made known to the churches in the towns from which they had been separated. My uncle, learning of my mother's location, had written to her, and her distress was due to the fact that she could not read Armenian in which the letter had been written.

The family was conversant in Turkish only, and therefore she could not read this very important letter. (The subject of the language will be discussed in a later chapter.)

As the two young girls were engrossed with my mother's upsetting dilemma, from the nearby walkway, there appeared two young Ottoman officers walking briskly, but then slower as they approached the young ladies. Smiles were exchanged but no words were spoken as it would not have been appropriate.

My mother's description of one of the officers remains vivid in my mind:

The officer she described was to become my father.

I could not hope to fully describe her impressions of her first sight of my father, but I hope the following will be adequate:

The 'Chosen One,' was taller than his fellow officer, and on the head of his youthful, handsome face, he wore a most striking *kalpak* (the headgear worn by Ottoman officers). It was in the shape of a *fez* but made from lamb's fur, with lustrous closely curled wool. His gray uniform had a high collar, buttoned close to his neck, with a gold-colored tassel resting on each shoulder. A gold sash was neatly wrapped around his slim waist, to which a metal brace was attached, and held a long encased sword, carried on his left side. His knickers-shaped trousers were fitted into long, shiny boots. As my mother would describe him to me, her eyes would glisten with the memories of her first sight of this princely young man. The girls giggled at each other, and whispered the comments which only young girls can make. Ah, who were they? Could the girls hope to make the acquaintance of these two dashing officers?

We know of the results but how it came about, are unknown. One of the two officers was Butrus Nakas (Nakkash), and the other, as mentioned, was my father; and each of them was a Christian Süryani! It would appear that only Hollywood could create such a script, but this narrative is not the creation of a scriptwriter, yet it occurred just as you are reading it.

The exact circumstances remain unknown, but that glorious day did arrive when the beautiful refugee girl and the Ottoman officer were introduced through family and friends, and one day, in the same garden, on a sunny afternoon and on the same bench, this beautiful story began.

The demure young girl was seated next to this handsome officer, close, but not too close, and she slowly removed the letter from its wrinkled envelope as her hands trembled in anticipation of what her brother had written to her. The officer read the Armenian correspondence aloud, and translated each sentence into (Ottoman) Turkish. Obviously, its content cannot be literally repeated here, my clear memory of my mother's recollection is as follows:

Expressions of love and longing for his sister, Zabel; his wishes for her well-being; his *returning* to their home in Balikesir (the significance of the RETURN TO THEIR HOME will be discussed in a later chapter); his asking my destitute mother for money (!); and then the most disturbing news: He, my uncle Minas, was preparing to travel to the city of Izmir (where the Greeks and Turks were engaged in severe battle), with the intention of joining the *Greek* Army *to fight against the Turks!*

It could be argued that what else could he do, after what the Turks had done? Yes, it is debatable, but should we not consider if not even respect, the thousands of German-Americans and Italian-Americans who wore military uniforms and waged war upon the countries of their ancestral homelands, *in defense* of the United States? My uncle's joining the enemy camp, was reminiscent of the Armenian Revolutionary onslaught upon *their* homeland!

In spite of her hardships, my mother was filled with anger at what she saw as her brother's betrayal, ripped the letter into pieces as though it might erase what she had just heard.

Now, what? No need for a script, for even during a war, the desire for happiness and affection is an inherent quality of human existence; especially so for lonely, young people.

From this point on, much is unknown. But the young couple was attracted to each other, fell in love, and the officer obtained permission from his commanding officer to marry the girl and bring her to his residence. Her 'family,' was devastated; how could she do such a thing?! Dear Reader, before you think gratitude demanded that she marry their son, consider this: During the period in which she had resided in their home, there had been a time when the entire family had been struck by a serious illness (cause unknown), and my mother, to the best of her abilities, had fully devoted herself to take care of them until they were restored to health.

In addition, from the onset of her stay, she had labored as a seamstress and assisted her 'family' financially, within her capacity. Alas, love for the family's son (the kind of love which is needed for a mutually happy marriage) had not been able to blossom in her heart.

Separation occurred and the young couple were married (which clergy, unknown), and began life as husband and wife.

About a year later, the war was coming to a conclusion, but the major cities of Turkey were under foreign military control. The city of Aleppo, which had been under Ottoman administration, became a city where English and French were now spoken along with the indigenous languages of Turkish, Arabic, and Armenian. Political and military conditions in the country required a bevy of interpreters who had command of these languages in translating discourse and documents.

My father was transferred to the major city of Aleppo, and life for the young couple became very comfortable indeed; they found themselves wanting for very little. Nevertheless, the Ottoman Empire faced not only a catastrophic war, but the existence of the Sultanate was threatened twofold: foreign powers as well as an increasing contingent of young Ottoman officers (from which began the Young Turks movement), driven by the inspirational leadership of Mustafa Kemal, who had the vision of establishing a new secular nation. His incomparable accomplishment, in extricating the Turkish homeland from an ancient, indolent, monarchy into a democratic Republic, brought to him the name of Ataturk: Father of the Turks. He is recognized as one of the world's greatest nation builders of the past millennium. Separation of Church (or religion), from State, recognition of women's rights, changing the Arabic script into the Latin alphabet, initiating the Western style of dress, education for everyone, Western classical arts, democratic elections, a free market system, and so much more, brought the Republic of Turkey into existence, and he as the architect of the new, dynamic nation, became its first elected President.

Let us now briefly return to Aleppo.

The winds of uncertainty blew throughout the land. As countless people of many cultures and languages had done before, the peoples of the dying empire began to seek a fresh start in that *new world* known as America.

Father's command of several languages allowed my parents' access to valuable information about wide-spread immigration to the United States of America, and they, too, yearned for a life of peace and opportunity. But insufficient funds seemed to make their dream unattainable. Once again, as if by Divine Will, destiny brought a totally unexpected turn of events which made each of them supremely happy, while at the same time crushed with sorrow (some names and specific details are unknown), but the opportunity was as follows: My father, because of his important work, befriended an Armenian gentleman named Nardikian, with a brother who had immigrated to the United States before the war had begun. The brother in the United States was eager to find a young lady (Armenian) from Turkey, with the intention of marrying her (it was common practice then); the brother in Turkey did indeed meet a young Armenian woman who agreed to the proposal, and the brother offered to pay my father's passage (by ship) to the United States if he would accompany the young lady to America to meet her husband-to-be.

The bride's expenses were paid by the brothers. My father's passage to the United States was now assured, but *how* would he leave his wife of one year, alone?

The chronology is unknown; however, despite the pain such separation was sure to cause, my mother urged my father to accept this rare opportunity with the hope that in the near future she would join her husband in the New World.

To expedite their departures, my father, now that his military service had ended, obtained his passport under the name of Nardikian, as the third 'brother" and the escort of the lady only known as Feride (her first name).

The trail of events I've narrated until now is only one of the millions of those whose lives were torn apart by a world-war. Here was a young, educated man who had to leave his wife and escort a lady to America in order for her to marry a man whom she had not met in person. Joy, sorrow, anticipation, uncertainty, hope, and all the human emotions rampaged in the minds and hearts of my future parents. Separation was most painful, and their tearful embraces reminded them once again of the horrific after-effects of war.

Because of the foreign presence in the land, French passports were obtained in the city of Beirut (capital of present-day Lebanon), and my father's passport, written mostly in French, shows: Name: Georges Nordigian; Departure date: September 13th, 1920; Purpose of Trip: To join his brother in Troy, New York. Additional identity information is also shown.

It was in the town of Troy, New York, where my father and the bride-to-be, Feride, met for the first time her future husband. Though much is unknown, what we do know is that the couple indeed married in an Armenian Church in Troy, where there had been a sizeable Armenian community, and afterwards lived happily ever after. (Surely, that is the best conclusion for that story, isn't it?)

My mother, upon my father's journey to America to escort the would-be bride, had become alone once again. She secured residence in an orphanage school for young Armenian women, and during her stay learned to speak the Armenian language, which was to become a magnificent surprise for my father when they were reunited one year later. (Why she could not speak Armenian and spoke only Turkish, will be discussed in a later chapter.)

If there had been numerous correspondences between my parents is not known, but as it will be described in the next chapter, my father did, during the year of separation, communicate to his bride his difficult life in the new world, and that he was determined to raise the money which would pay for my mother's passage to the United States of America.

Their dream was eventually fulfilled. One year later, my mother, named Izabel Nordikian on her French passport, shows departure: June 4th, 1921; Purpose of her trip: To rejoin her husband in New York, U.S.A.

Their original passports are still in existence, and at this time, these documents are included in my unique exhibition, which in 1998 was *given* to the National Library in Ankara, Turkey (this will be described in a later chapter).

III. Establishing a new life in the New World, ca. 1920.

My father, as a young emigrant in a different county, with customs unfamiliar to him, faced a traumatic life, far beyond what he could have anticipated. His command of English presented him with a major advantage, nevertheless the proverbial *streets of gold* were nowhere to be found. His medical education would not be an asset to him, as contacts and further professional training were not available to my father. But he did befriend numerous Armenians residing in town (Troy, New York).

Among his first needs were a job, a place to live, and a haircut. At this point the haircut is of major significance, for it paved the way for yet another unexpected opportunity. There had been two Armenian barbers in Troy, who had been bitter enemies, their enmity exasperated by the fact that their shops faced each other on opposite sides of the same street. (Again, names and specifics are unknown.) One of the barbers was disliked by the small but closely linked Armenian community, to the extent that my father had been advised not to frequent his shop because he was unfriendly and obnoxious to boot. But my father ignored the apparently good advice, and one day entered the establishment of the "nasty," barber for a haircut. Because of this "momentous" decision, a mutual friendship developed and the barber procured a room for rent and a job for the young emigrant!

The once-upon-a-time dashing, educated, Ottoman military officer found himself working as a dishwasher in a restaurant, in America. There was always a need for dishwashers. Demeaning? No, not at all, consider this: for six days a week he was assured of a hot meal, and he was paid a salary in 'American money!' On his day off, for ten cents he would go to a movie with a loaf of bread, and remain in the theater all day.

One day, for whatever reason, his boss declared, "You are fired!"

My father smiled politely.

That evening, however, in his room, he turned the pages of his dictionary and found the definition of the word: Fired.

Seeking no logical connection, the next morning he *returned* to his job!

Father Tashji continued to work hard wherever he could, paid his rent on time, but deprived himself of the many comforts and pleasures of most people. With his savings, one dollar became two, ten became one hundred, and when he learned he could earn extra money, he worked on his day off, as well. Determination and the labor of one year accumulated enough money for his wife's third-class ticket by ship, to join her husband.

In 1921, my mother arrived in the United States, at a time when the emigration quota into the country was about to be filled. Her ship docked in the city of Providence, Rhode Island, where, for the slightest reason, emigrants could be denied entry.

Getting time off from his job, my father was reunited with his bride; however, their exuberance was imperiled due to the fact that the new arrival had developed a bad cough!

My father pleaded desperately, "Try not to cough! If the examiner sees you coughing, he will send you back!"

The line became shorter while the pressure and the tension became uncontrollable. Finally, it was her turn; the examiner was a huge, tall and hefty man, and anything but friendly. He growled, "Why the hell is she coughing?!"

My father hurried to reply, "It's because she is excited, sir."

After what appeared to be endless questions, the examiner lifted a large stamp and pressed it on top of the entry application form. My father held his breath as he struggled to read it from the distance: Dear God, what word would appear?

The stamp was removed, and there it was, in large black letters: ADMIT. Father burst into tears and Mother assumed the worst. When she was told the magnificent news, she began to cough again. My father, on the verge of hysteria, grabbed her arm and rushed her away before the examiner took notice. God be praised, fulfillment of their dream was at hand!

In Troy, New York, the joyous young couple viewed their single room as a luxurious mansion, simply because they were once again in each other's arms. At that time in Troy, a large textile company named Kaloote & Peabody, manufactured the famous Arrow shirts, collars, and neck ties. It was perfect for Izabel, since she could create magic with a needle and thread. Their joy was supreme. In addition, she surprised my father with that she had managed to learn Armenian, in Turkey, during their year of separation.

But their happiness was to endure many challenges. Izabel could not speak English, and had difficulty at work, more so when trying to communicate with strangers. However, even in 1921 and for years thereafter, there had been a sizeable Armenian community in Troy. The grocer, the butcher, tailor, even the mailman, the doctor, of course the Church, and all of their newly-made friends, were of Armenian background. As a result, for the rest of her life, her English remained poor. There were no Sűryani in Troy; they first settled in Worchester, Mass., then New Jersey.

Work had become my parents' partner and it was not long before Father was removed from the kitchen and brought into the dining room of better hotels, to work as a waiter (owing to his multi-lingual skills and personality). For the young couple this became a major promotion. During a period when work was scarce, my father's earnings were quite substantial.

Father used to tell me that every evening in their room, he would empty his pockets onto a table to show his wife his earnings for the day: five, ten, fifteen, twenty dollars, and more. A larger apartment and a savings account at the bank became the fruits of their labor. Their combined earnings, even at that time, increased their savings dramatically.

It was to take four years of tireless work, when the American Dream became fulfilled: Home Ownership! They purchased a two family house, which stands to this day with the same address: 230, 10th Street. There were neighbors next door, across the street, all over town – the Armenians were everywhere.

In my desire to maintain accuracy, the following are some of the families with whom our parents shared much time and friendship: Papazian, Chakmakian (both of whom were cousins of Mother, in Balikesir), Masrobian, Sarkissian, Tutunjian, Quinones (an Armenian married to a Cuban), Ganimian, and Kachajian among many others.

The latter two families became important during the young adult years of the author, which took place in New York City.

Life for the entire community shared a common scenario: adjusting to a new way of life, work, raising of children, family problems, and the ubiquitous gossip.

Everyone knew just about everything of the lives of their neighbors. During that period, the only other cities that had Armenian communities were the towns near Boston, Mass., and towns in Rhode Island. The enormous movement of Armenians to California and other states occurred many years later. My parents' first home had a tenant, renting a large apartment on the second floor. It was an Armenian who spoke only Turkish (the subject of language is extremely important, but not here, I have not forgotten); daily visits, keeping home, raising children, church picnics and social gatherings, and the resurgence of contentious Armenian political parties (nothing to do with *American* politics), all these were permanent components of Armenian life in Troy, New York.

In 1927, the Tashji family became three in number, as their first son George (Terrence) was born. After a few months, Mother felt the need to return to work; occasionally she would bring her work for the company into our home. When she would go to the factory, she would leave her baby in the care of her tenant. It was during that time Terry (he preferred his chosen name), became exposed to the Turkish language from his caretaker. As a result, my parents began speaking to him in Turkish.

Five years were to pass until their second child was born, and though each had yearned for a baby girl, it was not to be. Their second son was named Edward, and resembled his father just as Terry resembled our mother. With two children, Mother performed her job duties at home. Her sewing talents kept her busy and eventually some of her female friends would be critical of her for 'neglecting' her children. But more complaints were to follow; Father had been very efficient at construction and home repairs, and as a result our home was always in good condition. The stone front entrance to the front door stands to this day. When our parents brought our private telephones, they could not call their friends because none of them had a telephone! They had become the envy of their neighbors. Hence, our parents were always considered as being wealthy, which of course they were not. Hard work produced their first automobile!

* * *

IV. An American Home Filled With the Culture and Languages of Turkey.

Mother and Father Tashji would not allow envious neighbors disrupt their domestic tranquility; they had enough problems trying to make a living while raising their two sons.

Our home had become an extension of their previous life in Ottoman Turkey (other than the added, modern conveniences), pertaining to languages, foods, music, family relationships, and the inherent hospitality shown to constant visitors. Who can really explain it? My parents spoke to Terry in Turkish, to me they spoke in Armenian, and my brother and I spoke to each other in English.

Eventually, as we grew older, everyone understood what was being said, regardless of which language was being spoken. The major differences of the brothers' personalities became very evident during the early years, and as a result it developed into confrontational exchanges. Among the many differences was the attitude of each son toward their parents and their home life. If I seem to suggest here that my older brother was a devil and I was an angel (which definitely is not my intention), then maybe one day Terry in his book might describe me as a 'devil,' and I surely would not want that to happen. Five years of separation in age, can make a significant difference upon young children, especially among boys. Hence, I had always been closer to my parents, and our home life, whereas Terry was more the 'normal and mischievous' young boy, who always kept our lives interesting.

Spending more time in our home presented me with the valuable opportunity of listening to the conversations of my parents between each other and with countless visitors. My father maintained, for many years, a constant correspondence with this 'Urfali' (a native of Urfa, Turkey) Sűryani friends, all of whom had settled in the Boston area. Among these families were: Peter Barsoum (the priest of our first Syrian-Orthodox church in Worcester), Yacoub Tashji (no relation) Ibrahim Kurkgy, Albert Chavoor, Sait Balli, and others whose names I do not remember. Conversations with most of the Armenians would be in Armenian, but with the Sűryanis, was mostly in Turkish.

Even as a child, I had learned from these conversations that there existed a bitter animosity on the part of the Armenians toward the Turkish people. Who could blame them after their suffering in their war-torn homeland? Interestingly, however, this was not the case with the Sűryani families. I DO NOT REMEMBER ANY HOSTILE OR HATEFUL COMMENTS from our Suryani friends, for the Turks. In fact they spoke Turkish freely, and in spite of their suffering in the major war, they always yearned for *"memleketimiz"* (our homeland)!

Why the Süryani did not display toward the Turkish people the same bitter hatred that the Armenians had always (and continue to this day), vehemently expressed, remained inexplicable to me as a child. After all, the Sűryani also suffered the ravages of war; how could two Christian communities be so philosophically different?

But to a young boy, political conflicts, war, ethnic hatreds, and all that "stuff" which grown-ups were always talking about, certainly were not important. Toys, games, the movies ... now these were most worthy of my interest. The only thing I remember as a child was that every Thanksgiving Day we had turkey for dinner, which was all I had known about Turkey. But the "seeds" had been planted while totally unaware of the effects upon me of the many statements by countless people.

In our home our parents spoke to each other in Turkish, the phonograph always played Turkish music, some Arabic, and very few Armenian recordings. When guests would visit and after dinner was finished, the women would remain in the kitchen and the men in the living room would inevitably discuss political issues and the war in Ottoman Turkey. My father was always diplomatic in his opinions when they differed with those of his Armenian guests. Father was always conciliatory, found fault on all sides, and emphasized the need for not being mired in animosity toward their former homeland. Armenian guests could never accept such a "bizarre" outlook, but after having been served such a delicious dinner (mother's Turkish cooking was a work of art), no one would dare engage in a futile debate; after all, Turkish coffee was about to be served, and politics could wait.

Our early home years in Troy, New York, had many similarities to family life in many Armenian and other ethnic homes, raising children, financial difficulties, maintaining cultures, language, and religion had been a major concern of families starting a new life in the United States. The attitude of our parents toward Turkey, and the Turkish people was manifestly contrary to the feelings in other Armenian homes; we have referred to this earlier. But another unique feature existed in our home, and that was the daily usage of three languages; English, Turkish, and Armenian.

With the birth of their first son, Terrence George Tashji, happiness was intermingled with worry, hard-work, and the uncertainty for the future. As the weeks became months, our parents became aware of an inescapable condition which had been transplanted from their former homeland: the bitter hatred by the Armenians toward anything Turkish. But our parents had been, and always remained, void of all animosity and as a result they were unable to 'fit' into the community. With numerous friendly Armenian families, it was only the Mesrobian family with whom they had spoken in Turkish. In addition to this sad condition, the Armenian political parties (which had caused havoc in Ottoman-Turkey), were transplanted in Troy, as well as other cities where the Armenians had settled. Mother and Father Tashji were determined not to infest their son with hatred and the same determination would be extended to their *daughter* whose arrival was still part of the future.

It was mentioned earlier that both of my parents spoke Turkish and Armenian, together with the other languages spoken by my father. Each of them worked very hard to obtain the American dream of home-ownership. In time, the fruits of their labors indeed brought to them their own home in Troy, New York; a two-family house which stands to this day. The apartment on the second floor of the dwelling was rented to a Turkish-speaking Armenian family, and as a result my older brother, Terry, began to learn the Turkish language. The reason being, when our mother went to work (I had not been born yet), she would leave her son with the lady tenant until she returned from her work. This attentive lady communicated with Terry in the Turkish language and as a result, it prompted my parents to do the same.

Five years later, on February 7, 1932, Edward became the fourth Tashji, and his first language (of the three which he eventually spoke), became the ancient Armenian language. Mother had to leave her employment but continued working for the Arrow Shirt company from home. Another five years had passed when for financial reasons Father Tashji began to consider moving the family to the City of New York, the destination of hundreds of thousands of immigrants arriving from all over the world.

While Mother had maintained our home in Troy, working and raising her two sons, Father found work in several exclusive hotels in New York City. Trying to save a portion of his income, he took residence in a furnished apartment. But unexpectedly bad times struck our family and resulted in the selling of the car and a foreclosure on our home. Mother Tashji departed from Troy by selling whatever she could, said her sad farewells to her friends, and with her two sons, moved to New York city to join our father. The exact date is unknown, but I was about six years of age, and Terry eleven.

We settled in our father's rented apartment in a two-family house owned by a Sűryani family, Mr. Kerim Bazaz and his wife Lucy Bazaz , located at 16th Street, in New York City.

The following several years found our parents working hard, my being entered into Saint Francis Xavier Parochial School and Terry into public schools. I continued at my school when the family moved to 15th street in Manhattan, and from there to Bank Street, in lower Manhattan. Our apartments had been furnished by our parents, and a continuous friendship continued with several Armenian families who also lived in the New York area. Father maintained his friendship with his Sűryani friends residing in the Boston area. House guests, dinners, conversations, music played on the phonograph, and years of various health problems on my part, were among the early memories of our lives in New York City. American citizenship now became very important.

In time both our parents became American citizens, for which they were deeply proud. But citizenship came to our mother with difficulty. Lacking the ability to speak English, she was advised to go to night school to learn the language. Again, being surrounded by Armenian friends, who needed to learn English? Mother's working for years in the garment industry had given her rudimentary introduction to the English language. The problem was that the people with whom she "spoke" on a daily basis, could not speak English either; so, Mother

Tashji, on two or three evenings of each week, attended adult-language classes in a nearby public school. I will never forget her notebook and pencils, and her coming home and uttering, "How the hell can I learn to speak this language?!"

Our father had obtained his citizenship earlier, without any difficulty, but this was not the situation for our mother. It was while Terry was in the U.S. Army towards the end of the Second World War, when our parents had gone to the office of Immigration and Naturalization. During that decisive event, one humorous story stands out: My mother had been aware of the word jail, but when the examiner asked her, "Have you ever been in prison?" with emphatic pride she replied, "Yes!"

Noticing the obvious alarm on the face of the examiner, my father came to the rescue by stating she had never been incarcerated. There appeared a hint of a smile on the examiner's face, but mother Tashji made her final appeal: "Me good American – My son in American Army! – Me good American!"

Several weeks later, mother became a proud naturalized citizen of the United States of America.

Our home life in the city was similar to our early childhood in Troy. My being close to my family, kept me at home more than my brother, and as a result of spending time with our frequent visitors, I became more aware of the Armenian animosity toward anything Turkish. There was one exception, and that was the Ganimian family with whom our family had been very friendly in Troy. The parents, Nishan and Nevart, were Turkish-speaking and their two daughters and son, all of whom had been born in Troy, were familiar with Turkish and Armenian. Father Nishan had played a Turkish instrument called the *ut,* an ancient stringed instrument from which evolved the modern guitar. Their son, Charles, began to learn to play the violin, but as he grew he became interested in the *ut,* and with his father's assistance, he would listen to many Turkish recordings. At that period no one could have foreseen that in his adult life, Chick, as he was called, would become the most talented and successful American-born *utist* in the United States. With the close friendship between the two families, Turkish music, foods, and language, became an integral part of our home-life. But any interest in the country or the people of Turkey was not to be found in my consciousness. I had learned of Armenian hatred for all things

Turkish <u>outside</u> our home, and yet much of Turkish culture was to be found in our home. In fact we had never even met a Turkish person. It was our love for Turkish music and my friendship with Chick that my interest in <u>all</u> things Turkish evolved.

V. As a teenager, first association with Turks. An Armenian Absurdity.

Our beloved hard working parents achieved their second American Dream: a beautiful one-family English Tudor, in Saint Albans, in the Borough of Queens, New York. This major event in our lives became the unexpected extension of our affection for Turkey and her people. It appeared to me years later, that all of it had been predestined, because had we not moved to Saint Albans, the subsequent events extending through many years would not have occurred, and therefore our truly amazing story could not have been written.

From Troy to New York City, extending to the suburb of Saint Albans, New York, our family-life continued the same scenario; work, children, occasional illnesses, culture, languages, frequent visitors on the week-ends, coupled with the problems which are prevalent in most homes, brought us into adulthood.

My brother Terry, contrary to all predictions, married a lovely girl named, Marie Louis Abdullah, who was born of magnificent Lebanese parents. They remain married to this day, the parents of four beautiful daughters and the grandparents of eight beautiful grandchildren. (As a proud uncle I could not describe them any other way.)

After Terry's marriage, Edward became the next "target" of my parents, whom they wished to see happily married. But as a teenager, marriage was somewhere in the distant future. He was interested in tape recorders, Turkish music, and obtaining a *darbuka,* a Turkish drum played on the lap, struck with hands and fingers. As a child, I remember listening to our Turkish and Arabic recordings and "accompanying" the music as I used the side of our phonograph or table, as my "drum". After much pleading, my parents purchased for me my first (of many) *darbuka,* and I played it almost every day; my parents were indeed very patient. One day, during a visit to the Ganimian home, we learned Chick had become proficient with his *ut* instrument, and revealed to us his desire to form a musical band. I was exuberant in my support and offered myself as the drummer of the band. Soon thereafter we formed the *first* Middle-Eastern Band in New York City. It was called: *Nor*

Ikes, Armenian for sunrise. We formed a five-piece band consisting of Turkish and Western instruments, played by young men born in the United States, and like myself, the children of Armenian families. During that time, the early fifties, an organized and talented group of young musicians, was a rarity, and the *Nor Ikes* became very well known and in great demand. Our repertoire included Turkish, Armenian, Arabic, and some Greek, dances and songs. As it was in my home, the Ganimian family spoke Turkish and as a result they favored Turkish music. This prompted Chick to learn many Turkish vocals, dances, instrumentals, as well as classical Turkish compositions. Our audiences were primarily within the Armenian and the Suryani, (Syrian Orthodox) communities. My joy was supreme! To perform for live audiences that were never under one hundred people, became a major challenge to a young man (the author), whose social interaction had occurred only with house guests. But there he was, playing a music he loved, on a Turkish drum which Americans had never before seen: playing his drum with rhythmic accuracy. None of these amazing young men could read a single note of music, they learned by ear, playing a music dissimilar to American or any Western music. We became professionals! To play the music we enjoyed and get paid for it was more than we could expect. We became members of the American Musicians Union; it was then and continues to be today: Local 802. Our vocabulary included the word *gig,* a term still used today, referring to a musical engagement or performance. My original union card, now fifty years later, can be found within my exhibition now housed in the National Library, in Ankara, capital of Turkey. This will be included in a later chapter.

What follows is an actual incident which I am not able to prove but swear to its veracity. At the age of approximately eighteen, my first exposure to extreme Armenian absurdity took place.

Our group was engaged to play music for a church-sponsored social function at an establishment still to be found in the Bronx section of New York City, called The Audubon Ball Room. For many years it had been a popular place for social activities. With an audience of over two hundred men, women and children, everything had proceeded very well. At one point our leader, Chick, began to play an old favorite Turkish vocal: it was a song which I had known for many years and had sung at home. Without prior rehearsal or permission from Chick, and with my drum under my left arm, I stood up and approached a standing microphone, and at the proper moment, began to sing the song in TURKISH.

Our group was momentarily shocked, and all of a sudden many faces turned to the stage, but it lasted only so briefly. The dancing continued and the favorable reaction of the audience touched our musicians in a most positive way, smiles were everywhere while the people clapped in unison. I had sung three verses and we concluded to a resounding applause, even our temperamental Chick approved, it was a success.

Then it happened – as our group took a break, a gentleman approached me, appeared to be friendly and with a slight smile, speaking in Armenian he said the following: “My son, your song was very well done, everyone enjoyed it. But hereafter when you play Turkish songs, play *the music only,* because you are not permitted to sing the words IN Turkish.”

There is no historian who can refer to the event which I have just revealed, because it happened to *me* and God is my only witness. At about 18 years of age, I had understood what a member of the Church Board of Directors had said to me, but at that time I could not fully grasp the significance of his convoluted statement. To accept, or permit, Turkish music played with Turkish instruments, but to *prohibit* vocals sung IN Turkish was my first experience with the absurdity of and the illogical position of the Armenian community. The absurdities were to continue throughout my adult life. That first event must have left an indelible image in my mind for me to recall it vividly even fifty years later.

During our future musical career we were careful not to “upset” our Armenian audiences. When we performed before Sűryani, Sephardic Jews, or at times, American audiences, we always played *our* music without fear of any negative reaction, in fact our Turkish music was always overwhelmingly *well received*, I am proud to emphasize. One future Sűryani function brought our group and one from their community to perform at the *same* function; it became my “escape.”

With talent, public recognition, and fame, whether it is in Hollywood or *Nor Ikes* band, artists can become obnoxious egotists. So it was with Chick Ganimian, even though his fame became established years after our group was dissolved. He and I had problems unlike the rest of our band, due to the fact I resented his brash treatment of people, which worsened when he drank. My "escape" occurred one day when our Sűryani church in New Jersey held a social function with our group performing at different sessions with another group of three musicians called *The Garabed Boys*.

At the very outset when I heard the music of this group, I remember how immensely pleased I was because they performed in Turkish. The small group was led by John Garabed, who was a master violinist. It would require many pages to describe the unique talent and impeccable personality of my new friend, John Garabed. He studied and performed classical Turkish music to a degree unequaled by any other American-born musician. With his cousin Jack Garabed, who played the *ut* and the *kanun* (an ancient Turkish stringed instrument), and Harry Esehak, who played the *ut* and the *darbuka* (the Turkish drum), this group of three, in talent, character and repertoire, was far superior to the group I belonged. I wanted so much to be associated with the Garabed group, and after extensive negotiations with Chick, he permitted me to perform with both groups on condition that upon conflicting dates I would choose to remain with the *Nor Ikes*.

My supreme joy was short-lived, as the arrangement proved to be a disaster. At a future function when both groups were brought together again, and while on stage, Chick, who reeked of liquor, assaulted John and accused him of "stealing" me. It was a disgraceful incident and my only solution was to side myself with the truly professional musicians and so I remained with the Garabed group for the rest of the concert. Many years of friendship continued in our group of four as we performed for our Sűryani community. John had been an inspiration to me and the memories of my beloved "brothers" will remain in my heart for as long as I live. All three, I am saddened to say, are no longer with us. Two important topics must be included in my reference to the Garabed group, events which have affected me deeply:

1 – During numerous performances of the Garabed group, a fifth musician would join our group: Mr. Tarik Bulut, a Turkish gentleman of extraordinary talent, as a composer, musician of all instruments, and a teacher of Turkish music and history. Tarik was to become the very first Turk with whom I had become very friendly; to this day we refer to each other as *kardeşim,* Turkish word for *my brother*.

There will be need for me to refer to Tarik in the following chapters; therefore briefly I'd like to introduce the person whom I am honored to refer as *kardeşim*: Tarik had come to the United States from Turkey working for the Turkish Information Office in New York City, in the early '50s. He had studied at the prestigious Juilliard School of Music, and devoted his life to music and his Turkish heritage. He married Frances, an Italian-American Roman Catholic beauty. Frances and Tarik had two sons and, eventually, retired to Florida. One of Tarik's countless musical achievements had to be his writing the music for an American orchestra during a historic performance. It was the celebration of the 50th Anniversary of the musical career of one of Turkey's most renowned *kanun* players, Master Ahmet Yatman. Two orchestras, one American one Middle Eastern, performed classical and contemporary Turkish music to an audience of over 500 people. With Tarik's genius, an American orchestra played Turkish selections in accompaniment with a Middle Eastern orchestra. The latter group was comprised of Armenian, Greek, Jewish, Syrian Orthodox, Arabic and Turkish musicians; truly representative of the harmony among ethnic and religious entities in Ottoman Turkey. This harmonious relationship continues to this day in the Republic of Turkey. Photographs of this historic concert are on display in my exhibition in Ankara, Turkey.

2 – John Garabed left a legacy of love and kindness to his family, his Syrian Orthodox Church, and his countless friends. His demise crushed me and I regret that my contacts with his family did not continue, but in 1999 a totally unexpected development took place. John's daughter, Marilyn (now Mrs. Bello), made contact with me by telephone, searching for a final "contact" with her father. John was revered by his entire family and by everyone who knew him. But Marilyn had maintained a keen interest in her father's music and to this day has kept his violin. She was searching for the proverbial "needle in the haystack," that being a recording made by her father many years ago. It was an LP recording called *In an Egyptian Garden*, and after searching at length for a copy of her father's music, she was advised to reach out to me in a final attempt to secure that recording. Being very emotional (no apologies please!), my eyes moistened as I revealed that the record she was seeking was in my possession. It was obvious that she too became emotional as she attempted to express her gratitude for what I had proposed. In less than a week, I had recorded on a cassette tape both

sides of the LP recording. Together with a color photocopy of the jacket, I prepared a list of the selections, as well as a personal letter describing my years of friendship with – and my love for – her father. Need I describe her supreme joy? I am deeply happy and honored to have been able to offer Mrs. Marilyn Garabed Bello, and her family, a treasure of memories of her beloved father, and my beloved *brother*, John Garabed.

My autobiography has referred at length to several people, whom I believe affected my youth and our mutual experiences which years later were to have a significant place in a most unique story.

One final comment must be made about my friend Chick Ganimian, my wife's cousin. Though born in America, Chick became a master of the Turkish *ut.* He incorporated his instrument and music into American jazz, and performed with numerous American orchestras on stage, clubs and recordings. In spite of our personality clashes, I remain proud that I had been a part of his initial music career. He has also passed away, and I miss him deeply – Chick remains in my heart. As in the case of John Garabed, with a few sentences I have paid tribute to two talented musicians who devoted their lives and their artistry to the music of their ancestral homeland, Turkey. There will be other references to the subject of music and related events in later chapters, but now we must return to our home in Saint Albans, Queens, New York where two major events pertinent to this book took place.

The very first Turkish person that visited our home in Saint Albans was a wrestler named Yusuf Şűkrű Gűrbűz. My brother had gone to a wrestling match in which Yusuf (the name we used to call him), was to compete. Being the amiable chap that he was, my brother Terry went to the wrestling arena and at the conclusion of the match, he introduced himself to Yusuf in Turkish and an immediate friendship developed. Since Yusuf had recently arrived in New York, he spoke no English, but Terry had become very helpful to him, especially in translation and driving him to the many places he needed to go. Soon after their meeting, Terry brought his new friend to our home; for Yusuf, it was like entering paradise. First, he was embraced by our mother, who exclaimed: *"Hoş geldin oğlum!"* (Turkish for: Welcome, my son.)

His senses brought to him the magnificent aroma of Turkish cooking, as well as the melodic sounds of Turkish music heard from the stereo. Our first impression of him was his size: when I stood next to him, you could not see me. That night, there were no leftovers for us to enjoy the next day. Our family had become Yusuf's family, and though he remained close to his parents, the subsequent years of friendship eased his longing for his family in Turkey. His wrestling career lasted a short time due to the fact that wrestling, as it is today, was a grotesque farce, and when Yusuf was told that he had to lose when ordered, he knew he had to leave the "sport." He eventually settled in a suburb of Chicago and married a lovely American lady, named Anne. He continued the trade he had learned in Turkey, metal foundry. Our close friendship continued for many years, until they also passed away.

It had been at a social function where Terry had met a Turkish gentleman with whom a friendship of many years was to develop. During the early 1950's, Oğuz Reha Tűrkkan, Ph.D., and his wife, Gűntekin Tűrkkan, became friends of our family and were overjoyed by the affection displayed by our parents. Doctor Tűrkkan had degrees in Law and experimental Psychology, and had taught at Columbia University. Our friendship continued to the present time.

During this period of my youth, my profound and extraordinary interest in anything Turkish had not yet evolved, but in order to reveal the introductory events, we must briefly return to the interrelationship of three families: Ours, the Ganimian, and the Kachajian, families. The many years of friendship had begun in Troy, New York, before I was born. The Ganimians eventually moved to the City of New York, as we had, and the Kachajian family had moved to the Boston area. Mr. George Kachajian was the brother of Mrs. Newart Ganimian, and our contacts with the Kachajians continued only as a result of our close relationship with the Ganimian family. George and Aznif Kachajian had five children, the youngest named Mary, born in Watertown, Massachusetts. When Mary was three years of age, she lost her father, and her saintly mother was left with five children and destitute. Upon his death, mother Aznif pleaded with the local Armenian Church to bury her husband, but the church *refused,* citing lack of funds. Then, however, a local Protestant church performed a humanitarian gesture, and the father was buried with a Christian service, *all* expenses paid. The young mother, who was filled with grief for her family's loss, became extremely angry at her church for demanding money first. As a result, she eventually had all five of her children baptized in the Protestant Church. In spite of the extreme difficulties faced by the family, mother Aznif kept her family together.

Years later, my mother, Mrs. Kachajian, and her sister-in-law Mrs. Newart Ganimian, "conspired" to arrange an introduction of Mary to this writer. One day Mary and her mother had visited Aunt Newart's home in New York, which resulted in a visit to our home in Saint Albans. Unfortunately, the cordial visit did not turn out the way the "conspirators" had hoped.

Again I ask: who can explain it?

This entire scenario was repeated three years later, and this time – BINGO! On May 4th, 1958, Mary and Edward were married in the Syrian Orthodox Church in West New York, New Jersey. When something is predestined, there can be no logical answer to why Mary would agree to live in the same house with her in-laws, far from her family's home. In fact, she became my parents' beloved daughter. Four days after our first wedding anniversary, my wife lost her beloved mother, and six months later, I lost my father – 1959 was a devastating year.

Our lives in our Saint Albans home, continued with mutual love, harmony, and of course from time to time we also had a sprinkling of "My son was not like this before he got married!"

Naturally there had not been any reason to doubt the love of my mother and my wife, but though the early years could not reveal the extreme hardships which my wife and I had to endure, I can state at this time that my wife Mary took care of my aging mother – her mother-in-law – in a manner which most women would not care for a declining parent. Because of Mary's patient efforts, I was able to fulfill my obligations of a loving son to my beloved mother. But all in all, our home was a happy place where my mother lived comfortably and Mary and I continued working, tending to our home and frequent guests.

One evening, when Mary returned from work (she was the assistant manager of a supermarket), she was noticeably excited when she announced: "Mom, I found a Turkish family here in Saint Albans!"

A Turkish Naval Officer, Dr. Sedat Derinsu and his wife Meliha, had rented an apartment near the Saint Albans Naval Hospital. He had worked there for one year after which he had to return to his

Naval post in Turkey. After a brief conversation – even then Mary could communicate in Turkish – by telephone, we invited them to our home. A few days later the young Turkish couple visited us and we became mother, sister, and brother, to complete strangers; all we knew about them was that they were *Turkish.* From my mother's exquisite Turkish cooking, to our speaking in Turkish, to our playing Turkish music, caused our guests to feel as though they were with their families in Istanbul. But their stay in the United States was coming to an end and their departure was truly sad for all of us.

One year was to pass by when Mary, while at work, noticed with delight two Naval officers sporting the Turkish star and crescent emblem on their caps. As it had been with the Derinsu couple, we now had two more Turkish Naval doctors with their families, here, for one year's work at the Naval Hospital. Doctor Osman Köksal, his pregnant wife Şadan, together with their five-year-old daughter, Bahar, rented a comfortable apartment near the Naval Hospital. Renting a second apartment in the same building were Dr. Naci Barut, his wife Gűl, and their four-year-old daughter Pınar. 1959 had crushed our hearts with the loss of two family members, but the arrival of two Turkish families brought to us the strength and the comfort which we dearly sought.

The countless magnificent memories going back in time to forty-one years can not be described here; suffice it to say we met as strangers but our three families merged into one. Again we became mother, sister, and brother, to these families who yearned for the love of their respective families in Turkey. So close was our relationship, that the Köksal family asked "Mom," as they called my mother, to choose a name for their newly-born daughter. "Mom" told them that in Balikesir, her birthplace (in Ottoman Turkey), the name Ceylân (pronounced Jeylan in Turkish, meaning: gazelle), had been a favored name.

To this day Ceylân lives in Istanbul with her family, and she is as beautiful as her name. Our humble home served as a temple to humanity, where love in its quintessential form had manifested: My beloved mother had lost her entire family during the catastrophic upheaval within Ottoman Turkey, and yet a day came when with open arms and motherly kisses, she welcomed the children of the former "enemy"!

Our Turkish *relatives* had now increased to three families. Just as it had been in Ottoman Turkey, as it continues to this day in the Republic of Turkey, so it was in our home in Saint Albans, New York: We celebrated our mutual religious holidays together, as well as our national holidays and birthdays. As family stories were exchanged, the joys and sorrows of our parents' experiences in Ottoman Turkey, together with our mutual love, our families served as living proof of the harmonious relationship among our peoples: Turkish, Armenian, and Sűryani (Syrian Orthodox).

I am compelled to repeat here that the pages up to this point have revealed events which spiraled the author from the inception of his interest in the culture and history of the Turkish people and its homeland, to the subsequent years of work on behalf of the nation whom my Armenian co-religionists despise beyond all comprehension: One phase of this spiral has led to another, culminating with *forty years* of effort in the defense of the Turkish people.

VI. Five Naval doctors and their families become our relatives.

This factual autobiography hopes to preserve the unique philosophy of (as well as some of the efforts) of the author with the firm affirmation that hate causes additional hatred, which is contrary to the teachings of the God of *all* Mankind. How the Armenian community in the United States can profess to be faithful Christians, while at the same time they are consumed with hate as they convey their hatred to each succeeding generation of innocent minds, is beyond the comprehension of logical thought.

The spiral continues: Our three Turkish families became five when at the end of their one-year stay in our country, the time approached when the initial two families had to return to their homeland. The two Naval doctors were to be replaced by other Turkish Naval doctors and their families, and had arranged to occupy the vacated apartments. Dr. Oktay Cumhur Akkent and his wife, Ayla, took the former residence of Dr. Köksal, whose wife had given birth to a beautiful baby girl. A major problem developed when the second family could not occupy the Baruts' apartment because of a delay in receiving orders from superior officers in Turkey. Dr. Selâhattin Büyükünal, his wife Ayhan, and their nine-year-old son, Cenk, upon arrival in Saint Albans, found themselves without a residence. The Akkent apartment had no space for three other people and the hospital had no immediate facility for the family who had no one here, in the United States. But there was indeed "a mother, sister, and brother," filled with supreme joy of welcoming the young family to stay at our home until their apartment became available. No one knew each other, other than how we were described by the Akkent couple. It was a cold and wintry day when our three guests came to our home for the first time. Their child appeared nervous; the parents seemed anxious and felt they were disrupting our comfort. Our home was a one-family brick, English Tudor structure with spacious rooms and sleeping rooms for their use. The three of them were noticeably exhausted after a long flight from Turkey. During our initial greetings, I could not have imagined the brotherly love that was to evolve between our families. In every respect, we became indeed *one* family: a mother, sisters, brothers, and a grandson.

At the very outset our guests heard the following words spoken by my mother in Turkish: "Welcome, my children, this is your home."

As she embraced each of them, Mary and I awaited our turn to welcome them to their new home. Our home was warm, the aroma of Turkish cooking, the sound of classical Turkish music, and the comforting sound of each word we spoke, brought to them an immediate relief of their worry. Before we took them upstairs to their bedrooms, we showed them the kitchen, and I declared in my somewhat faltering Turkish, "This is the refrigerator, whenever you feel hungry, you will open this door and help yourselves to whatever you desire."

Their stay in our home lasted one month before their apartment became available. *Our mutual love has become irreversible.*

During early 1960, we had arranged a magnificent gathering in our home, during which we would say goodbye to the Köksal and Barut families, while we welcomed the Akkent and the Büyükünal families. The event was filled with deep emotion, tears, and recorded statements on my tape recorder. As an unusual surprise, we had invited Mr. Harry Esehak and his wife, May; Harry played the *ut,* a stringed ancient Turkish instrument, for the pleasure of the four families. The buffet was filled with Turkish foods, pastries, a floral centerpiece, with an American and Turkish flag in place, and with red and white tapers, completing a magnificent presentation. The evening of joy and sorrow finally came to an end with dry eyes nowhere to be seen. The Turkish "navy" departed, while a new contingent of the Turkish "navy" returned to share our lives for another year. It was a matter of similar personalities between Dr. Selâhattin and me which brought us together emotionally. Both of us very close to our families, we were excitable, punctual, polite, soft spoken, extremely hospitable and very useful in the kitchen. Paradoxically our differences caused no adverse effect upon our "kardeşlik," Turkish word for brotherhood: we were born and raised on opposite ends of the world, our national, religious, and ethnic backgrounds were different. He was a Naval officer, I served nowhere because of poor health; he had been a doctor, I had studied hotel management; he attained the rank of Captain, I became a restaurant manager in several exclusive New York hotels. Nonetheless, we were true brothers.

Another major difference between us was, Selâhattin had been a heavy smoker, and I, during those years, and up to the present time of forty years later, find smoking repulsive and self-destructive. But it could not lessen my love and high esteem for *kardeşim* Dr. Selâhattin Büyükünal. His wife, our *sister* Ayhan, became interested in the life of my mother and her war-time experiences, to the extent that many nights when everyone had gone to sleep, "Mom" and Ayhan would sit near each other and Ayhan would bring to paper my mother's memories. Her notes became a book published in Turkey, for which she won an award by the Turkish Ministry of Culture.

The Barut apartment became vacated and our beloved guests moved in. Each day as I would bring Mary home from work (in those years we had no car, besides, neither of us could drive), I without fail would first stop at my *brother's* home and have Turkish coffee with Selâhattin and Ayhan, exchanging our daily events. This continued with weekend visits that would include the Akkents. The months passed by so rapidly that we could not believe our separation was drawing near. With one month remaining before their return to Turkey, someone suggested we spend our "final" months together – and we did.

One evening, as I was alone, I prepared an ad-lib statement on tape, expressing our eternal love and our deep sorrow for their departure. For added effect (there just had to be one!), at the beginning and end of the recording, I recorded the sound of a ticking clock. I had given a copy of my emotional farewell to our departing family. Selâhattin had reciprocated with his own very emotional comments recorded in private.

The days passed quickly as the sadness in our home became increasingly noticeable. A final dinner with our three families, gifts sent to relatives in Turkey, packing, tearful embraces, and then the unavoidable separation. One final gesture of love had to be expressed, something which caused total surprise and a bevy of emotional responses: As their vehicles were about to move, we emptied two saucepans of water onto the street, as a symbolic wish for a safe journey.

So was the custom of Ottoman Turkey, so it is continued in Turkey today, and so it did in Saint Albans, Queens, New York….

Toward the end of 1961 our close relationships with five Turkish Naval Medical Officers and their families came to an end, as each of the families had returned to Turkey. Nevertheless, our contacts with each family continue to this day by mail, as each letter would serve to remember the many memories cherished by each of our families. Most of the correspondence has been between *kardeşim* Selâhattin and me, which surprised no one because of the similarity of our character, I believe. Each of our brothers would write to us in Turkish and I would respond with "Sevgili Kardeşim," (my beloved brother) followed by a first name. But the remainder of my correspondence was always written in English. When it had begun, I can not say, but a day came when following the salutation I would write a few words, then a few sentences, and eventually, *the entire letter in Turkish.* Selâhattin had left me a Turkish dictionary which had assisted me in my Turkish composition. But there is a major difference between writing to my "brother" about family matters, and the expression of serious opinions to high ranking officials and the Turkish media on issues of historical significance. As I have earlier referred to the predestined events of my life, my dependence on the Turkish dictionary, in time, became less necessary. To say I have taught myself to speak and write the Turkish language is not an exaggeration. My volumes of composition and poetry IN Turkish is evidence of my humble efforts. If I stated here that I am convinced one of the world's most beautiful languages is Turkish, would you be surprised?

If I may digress from the continuity of this book, years later at countless social functions, meetings, and conferences, untold numbers of Turks have asked me the same question which has filled me with deep emotion. The question to the present time continues to be: "How long has it been since you've left Istanbul?"

Instead of the word, Istanbul, had Turkey been mentioned, I'd not feel so honored, because my diction, my vocabulary, and my discourse, reveal knowledge of the modern Turkish language. In addition, at the outset, I am thought to have been born in Turkey and have married an American lady. The latter of course, is true.

With the departure of the Akkent and the Büyükünal families, the number of our families in Turkey, increased to five. The fifth family had comprised of Selâhattin's close friend Dr.Yılmaz Gerelioğlu, his wife Yurdakul, and their sons Canpek and Gerçek. Yilmaz had come to work for one year at the Naval Hospital and since he and Selâhattin had been close friends since their years in the Navy and Medical school, they occupied one of the vacant apartments. As it had been during the previous years, much of our time was spent in each other's company.

Again, one year later, another tearful separation, and another saucepan of water spilled on the road just as they drove away.

Our years of letters and phone calls continued the deep love and the yearning among our families. With each correspondence from Turkey, we were asked: *"Ne zaman geliyorsunuz? Bekliyoruz!* (When are you coming? We are waiting!)" For years our families had repeated to us with sincere longing, their wish for our return to our *Anavatan* (our Motherland). My mother had never returned to the land of her birth after leaving at the conclusion of the war. Her dream had always been to set foot on Turkish soil and to see the Turkish sky, just once more.

The time came when Mary and I were assured of six weeks vacation during the summer, so we hoped to fulfill her life's dream. However, nothing we said to Mom would enable her to fly – she was deathly afraid. As August of 1968 drew closer, no one could have envisioned the monumental impact upon our lives, especially mine! My mother at the time was able to care for herself, also, Terry would visit her frequently, and we were free of that worry. There was so much to be done: shopping for clothes, gifts for our families in Turkey, airline tickets, passports – after all, Ed was always early and precise about everything! He was *determined* to be at the airport *three hours* before the scheduled departure. Up to that time there were no direct non-stop flights with Turkish Airlines. Everyone had to be informed, time of arrival, flight number, Turkish Airlines from Frankfurt to Istanbul… when would we sleep, WHO would sleep?! MARY! Where are the keys?!

Ah, but of course nothing was forgotten.

Prior to 1968 there had been only two major projects which I had composed, noted as my very first written position on the subject of the Turkish Nation. The first had been a pro-Turkish letter written to an Armenian newspaper (a copy of which was not kept), and the second, in November of 1965, I had written (typed), three pages to the incumbent President of Turkey, his Excellency Cemal Gűrsel. This had been a correspondence from a thirty-three year old man, hoping to express his love for all things Turkish, to the President of Turkey. It was the latter correspondence which I took along during our first visit to Turkey. My loved ones had joked, saying that it would be impossible for the President to personally reply to a letter from an unknown American; it seemed illogical at that time. But I had felt at least someone would read my sincere feelings. Now, the predetermined course of events began and nothing was to alter the inexplicable direction we were about to follow.

As we flew in the plane, Mary and I were filled with an excitement the likes of which we had never experienced before. Sleep had not even entered my mind. The Turkish 707 landed safely to a joyous applause by the passengers. With each step we looked near and far, searching for a familiar face …

Suddenly Mary exclaimed: "Look there! It's Oktay!"

Then we saw Selâhattin, Ayhan, Ayla, Osman, Şadan, Naci, Gűl, the children, even Varojen, Selâhattin's Armenian friend. They were all here! Oktay gave Mary flowers and behind him were several newspaper reporters with cameras flashing! *Cameras flashing?* But … what was happening?

When they began asking me questions, I realized that their words were not foreign to me; I understood their questions, with the first one being: "Why did you come to Turkey?"

Despite my deeply emotional state, by the grace of God, I replied in a calm, clear, and audible voice. Yes, they understood each word, all of it in Turkish. I shall not forget those moments for the rest of my life….

Everyone was impatient for our kisses, our embraces, and of course everyone was in tears. Our joy was supreme.

At this point, however, I have to take a moment and add a brief introduction to Mr. Varojen Margosyan: Varojen and his wife, who had a son, Aret, were ethnic Armenians, who were born in and lived their entire lives as peaceful *Turkish citizens*. So close were the Büyükünal and Margosyan families that several years earlier when Selâhattin had become seriously ill, he said the following to Varojen: "If I die, I entrust my family to YOU for safekeeping; promise me you will take care of them!" Of course Varojen had promised without a second's hesitation. Thankfully, though, in time Selâhattin had recovered. The two friends remained as inseparable as were their families. Varojen had been a master auto mechanic who had begun his business on a humble level but expanded to become very successful. He and his family became included in our ever-growing family, and during their visits to New York they had stayed in our home.

VII.... The President has granted you an audience ....

Excitement would not even permit fatigue. Turkish television was still in its early years, but the print media covered our visit extensively from the first day. Our passports were stamped: *Giriş* (entry), our luggage was secured, and as prearranged by the families, we began to drive to Oktay's home.

While his wife Ayla was driving, Oktay spoke the following words: "Edward, we have a surprise for you, the President has granted each of you an audience."

Surely he had to be joking and I dismissed his statement by replying casually, "How is the weather in Istanbul?"

Oktay became agitated by my indifference and repeated with emphasis each word he uttered: "I told you the *President* has agreed to meet with you!"

It was only then that the meaning of what he had said, struck at me, and still my cognitive process was unable to accept what I had just heard.

As we continued our drive to the Akkent home, our questions were endless but the answers could not hope to become clear in my mind. How and why were we being so greatly honored? There was so much I needed to ask, so much confusion in my mind, and how could I be expected to speak with countless relatives and friends of our four families? And as if this difficult challenge of behaving normally, were not enough, I was expected to converse with high ranking Turkish officials! *What? Who? Me?!* Me, Edward, who at the age of sixteen could not speak a single word of Turkish, will now have to face the President of Turkey. How could I begin to express my love for my ancestral and cultural homeland? Would my adlib comments and opinions merit the interest of the many people with whom we were to have private conversations? Was this really happening?

Rather than devote more time and space to the unbelievable effort Dr. Oktay Akkent had spent with government offices, the media, and arranging meetings with officials, I will, instead, reveal the program which had been prepared for us. Everyone knew how Oktay had worked, and all agreed only he could have achieved so much in such a short time.

Anyone who has ever had any need to spend time in a governmental office or agency will know well how difficult and even exasperating an experience this can be. Oktay was renowned for having the capacity for getting complicated matters resolved. His expertise included arranging meetings with government officials, interviews, media contacts, and much more, thus he took charge of our itinerary. His involvement meant we had to spend far more time with him than we were able to be with our other three families. Please bear in mind that the telephone never stopped ringing because friends and relatives of our families were emphatically requesting us to visit their homes. Mary and I immediately learned that without exception, Turkish hospitality is and remains for all time, *unequalled.* If we even tried to assist with the dishes, we were made to feel as though we were offending our hosts. With all you have read of the author so far, can you imagine how we must have felt when the following program – on paper – was given to us by Oktay *kardeşim:* His Excellency President Cevdet Sunay will receive us at his summer residence in Istanbul. – The Mayor of Istanbul, Fahri Atabey, at his offices. – The Armenian Patriarch (the late) Şnork Kalutsyan, Patriarch of the Armenian Church…-- The Grand Mufti of Istanbul (he being the highest Muslim cleric) … -- Zeki Mű̃ren, Turkey's most beloved vocalist … -- then famous female vocalist Safiye Ayla … --

The list goes on, encompassing a veritable roster of the movers and shakers of Turkish society. Indeed my wife and I were given invitations to visit numerous magnificent museums, awe-inspiring mosques and former palaces of the sultans; and in each instance we were given private admission and a personal guide. We were then flown to Ankara, the nation's capital, met at the airport by officials who introduced us to a couple, a husband and wife, who were to serve as our hosts.

Two cars with drivers took us and our hosts to our hotel in the center of the city. Sight-seeing, beautiful restaurants, impeccable service, delectable cuisine, and warm hospitality which defies description. Sorry! We had no time for shopping. Was this all a dream? I feared I was about to wake up.

The next morning, the most unforgettable day of our lives was about to begin: After an excellent breakfast with our hosts, we were escorted to the expansive mausoleum of the Founder of the Turkish Republic, the immortal Mustafa Kemal Atatűrk. It was a warm, sunny afternoon in Ankara; we were standing on sacred ground. The land surrounding the massive mausoleum was about the size of an American football field. We pulled up in front of the white marble steps, walked up to the upper level where during national holidays and major memorial ceremonies, many thousands of citizens would be in attendance. We were welcomed by a three-star general, security officers, a protocol officer, and our hosts. We noticed a large bouquet of flowers carried by one of the officers, with a broad red and white ribbon attached to the arrangement. On the ribbon I read the letters: *Taşçı* (our name spelled in Turkish). Our entourage had invited us to participate in a private but very respectful solemn memorial procession along the entire length of the approach to the huge structure which housed the marble mausoleum.

We entered and approached the marble site as the officer placed the flowers in front of the monument. We all bowed our heads and recited our prayers. From here we were taken to a nearby room where a large Book of Honor had been placed. It was here where kings, presidents, and heads of state, would, on behalf of their nations, record their messages of respect and friendship for the people and government of Turkey….

At that moment, I was left breathless. I'd been invited to write my own thoughts in that special Book of Honor! As best as I can now, 32 years after the fact, my words, written in English, were as follows: "We, as the children of parents of Armenian and Sűryani (Syrian Orthodox) background, in their name have come to our *Anavatan* (Motherland), expressing our profound respects and love for Turkey and her people." After which I signed both our names. All that has been described above can be confirmed by news articles and photographs in my possession and in my exhibition which will be described later.

As spectacular as the visit to Ankara was, this served as a prelude to truly amazing events which were to follow us during our future trips to our *homeland,* Turkey. The following day, our warm and gracious hosts escorted us to the airport for our next stop, the beautiful city of Izmir, on the coast of the Aegean Sea. Our goodbyes included our farewell embraces and sincere expressions of gratitude for their friendship and hospitality. We boarded our plane en-route to Izmir.

When we arrived, officials were again waiting for us near the terminal building. We were introduced to our host, who this time was a young representative of the Ministry of Culture. The scenario was about to repeat itself: an automobile with its driver, to a beautiful hotel in the city, everything attended by our young host, brought to our special suite with an overwhelming view of the Aegean Sea. A brief rest and down to the lobby and our host took us for dinner. The most inspiring event which took place during this visit to Izmir, took place the following day.

Months before our historic trip to Turkey, Dr. Akkent had asked me to reveal the places we would like to visit. Together with Istanbul, Ankara, and Izmir, I had mentioned that we would be extremely happy to visit *Efes* (Ephesus), which is the site of the Blessed Virgin Mary. The home which stands on a high mountain near the City of Izmir has been the destination of hundreds of thousands of visitors to the Turkish homeland. It took about two hours, but driving on winding narrow roads up a precarious mountain was frightening, to say the least.

At the site there were many tourists from many countries, and along the gardens leading to Her home, were several encased large signs in various languages, revealing the authenticity of the small stone house. As we entered its premises we felt a divine presence; the single room had no furnishings and a simple but beautiful altar was prepared with flowers, candles, and discarded canes, crutches placed against a wall, as many examples of proven miracles. As Christians we felt we had been touched by the hand of God. Among many of the amazing facts we learned was that the Turks who are predominantly of the Moslem faith, recognize the Blessed Virgin Mary as the mother of Jesus Christ and as a result, Turks make a religious pilgrimage to this holy edifice.

The following day, the government's invitation was to come to an end. We were told Dr. Büyükünal and his family was driving from the Turkish Naval Base of Iskenderun, to take us by car to the city of Balikesir.

Balikesir is the city where my saintly beloved mother was born – at that time in the early 1900s, it had been a small town. You can imagine my excitement at the mere thought of arriving at where my mother was born and played as a child in the home of her family. It had to be toward the end of August, 1968, when in the quiet corner of the cocktail lounge of our hotel, late at night, our Turkish hosts brought their wonderful welcome to us, to an end. Dr. Büyükünal and his wife Ayhan (their son Cenk was fast asleep after a long car trip from Iskenderun), my wife Mary, and I, were seated sipping our Turkish coffee and tea. It was a deeply emotional encounter for each of us. Though our visit to Izmir had been brief, we had become close friends and now they were about to *surrender* to us another couple who had already been in our hearts and memories. At the conclusion of our long conversation, we stood up, smiles filled with moist eyes, we embraced, kissed each other on both cheeks, and sadly went to our rooms.

The next morning, after a splendid breakfast, we spoke our final farewells, filled Selâhattin's car with our luggage and departed for Balikesir. His car had been purchased in New York during their year in Saint Albans. It was a big 1955 Chevrolet, still in excellent condition. The four-hour drive was pleasant as we viewed the Turkish towns and countryside near the Aegean Sea. The trip was uneventful except for one unforgettable incident. It never received attention in the Turkish media, and regrettably, in my voluminous writings I have never given it the recognition which it truly deserved. However, this *insignificant* event has remained in my heart, mind and soul ever since 1968, and now I offer it in the recognition it deserves: during our drive, in the distance, we could see a landscape of luxuriant vegetation; it was one of Turkey's many vineyards, a massive plantation of grapevines. Certainly the most delicious and sweetest grapes are grown in the rich soil of the Turkish homeland. The road at one point became narrow so that from within the car we could see a person seated amidst the huge field.

Selâhattin brought his car to a slow stop and we could see the person was a middle-aged woman filling her baskets with grapes. Dr, Selâhattin Büyükünal stepped out of the car and got close enough to converse with the smiling villager, greeting her with "Iyi gǘnler, teyzeciğim (good day beloved aunt)!"

After a brief exchange, my brother informed the gentle lady with the angelic face that he and his family were escorting their American guests to Balikesir so that we would visit the birthplace of my mother (mentioning that we were the children of Armenian and Syrian Orthodox parents who were born in her homeland).

Selâhattin had requested to purchase some grapes for us to taste. The gentle lady then became agitated, her expression angry as she exclaimed: *"Satmak ne demek* (what do you mean sell?)" She then continued, "They are our guests, our children, I CANNOT SELL THEM MY GRAPES!"

By this time we had all spilled out of the car, received her enormous gift, expressed our deep appreciation, and then resumed our journey. My beloved *köylü teyzeciğim* (my beloved provincial aunt), the heart and soul of the Turkish Nation, I do not know your name and most likely our paths will never cross again, but before the world I acknowledge your kindness and loving, pure heart, because in August of 1968, I became your loving SON.

Without our knowledge, Selâhattin had communicated with the office of the Mayor of Balikesir, giving information of our first visit to our ancestral homeland, and requested a few minutes of the Mayor's time by receiving us at his office. As we drove we saw the first of many road signs which introduced: Balikesir!

We located our hotel in the center of the city; it was spacious, modern and clean – indeed our accommodations were perfect. After the necessities were concluded we were driven to the office of the Mayor, a tall, white-haired, erect, and most cordial person with that inherent, warm Turkish smile. Also a great host, he drove us in his car and gave us an insightful tour of what had become a major city.

As had happened many times before, our day was filled with sight-seeing, brief conversations with officials and citizens who displayed varied emotions. It was comprised with the initial quality of Turkish hospitality, but more so, that the people in Balikesir were speaking to American visitors IN Turkish. Many believed that I had been born in Turkey, immigrated to the United States and returned with my American wife. It is important to remember that, other than the letter I had written to the former Turkish President, my efforts on behalf of the Turkish nation were non-existent and the only "documentation" we had were magazine and newspaper articles which had been printed since our arrival in Turkey. When it proved to be informative, my *brother* Selâhattin would eagerly show them to our hosts.

We were eventually driven back to the Mayor's office, where he astonished us by presenting us with gifts. For my mother, he presented us with the world-famous Turkish towels, and for our home, a hand-painted miniature arrangement of flowers on glass and gold-filling, framed with mahogany. This beautiful work of art hangs on our living room wall to this day, in our most unique "Ottoman" and Turkish home. Though President John Kennedy had never visited Turkey, the Turkish people loved him and when he died, it was mourned as a national tragedy. We had taken with us several Kennedy one-dollar coins, so we gave one to the Mayor as a *hatira* (keepsake), which he deeply appreciated.

Then… departure … expressions of appreciation and affection, return to our hotel rooms and preparation for our exit from my beloved city of Balikesir.

I wonder if I will see her again.

Our journey back to Istanbul included an overnight visit to the heavenly resort of Yalova, which rests on the shore of the Sea of Marmara. The landscape, the color and calm of the sea, the hotels and accommodations, were as welcoming as the people. It reminded us of our visit to *Kuşadası* (Island of Birds), near Izmir, on the Aegean Coast. Time and distance certainly had prevented our visiting the birth places of the rest of our families, namely: Şanliurfa, Adiyaman, and Harput (Elâziğ).

One evening we were taken to the home of a close friend of many years: Dr. Zeki Uygur and his wife, Ayla (same name as Oktay's wife). Zeki, too, was a doctor in the Turkish Navy. Our visit was a heart-warming introduction and our friendship was to extend to our home in Saint Albans, New York. Our enchanting trip to the homeland of many ancient civilizations was about to come to an end as our departure drew close. Without the photographs and media stories in our possession, we would not have been able to prove the events of the previous six weeks.

The preparations for our return to home in the United States were completed, and the very final day of our historic trip to Turkey, brought yet one more surprise: I have described my 1965 letter to the incumbent President of Turkey; no response was ever received to my correspondence, which surely proved the predictions of my family. The lack of a reply had not disappointed me; after all, he was the President. Just because a reply was not received, did not mean there was no *response*. For as it turned out, there indeed was a magnificent "reply."

The day before our departure, an honored guest arrived at the Akkent home; it was Senator Sadi Koçaş, the author of a book on Turkish-Armenian history and relations. He greeted us with much respect and deep affection. He told us that the President (the late Cemal Gürsel) had indeed received my letter, that he was extremely moved by my statements, and had requested a book be written on the subject. And then the Senator assured us that my letter, which had been in its entirety printed in the book, was responsible for this book coming into existence!

He presented me with an inscribed copy of his book and during a long conversation I urged him to have the book translated into other languages. Concerned about my safety, he had not included my name at the end of the letter; whereupon I insisted it be added in any future printing. He then revealed that after searching for us for three years, they'd been delighted to find us in Istanbul.

As honored and pleased as we were for having the Senator visit us at the home of our hosts, without any exaggeration I can state that he was equally—if not more—pleased to meet face to face with the young writer whose letter had affected high ranking Turkish officials, and as a result a 309 page historical compilation was published in 1967. Not only was my humble letter printed in full, but in addition, within the front pages of the book the author kindly refers to us in a most complimentary manner and states clearly that my letter was indeed the reason for the book to be written. It was far beyond my ability to express to this soft-spoken gentleman the extent of my gratitude and appreciation; especially in Turkish.

And then, another departure, with promises to stay in touch.

The next morning Mary and I were at the airport with our luggage and members of our families to see us off. *Kardeşim* Oktay came running towards us with extended hands. He had left his office in order to personally obtain photographs which he wanted to place in our hands. Together with the priceless pictures, he gave a photo album showcasing a magnificent copper image of the Ayasofya Museum on the cover, depicted in a three-dimensional engraving. To this day, it remains as one of our most cherished possessions, displaying some of our most unforgettable memories. There was no time to view the photos as it was time to enter the passenger gate.

After our final embraces and kisses for our beloved families, Bűyűkűnal, Akkent, Köksal, and Barut, our steps slowly directed us on board the plane. We found our seats and the swirl of countless memories began to take hold of our senses. Ah, the pictures! We had to see what had been recorded on film, how else would anyone believe this truly unbelievable experience? There they were: The ceremony at *Anıt Kabir* (Ataturk's mausoleum); signing the Book of Honor; the Armenian Patriarch; Zeki Műren; Safiye Ayla; President Cevdet Sunay, and so much more – it was all there! No, this whole trip had not been a dream.

Questions gathered in my mind. Will the Armenians say that I was used by the Turks for propaganda services? No, impossible. I had nothing to offer Turkey other than my faithful LOVE. In America, I had no wealth, no fame, and no means of influencing the Turkish nation in any way. Therefore, it had to be the inherent quality of the Turkish heart to receive love freely and offer it in return, just for one … humble … letter.

VIII. Returning home, the magnitude of my affection becomes supreme.

The previous chapter has described MOST of the significant events which had taken place during our first visit to our ancestral, cultural and historical homeland, the Republic of Turkey. But what of the rest – the many people, the places? Do I not have an obligation to so many individuals for their kindness and sincere friendship? I believe I do; they also deserve the recognition of the world's attention, for within the period of our visit to Turkey *'sevgi,'* and *'kardeşlik,'* literally translated: love, and brotherhood/siblinghood, prevailed everywhere we went. All that was known about my wife and me was that we were the children born of two families whose land of birth had been the nation to which WE referred to as 'Anavatanimiz,' (our Motherland) and this public pronouncement had been expressed in Turkish. The response of the Turkish Government, media, and the people, as overwhelming as it was, proved to be merely a prelude to unimaginable countless events that were yet to occur.

I have never attempted to explain to anyone the many inexplicable circumstances that have had an effect on the development of my interest in and love for the Turkish people. For years, through extensive, personal meditation, I have tried to comprehend my feelings and perspectives pertaining to Turkish-Armenian history. As objectively as possible I have considered all angles and the only logical conclusion I have arrived at is, that it has all been by the Will of God.

Had it not been for my letter of 1965, written to the late President Cemal Gürsel, then the suspicious, the cynical, and even the envious, would have just cause to say: My position towards the Turks has been predicated by the reception given to us in Turkey. But these negative minded individuals – including the Armenian "Hate Merchants" – would be wrong by THREE YEARS. My profound affection for the Turkish Nation and my condemnation of eternal hatred as manifested by the Armenians of the United States had been clearly stated in my letter of 1965. This simple fact cannot, and will never be refuted! My fundamental principles have been formulated by my God, my parents, and the humanity of the Turkish people.

Our return home to America had been filled with a multitude of emotions. How were we going to describe these extraordinary events and the reception Mary and I were given by the people and the government in Turkey? We were truly unable to comprehend the efforts of so many people, the monumental cost that was surely incurred, and the most bewildering question of all: WHY?

If *we* could not find the logical explanations, then how would we be able to make others understand? But the newspaper and magazine articles and pictures, said it all. Our many rolls of film – all developed – had revealed conclusively the story was true. All that happened was far beyond ordinary coincidence and as a result I was brought face to face with my destiny, and that was *to speak in defense of the Turkish people.* With specific attention to the Turkish-Armenian issue, my humble efforts would strive to refute the Armenian allegations against the Turkish Nation, while at the same time revealing the ubiquitous fraud perpetrated by the Armenian co-religionists upon the people, the history, and the culture of Ottoman Turkey as well as the Republic of Turkey.

This was not to be a simple endeavor; in fact, it could prove to be dangerous for my safety – as it will be described later in this chapter. Because the phrase "I am called a Friend of the Turks," had begun with the Turkish media, the author began to identify himself as a *Friend of the Turks.*

Well… what now? The author had his identification, had his destiny revealed to him, and he and his wife were given a reception the likes of which would be planned only for a Head of State. So… but… how do you begin? What is your program, your documentation, your supportive organization? Whom will you contact first?

These were the questions to which I had no answers. My "program" was in my head; my *documentation* were the valuable facts learned from my mother (certainly far from adequate) and as far as my "organization" … at that time I had only *one* close Turkish friend, and that was Mr. Tarik Bulut.

But the real work would begin NOW.

Not to be redundant, my belief was that a Divine intervention had preceded my perception of my own destiny. This was once again manifested one day when at our home in Bayside, Queens, after our return from Turkey, our door bell rang and it was Dr. Zeki Uygur; naturally we were overjoyed. Dr. Uygur, a Naval officer, had been brought to our home by his close friend Dr. Oktay Akkent when he (Akkent and his wife) had been in St. Albans for one year. That initial meeting had taken place before our trip to Turkey. We had become close friends and eventually Zeki also became my *kardeşim.* We had visited the Uygur family while we were in Istanbul during our first visit, at which time we were told he was planning to work in the United States. Zeki's wife, Ayla, and their two sons had remained in Istanbul while he secured residence here. After the return of the Akkent and Bűyűkűnal families to Turkey, we had lost contact with Dr Uygur. His time and energies were consumed with establishing his medical position with a hospital and a home for his family.

Zeki was a highly respected neurosurgeon who could have obtained a position at any prestigious hospital anywhere in the United States. But he had no way of knowing his choices had been influenced by *my* destiny: he obtained a position in a New York hospital and established residence in Bayside (a ten minute walk from our home), in which we had been living since 1961. If we had planned it that way, it most likely would not have materialized, but it was all prearranged by a greater power. For had it not been for our friendship and our proximity, the next phase of my destiny could not have taken place; a viable, active, and successful Turkish-American Social Organization, called the Anadolu Club. Dr. Zeki Uygur spoke to us about the organization of which he was a member, and invited us attend a forthcoming social function where we would be introduced to the members. There would be no possible method to describe my joy: what a great leap from one dear Turkish friend to an entire organization!

As if that was not miraculous enough, when I later learned *kardeşim* Tarik was a member of the same Anadolu Club, I had become ecstatically overjoyed. We had attended the function, speaking Turkish and made to feel very welcome. I applied for membership and was unanimously accepted. Thus, my "organization" had become a reality. My *work* had begun.

The English word for Anadolu is Anatolia, and its translation becomes "full of mothers." It could be considered an unusual name for the Asian region of the Turkish homeland, but it was most appropriate because during its ancient history many military conflicts took the young men and fathers into battle and all that was left behind was a land of grieving mothers. None was more devastating than the First World War when the Turkish people faced annihilation and the destruction of the sovereignty of the Turkish Nation. Historians have devoted their attention to the suffering of certain peoples, totally disregarding the millions of Turks who had perished. But let us return to the cultural organization of the Anadolu Club….

Not unlike other societies throughout our country, the organization of approximately fifty families, maintained its cultural and religious traditions by passing onto their children their pride in their ancestral heritage and language. Building bonds of friendship with our fellow Americans and creating closer relationships between the United States and the Republic of Turkey, had been among our priorities. The club became incorporated and the Board of Directors selected their "Friend of Turks" to be the Recording Secretary for the club. When letters needed to be written, I'd prepare them, and when requested, I'd prepare letters for our President, Dr. Hilmi Kodaman. Turkish national and religious holidays were celebrated with our members and guests gathering together, and often notable speakers would make speeches pertinent to the event being celebrated and commemorated. The ladies' branch of our club always worked very hard with preparing foods and the many arrangements necessary for a successful function. During our fifteen years of membership with the club, Mary and I would offer our assistance: by trays of food prepared by Mary, by setting-up, as well as our financial support. In addition, you might recall my description of my musical "career" during my youth; it proved to be beneficial in our club. Mr Tarik Bulut had accompanied our group during musical performances. Within the Anadolu Club, a dear friend, Mr. Sait Tűrkgűcű, had played a stringed instrument, and the author with his drum, our musical offerings were always well received. As the years passed by my joy never lessened, alas though, something was missing: *vital efforts*. My frequent speeches were always received with resounding applause, but within me there was a void: I felt that there was much more to be done.

During the ensuing years, while I continued my efforts within the Anadolu Club, numerous events of significance took place as my devotion to the Turkish people revealed itself through work and effective efforts. The following are but a few of the major occurrences worthy of mention here, as I regret I am compelled to omit many events and people with whom we had met during my early years of effort:

1. In the summer of 1968, while I was a departmental manager at the Commodore Hotel, in New York City (today the Grand Hyatt Hotel stands in its place), I had arranged a private meeting with a distinguished member of the Turkish-American community, Professor Talat Halman, who a few years later had become Turkey's first Minister of Culture. For such a highly respected gentleman, who had known me only through my writings, to give his time was for me an immeasurable honor.

2. I believe Turkey is the only country in the world which has a holiday named 'Çocuk Bayrami' or Children's Day, a day of joyous celebration and gift giving. Though the year was not recorded, once on a holiday, which is every April 23rd, the Anadolu Club had a party for about forty children who received gifts from a clown who gyrated in his colorful and comical costume entertaining the children and parents alike. Underneath the make-up and the huge round red nose, was none other than our *Friend of the Turks.*

3. After our return from Turkey, my first project was to write a letter to the President of Turkey, Cevdet Sunay. My letter of profound and respectful gratitude had to be published in Turkey (I am assuming), because my long letter wound up in the newspaper *Armenian Reporter,* which is published in Boston. With no commentary from the Editor, my letter had been released in its entirety. The Editor knew for certain the reaction that would follow.

The brutal condemnation of this writer was immediate.

The following issue of the newspaper in August of 1970, included letters from the readers who expressed repugnant statements in their letters to the Editor. I was branded a "traitor" to my people, together with vehement, hateful, and disgusting phrases which will not be repeated here. Since I had not and never would, subscribe to any publication printed by the Armenian "hate merchants" future issues of the *Armenian Reporter* did not come into my possession, and therefore other letters were not added to my collection. As hurt as I was, my position did not waver.

4. On July 9, 1972, a historic event took place in our home in Bayside. The Anadolu Club had invited and sponsored a group of about twenty musicians and vocalists who were respected members of Ankara Radio and State Symphony Orchestras, to perform in a few cities in the United States. While in the New York area, the group was housed in the homes of our club members. We had a spacious guest room with a queen-sized brass bed in our *Ottoman* home, and we offered to have two ladies or gentlemen to stay with us. My mother, who was living with us, was as overjoyed as we were when two famous vocalists were assigned to our home.

For a period of four days Elâ Altin and Gönűl Akin were our guests and we became sister and brother to them, while our mother became their loving mother. We decided to have a major welcome party; each member of the entire group and their host families were invited to our home for an unforgettable day: at least forty people in our huge finished basement; an enormous buffet with fresh flowers and tapers accenting the ferns, upon which were many platters of delicious Turkish foods; the color scheme was red and white; the bar was filled with refreshments of every taste; a large square cake with American and Turkish flags engraved with multi-colored sugar, with the Turkish inscription: *Welcome Ankara Radio, our beloved brothers and sisters;* on the turntable I played a recording of the Turkish National Anthem as everyone stood at attention, and I proceeded to unfurl first a small Turkish flag, continued with larger flags, and at the end a huge Turkish flag touched the emotions of many of our guests. *Very emotional these Turks* – there were tears everywhere. These consummate artists who had performed before heads of state and nobility were in awe for the manner in which we revealed our love for them; but there was more that would touch their hearts.

Fact is, these were distinguished people, talented artists, who were loved and applauded by countless audiences in many countries. Would it be possible for us to entertain such experienced professionals of classical and contemporary Turkish music?

First I read a prepared statement, in Turkish of course, and at its conclusion, followed by a resounding applause, Mr. Kutlu Payasli, who was the male vocalist and director, asked if he could have a page from which I had just read. I could not refuse him and as a result I have no copy of our warm welcome to the gathering. A magnificent surprise was to follow: I dimmed the lights and seated myself next to our record player housed in a wall stereo unit. My drum was beside me, on the floor, as I introduced our "program." Our guests heard a recording of Middle Eastern mode, an instrumental of graceful and slow melody of music, and as the music played no one anticipated what was about to happen.

Mary appeared in the center of the room dressed in a beautiful belly dancer's costume! It had been sewn by my mother, turquoise in color, a veil with a crown above it, and around her waist was a chain of gold colored circular discs which accented her movements. Expressions of astonishment were evident as everyone applauded. As we had rehearsed it, Mary kept the veil over her beautiful face until the selection ended. Then the second recording followed: a lively, rhythmic, dance instrumental. I played the drum as Mary performed her movements in unison with the rhythm. While the dance continued, Mary removed her veil, and again as prearranged, danced toward an elderly gentleman who was chosen to receive the veil and as she approached him, she began to wrap her veil around his head. This is considered as a gesture of good-natured respect. Mary had danced for thirty minutes non-stop!

The program ended with everyone on their feet, applauding, kissing, and embracing us. Our efforts were a supreme success! To say that our guests were extremely pleased would be an understatement. The party came to an end and other than our two house guests, everyone returned to their homes.

Eventually our guests returned to Turkey and our next encounter with the Ankara Radio group was to take place five years later. An evening of friendship and love between people who were meeting each other for the first time, thus ended with memories to last a lifetime. As it had been between our peoples for centuries in the Turkish homeland, as it continues to be, and so it was on this day in our home.

However, before we leave the reminiscing about Radio Ankara's visit to our home, the following needs to be mentioned: The day our guests had come to our home, they had given a concert in New

York City, and at its conclusion, their Director informed them that the entire group had been invited to the home of an *Armenian*. Several of the artists had become skeptical and their consternation was emphatic. The events as briefly described above, surely brought comfort and joy to their hearts. Finally, before they left our home, they decided to leave us a "hatira" (remembrance). Each member signed their autograph with a brief message, upon two lamp shades placed on our end tables. This magnificent expression of their love remains in place in our home. Since then many other honorable guests have also left us this symbol of affection and brotherhood.

5. The year was early 1976, when a member of the Anadolu Club and a dear friend, Mr. Iskender Necef, had informed me of the arrival from Turkey, of a group of young folk dancers who were to tour several American cities. Knowing of my position at the Commodore Hotel, he asked if he could secure rooms, at a reduced rate, for about 35 dancers and their escorts. My response of course had been affirmative and I proceeded to contact the reservation, housekeeping, and lobby departments, for assistance in expediting their arrival into the hotel. The necessary arrangements made quickly, VIP status assigned to the entire group, thirteen rooms were impeccably cleaned, and just before scheduled arrival, pitchers of iced water and flowers were placed in each room. But there was one other expression of welcome to our special guests: as the 37 young men and women entered their respective rooms, on the dresser they found a letter of welcome addressed to them and written in Turkish.

That welcome letter, written by me, together with the page of guest names and room numbers remain in my possession to this day – 24 years later.

The following morning I had breakfast prepared for the entire group, and as they were welcomed by Mr. Necef, he introduced the author to our young people. Addressing them in Turkish, I had identified myself, my background, and briefly, the conditions under which my parents had left their land of birth. There is no need to describe here the overwhelming gratitude of the group, and their tearful expressions of affection and respect for this stranger who had become their *Ağabey* (older brother). However, the next chapter of the FOTEM group must be recorded here, because it describes beyond any question a quintessential distinction between a philosophy of love and hate.

FOTEM was the abbreviated name in Turkish which described the folk-dance group which had represented Turkish folklore and folk music in many countries, and this was their first tour in the United States. On April 8, 1976, FOTEM was about to give its first program at Hunter College, in New York City. That evening with my wife and mother seated in our car, we drove toward the college theater. As we approached the college, we heard loud shouting voices and saw young individuals protesting the performance with their posters of anti-Turkish rhetoric, while walking in a circle at the nearby entrance. I drove very slowly, bring the car to a stop just a few yards away from the Armenian miscreants, and speaking slowly and clearly, shouted in Armenian the following: "You smelly dogs, go back to your homes!"

There was instant panic in our car; my mother and wife were on the verge of hysteria as they expected us to be attacked. The miscreants were shocked as they clearly understood my expletive, which was far milder than they deserved, but to calm the ladies in our car, I drove forward and proceeded to search for a public garage. My ladies were reluctant to return to the site of the demonstration, but I had assured them there was no need to worry. My words were proven to be correct for as we arrived at the theater entrance, we noticed all was quiet, several of our young Turkish people were standing near the steps, and the sidewalk was strewn with the torn placards which the Armenian "heroes" had surrendered before they ran away.

The theater was filled to capacity and eventually the lights were dimmed and as the music began, the curtains rose and the folk dancers appeared from either side of the stage carrying lighted candles as was the custom in the dance from Silifke, Turkey. Before the two groups met at the center of the stage, a large number of people from the audience, seated in the front rows, stood up with loud voices of alarm. In a short time the cause of the disturbance became noticeable to everyone other than the people seated in the rear of the theater. It was a putrid odor that had been released by a stink bomb placed by Armenian intruders who had entered with the audience. The disturbance and screams of fright increased and it was obvious the situation was to become a disaster. We had been seated in the center of the audience, and as I stood up, I told my ladies to remain in their seats, then ran toward the stage and made my way backstage. By this time all the dancers had left the stage, many of the young girls were crying and certain pandemonium was about to erupt. There was no way of foreseeing the result of my action, but something had to be done to restore order.

In a loud voice (and in Turkish) I shouted to the young people, "Kids, do return to the stage! Please continue with your program! DO NOT allow them to disrupt your performance, remember you are representing Turkey! Return to the stage!"

The music had begun, first a few and then the entire group of dancers relit their candles, took their positions, and entered the stage. The audience, seeing the return of the performers began to return to their seats, with continuous and loud applause for the courage of the young people. And there was one individual backstage, seated by himself, engulfed in tears.

Indeed, on that day, in New York City, hatred had been defeated by love.

Alas, yet one other dreadful occurrence was to devastate the young men and women of the FOTEM group. During their performance in numerous cities of the United States, the Turkish and American audiences had reacted to young folk dancers' performance with resounding applause. Theater critics in the media had given most favorable reviews of their two hour performances. The last city in which they had an engagement was Boston, Massachusetts. Upon hearing of their last destination before their return to New York City and the Commodore Hotel, negative thoughts entered my mind – I knew the Boston area had, and still does, a large Armenian community, and I anticipated trouble.

Once again my premonition proved to be correct. Much publicity had announced the performance and the Armenian *Frankenstein* monster of hate once again raised its head and performed its ugly deeds. The theater where the program was to take place began to receive phone calls and written messages which threatened to bomb the theater during the Turkish performance. The theater owners informed the police, the program directors, and the sponsors. The consensus of all parties concerned had been to cancel the performance. Many in the group were devastated as each young individual was unable to comprehend such maniacal hatred. How could they, they had never been taught to hate any ethnic group!

Thus, a very successful trip of cultural performances ended on a sad note brought upon by Armenian hate merchants.

On the next morning, filled with deep sorrow, the entire group returned to the Commodore Hotel in New York City. I had been informed of the events in Boston, and at once the wheels had begun turning in the head of this "friend of the Turks."

I would NOT allow this innocent group of talented young performers to fly back to Turkey with the painful memory of the abomination they had witnessed in Boston. My strategy had been carefully planned and I could only hope that the effort would be successful. The day for their return to Turkey had arrived, and that morning Mary and I drove to the hotel, parked in a garage, and took with us two items which were to be part of my strategy. At the hotel entrance I met the Bell Captain and requested he place our items in the luggage room until I returned to fetch them.

Mary and I then entered the lobby. The lobby was large but we were able to see many of the people seated in small groups chatting with each other while the check out were being completed. Several of the youngsters approached us, kissed us in Turkish fashion on both cheeks. Nevertheless, the distress on their faces was clearly evident. As I looked into the eyes of each boy and girl, their distress pierced my heart. Mary wished she could express her feelings in Turkish, but the little she knew at that time, did reveal her thoughts to the group. They were very grateful.

I proceeded to visit each group of the seated young people, three at one place, two at another, four elsewhere, and I sat down by each and every group and hoped I would not become emotional myself. I spoke to each group the following message: *Because you have not witnessed this behavior in Turkey, you have become rightfully upset. You must overcome your distress and realize that this is the situation in the United States; be proud of your most magnificent performances and how each of you has brought honor to our Turkish homeland! Consider the thousands of people, Turkish and American, who've honored you with such ovations and affection. And as for those few individuals who retain hatred in their hearts, pity them, because they will never be free of hate!*

Many of the young performers told us that in numerous cities from within the audiences, many Armenians had approached them with flowers and baskets of fruit, and sincere expressions of affection.

"Why should it be so different in Boston and in New York?" they asked me.

There was no time for lengthy answers, so all I could do was to jest lightly: "Maybe it's in the water."

Their smiles delighted my heart. In conclusion, I stated to each group: "Forget all unpleasant events and keep in your memories what you are about to see as you leave the hotel. Keep that memory in your hearts as our expression of our love for each of you! May God bless you all, our beloved sisters and brothers!"

The tearful embraces of separation began as each youngster reached for his or her luggage. Meanwhile I hurried to the bell captain and finding my belongings, proceeded to prepare my surprise. The young people finally began leaving the premises and what they saw outside was a large Turkish flag draped over the side of an evergreen tree, and next to it, placed on a tripod, they noticed a large poster with a message printed in Turkish.

The message proclaimed: "Happy and safe journey, our beloved sisters and brothers!"

When the bus was filled, from the sidewalk we heard loud voices shouting from within the bus, "Taşçı! Taşçı! Taşçı!"

Repeatedly they chanted our name in Turkish. Oh yes, I became very emotional as the bus started to move.

But the FOTEM chapter was not yet concluded. The bus departed and as we gathered our poster and flag, Mary and I returned to our car and commenced our return home. It had to be at least fifteen minutes later, while we were driving on the Long Island Expressway, further ahead on the highway in the right lane I noticed a bus which resembled the one in front of the hotel…

At this point, I must digress briefly. For many years I have, with strong conviction, believed that Divine Guidance has prepared me with an inexplicable love for all things Turkish. To assume all that has happened is pure coincidence is simply not possible for me to accept.

Let's return to the highway. That aforementioned bus was at a considerable distance from us, and deciding that this was not a coincidence, I accelerated. At last we were driving alongside the bus, on its left and we spotted our young performers. Maintaining the same speed as the bus, I shouted to Mary, "Quick, get the flag! Hold it outside the window, hurry!"

She reached for the flag, I opened her window, and holding it tightly, Mary unfurled the flag outside the moving vehicle.

The windows of the bus got crowded with those who had been seated on its right side. We saw some activity but could not determine what it was. Then, we saw it, there it was: They responded to our flag by lowering a small Turkish flag tied to a cord! Everyone was waving and as we greeted each other with our respective flags, the bus entered the exit, and continued onto another road as we remained driving straight.

A heart-warming moment which could never be forgotten. Indeed, once again, hatred had been defeated by love.

6. August of 1977 was the date of our second trip to our *Anavatan* (Motherland), and as it had been in 1968, my mother refused to fly. Though she was still able to take care of herself, we decided our second trip would last for four weeks only. Our anticipation and excitement were equal to our first trip, and as we arrived at the Ataturk Airport in Istanbul, we faced the same scenario which had greeted us during our first visit. Our four families together with other people greeted us at the airport, and once again we faced media cameras and many questions. My statements then reiterated my position which has remained firm and constant throughout the many years of my work on behalf of the Turkish people and the Turkish Nation. Specifically, we are living proof of the six centuries of brotherhood among the Turkish, Armenian, and Syrian Orthodox peoples.

There is no need to describe in detail our joyous reunion with our families, our visits to the many beautiful places in Istanbul, and Mary's complete delight in her hours of shopping tours. However, five significant events took place which remains indelibly recorded in our memories, to which I will briefly refer here:

a. Once again *kardeşim* (my brother) Dr. Oktay Cumhur Akkent, had performed the unattainable, which only he could achieve: We had been granted an audience with His Excellency, the President of the Turkish Republic, President Fahri Korutűrk at his summer residence in Istanbul. With his wife in attendance, the Honorable Haluk Bayűlken, who was the executive aide to the President, honored us with his company. We had had personal meetings with the Honorable Bayűlken many years ago in New York when he had served as Turkey's Permanent Representative to the United Nations. When we met at the President's residence, we embraced each other as in the fashion among the Turkish people. With Dr. Akkent in attendance, I had given the President information pertaining to my efforts within the Anadolu Club. He was noticeably affected by our work on behalf of the Turkish people. The warmth of and the cordial exchanges with our distinguished hosts filled us with unforgettable memories.

b. Another one of Dr. Akkent's successes was having Mary and I invited by Vice Admiral Sabahattin Ergin as his guests for luncheon at the Naval Military Training Academy located at Heybeliadasi, an island located near Istanbul. We were overwhelmed by the attention and warmth of the Admiral, officers, and the Naval personnel. After a formal and delectable luncheon, with a magnificent view of the Bosporus, accompanied by live music, we were given a tour of the Academy (the Admiral was the Commandant). As if the events just referred to were not enough to fill our hearts with joy and appreciation, the Admiral had a surprise for us far beyond any of our expectations. Docked in the harbor close to the Academy, sat the luxurious yacht which had been used by the Founder of the modern Republic of Turkey, the immortal Mustafa Kemal Ataturk.

All at once, a question I will never forget was asked by Vice Admiral Ergin: "How would you like to visit Atatürk's yacht, the Savarona?"

Our joy was beyond our ability to express. Just to be able to walk on the vessel where the architect of the modern Turkish State had spent time, would be for me and Mary an immeasurable source of happiness.

We boarded the Admiral's personal vessel, with five accompanying seamen, and Dr. Akkent. At that time the Savarona was not open to the public and had been restricted to everyone other than heads of state. The beguiling view of the blue waters of the Bosporus completed the magnificent rooms and facilities aboard the vessel. During the extensive tour one memorable occurrence took place and like so many others, will remain in our memories for as long as we live: as the Admiral escorted us into a beautifully furnished state room, Admiral Ergin suggested the following, "Our leader Kemal Ataturk had sat in this chair; wouldn't you like to sit in *his* chair?"

I considered it an honor I did not deserve, and responded, "Sir, I am not worthy to sit in the chair of the great Mustafa Kemal Ataturk! I thank you for the invitation, but I cannot accept it."

Yes indeed, it had been an unforgettable moment during an unforgettable event.

c. Dr. Akkent and his wife Ayla had a beautiful summer home on the Asian side of Istanbul, facing the Bosporus waterway. While we visited them in their home in Dragos, we were told their next door neighbor was the retired Prime Minister, His Excellency Nihat Erim. Dr. Akkent telephoned his distinguished neighbor, and requested a few minutes of his time to meet his guests from the United States. As it is inherent of Turkish hospitality, he extended us a warm welcome and together with his wife, received us in his home. They were deeply pleased as we were, and were amazed at my ability in speaking Turkish. This informal visit with the former Prime Minister, Nihat Erim, remains among our cherished memories. We were no head of state, no official, but to the Turkish people it made no difference: they reacted to our love for the Turkish Nation.

d. While we were staying at the home of *kardeşim* Dr. Selâhattin Bűyűkűnal and his wife Ayhan, a very special guest came to visit us: Elâ Altin, one of the vocalists who had stayed at our home in 1972, when the Ankara Radio artists had visited us. It was an emotional reunion. As we relived our memories, Elâ insisted we travel to Ankara for a reunion. To be able to meet our brothers and sisters of the Ankara Radio group would be a most desirable event. Mary was as eager for the reunion as I, and we promised Elâ we would go to Ankara for the reunion with as many of the group as possible. Contact was made with Gönűl Akin, who'd been with Elâ at our home, in 1972. Joy and excitement prevailed amongst all of us. We accepted Gönűl's invitation to stay at her home in Ankara, where most of our friends had their residences, and agreed to go to Ankara when Elâ would be there also.

e. Our visit to Ankara could last no more than three days because the Köksal and Barut families in Istanbul, were still waiting for our visit. To celebrate our reunion with the artists of Radio Ankara (five years had passed since the reception in our home), our friends arranged a beautiful dinner at an outdoor restaurant in the center of Ankara. We were embraced by more than 25 young men and women who proceeded to treat us like royalty. The entire gathering must have consisted of at least 35 people as many of our friends had brought their mates along. The reunion was magnificent: the food, the atmosphere, the warm affection shown to us, and the musical program they prepared for us. I am unable to conclude this recognition of our beloved friends without at least revealing the identity of the names I remember. Our sisters: Gönűl Akin, Elâ Altin, Zűhal Taçkin, Seyhan Tűtűn, Sema İleri. Our brothers: Kutlu Payasli, Hűseyin İleri, Cahit Ünyaylar, Turan Aşkin, Özay Gönlűm, Emin Aldemir, Orhan Özgediz, and Muzaffer Tűzűngűven.

I fear there might be others left out, and if so, I apologize to them if I have overlooked their names. The wonderful reunion and evening came to an end with tearful embraces of separation. The following day we left Ankara and returned to Istanbul for the conclusion of our second trip to Turkey. For obvious reasons space prohibits my referring—even briefly—to the countless meetings with many friendly people, our experiences, as well as the examples of the media coverage of our work becoming recognized by the general public.

So, finally, with our splendid memories, priceless photographs, and the press coverage in our possession, we prepared to return to the United States totally unaware of the countless endeavors and challenges that were yet to become the chapters of my life's work, this is my inexplicable story.

7. Our return home brought much good news to my mother who was very proud of the way we had been received in her homeland. But she had a disturbing story for us about which we had no information. Our visit to our cultural and historical homeland, together with our widely publicized comments pertaining to the anti-Turkish activities of the Armenians in the United States, had received, as we have said, extensive media coverage. This included the Armenian newspapers published in Istanbul, in which numerous articles had been printed. As a result and while we were still in Istanbul, my mother had received a phone call from a lady friend of our family (an Armenian), and in a furious, loud voice she had declared: "Your son has lost his mind!"

My beloved mother, very much alarmed, had inquired, "Why? What has he done?"

"Your crazy son has entered a mosque and prayed IN the mosque!"

A moment of silence had followed while my mother had struggled to gather her thoughts. She then asked for a repeat of the statement she had just heard. "Yes!" came the affirmation, "Yes, I read it in the New York Armenian newspaper; it says your son prayed IN a mosque!"

My mother had lost her temper and shouted back: "SO WHAT? WHAT IS WRONG WITH THAT? My son has prayed in God's home! And I love him!"

If my destiny had become evident to me after our first visit to Turkey, then there could not be any question – in my mind – that my conviction and dedication were now firmly and irrevocably instilled in my heart, my mind, and soul. Our participation in the Anadolu Club continued and my writings in support of Turkey on a multitude of subjects became my passion. At every social function of our club, people from other organizations as well as the Federation of Turkish American Associations, would participate and join their friends whether it was a conference, a concert, or any social activity. We had been introduced to many people, all of whom were deeply pleased – if not confused – that an Armenian couple worked tirelessly on behalf of the Turkish people and the Turkish nation.

The Turks were aware of my bitter condemnation of Armenian terrorism which manifested itself in the United States since 1973, when Armenian assassins began murdering Turkish diplomats in this country and in numerous countries around the world. One day at one of our functions, we were introduced to Dr. Bedri Gürbüzer, who had been active in the Turkish-American Federation. The recognition of this "Friend of Turks" had become far beyond what we could have imagined.

Many we had met for the first time would declare, "I know about you! I've read and heard much about your work, you are to be congratulated."

Dr. Gürbüzer was one of our generously complimentary friends. During our initial introduction, he asked me a question I'd never been asked before: Would I deliver a speech in public across the United Nation's building?

I was not only surprised, I was overwhelmed by the suggestion because I considered it an honor to address the Turkish-Americans, especially in public.

The information was as follows: The Federation, which is an umbrella organization comprising of 30 organizations, had prepared a public demonstration to condemn Armenian terrorism against innocent Turkish diplomats and citizens, worldwide.

At that time in 1983, a total of 35 Turkish and non-Turkish persons had been killed with many more injured, by a group of Armenian "hate merchants," who professed to be Christians. Without hesitation I accepted the proposal and having never made a public speech in my life before, I began to compose my speech, the first part in English, and the second in Turkish. The following is the English portion of my speech delivered on April 23rd, 1983, across the United Nations building in New York City:

"Ladies and Gentlemen,

At the outset, I wish to express to the organizers of this demonstration, my most profound appreciation and gratitude for extending to me the honor and privilege of addressing this gathering. My interest in and my affection for Turkey was indeed the greatest gift given to me by my beloved parents who left Turkey over 65 years ago. The magnitude of my love for all things Turkish cannot be measured here, but I am proud to say that as an American- born, I have dedicated myself to a lifetime of service on behalf of the Turkish Nation; mine has been a difficult task, when you consider my ancestry. I'm born of Armenian and Syrian-Orthodox parents, who came to America as a result of the First World War. For many years I have opposed the position of my Armenian co-religionists in their philosophy of hate against the Turkish people. Let me assure you, the scar which the Armenian people bear is the same scar upon my heart and soul. As I mourn the innocent Armenians who perished during those dark days, I also mourn with equal sincerity, the loss of our Turkish brothers and sisters who suffered untold hardships. Yes, brothers and sisters—because they were all the children of the same land, and the same nation.

This is neither the time nor the place to debate the events of that terrible period. But this is the time and place for me to say the world is witness to the results of Armenian fanaticism. The seed of hatred is responsible for the brutal attack upon Turkish representatives worldwide. The Turks' patience is unbelievable! There is no nation, no ethnic group which would not retaliate against those who spill innocent blood. The world is amazed and wonders for how long Turkey will endure in the savage attacks upon our people. The news media seem to be concerned with terrorism and yet it has failed to focus on Armenian terrorism against a staunch ally of the United States. There must be an arena *(author's note: at this point I had pointed to the United Nations Building),* for rational and constructive discourse. The civilized world cries out for their end of all terrorist activities.

The Western world, with America in particular, knows very little about Turkey and her true history. I'm proud to say that I have been and will continue to be a part of your history and culture. For I tell you I am living proof of the brotherhood between these ancestral families. As it was then, and as it is today, in Turkey. Let the hate merchants realize the Turkish and Armenian peoples have been and will remain for all time inseparable.

Now, with your indulgence, I'd like to say a few words in Turkish, please...."

By police estimate there were at least five thousand members of the Turkish-American community gathered for the peaceful but vociferous demonstration. My speech received continuous applause, but when with emphasis I shouted into the microphone *"Sevgili kardeşlerim!"* (My beloved brothers and sisters), then the resounding ovation and emotion of these gentle people, caused me to pause, and I could not continue.

Eventually, I went on in Turkish and at the end of each sentence a loud applause followed. At the conclusion of my address, 5000 voices shouted in unison: "TÜRKIYE!"

On the stage I was surrounded by people embracing me. Would it be fair to assume my singing songs as a teenager, prepared me for this supremely successful speech? I made my way to the rear of the stage and found a young man, standing, holding his son in his arms; he approached me, his face soaked with tears. "This is my son, Mehmet," he said softly.

Deeply touched, I replied in Turkish, "Thank you my brother, may your child never see the tragic events that our parents and grand-parents had witnessed."

We embraced and he departed. I did not learn his name and most likely we will never meet again.

8. *"Your dossier could be very valuable to Turkey."* One event of major significance had to occur before my first speech was made in public:

In early 1981 Mr. Kutlu Paşali (a member of the Ankara Radio artists referred to earlier), had come to the Washington D.C. area to present a concert. Through this visit, he and his wife had become close friends of Dr. Oğuz Turgut and his wife Ülker, a very active couple in Turkish-American affairs in the State of Maryland.

Kutlu evidently must have spoken extensively about us and as a result, when he came to New York for another concert, Mrs. Turgut wanted to join him and his wife, so that she could meet this "friend of Turks." Of course we said we would be happy to have them stay at our home. During their brief visit, I had presented numerous items from my enormous dossier, even in 1981, and with my oral presentation of my work, Mrs. Ülker Turgut who was meeting us for the first time, had become overwhelmed and emotional by my documentation and discourse. She insisted that Mary and I visit her home in Maryland and that I bring as much of my material as I could carry, because she wanted to introduce us to some of her close friends. The exact date of our visit to the Turgut home is unknown, but it had to be in 1981, when at their home we were introduced to many of her non-Turkish and Turkish friends. With about ten people in attendance, I was introduced and given the floor. Their expressions of compliments and praise need not be mentioned here, but their recognition of the educational benefits of my material, was for me of major significance. With emphasis on the Turkish-Armenian issue, Armenians' groundless allegations against Turkey, together with my reaction to stereotypical images of Turks, the guests had seen material they had not seen before. One gentleman spoke the words quoted at the beginning of this segment. The following morning the same gentleman phoned the Turgut home to thank us for an illuminating presentation, and appreciation on behalf of the Turkish Ambassador! Mr. Murat Sungar was one of the guests from the night before, and he was the Consular to the Turkish Ambassador to Washington, his Excellency Şükrü Elekdağ. That my dossier, my voluminous material, and my work could be valuable to Turkey became mentioned for the first time, by an official during an informal gathering.

9. On November of 1983, the incumbent Consul General of Turkey, the Hon. Aydin Tosun and his wife honored us by visiting our home. Because Armenian terrorism had by this date taken the lives of over seventy five innocent human beings, safety measures where followed even at the home of a friend of the Turks. For our dinner invitation we had also invited our mutual friends, Dr. Ata and Mrs. Erim, Mr. Orhan and Mrs. Gürsel, and Mr. Doğan and Mrs. Ak. Security personnel (there were three), entered our home first. The gentlemen had known us from our many visits to the Turkish Center, and were also aware that they were in the house of a *friend of the Turks*. Hence all they requested was to see if there was another entrance to our home. I showed them a second door which led to the side of the house, accessible from our kitchen. They remained in the kitchen where we fed them, watched television, and relaxed during the entire visit. In our finished basement, our guests were entertained by music, a fine dinner, and a review of my dossier which I had displayed on long tables. Once again amazements, appreciation, and praise, were expressed by our guests with one word which we heard for the first time: *"Sergi* (exhibition)."

The event ended with photographs, expressions of affection and gratitude from all parties present. The Consul General was deeply impressed by what he saw.

10. On August 4, 1984, I had prepared, for the first time, an extensive display of my dossier for presentation to several members of the Federation of Turkish American Associations, Inc.

Our basement had become an exhibition hall with six long tables filled with documents, journals, books, published articles, priceless 78" records, and many other examples of my work. In attendance were: Mr. Erol Gűrűn, the President of the Federation; Mr. Ergűn Kirlikovali, Mr. Iskender Necef, and their wives. After hours of review, the consensus was unanimous: the material was of extreme value, and since I had previously stated that I was willing to donate ninety percent of my material to the Turkish people, they agreed to create the first

Turkish Library in New York City, and our name was to be given to the library. I certainly revolted against such a proposal and thanked them for the honor. "Majority rules," I was told and my precious items which I had preserved for many years, were about to be given away! Large empty boxes were slowly filled with my most cherished possessions to be taken that evening to the Turkish Center in New York City.

I was at the same time very happy and proud, but also heartbroken that my precious material had been removed from my home. Slowly the tables were emptied and the story of that evening was printed in the August 22nd 1984 issue of the Turkish daily *Hűrriyet* newspaper. The lengthy article had urged the community to offer their books and other material to the forthcoming Library, which could be of immense value to the Turkish-American community as well as to Americans who lacked any knowledge of Turkish history and culture.

11. My efforts within the Anadolu Club continued uninterrupted and our efforts on behalf of the Turkish people manifested themselves in many forms; one of them had to be my extensive work in planning the meeting between representatives of the Federation of Turkish-American Associations, and the highly respected clergyman of the Antiochian-Orthodox Church, the very Reverend Paul Schneirla. A few sentences could not describe the time, the phone calls, the effort, and the financial cost, which my wife Mary and I had utilized in bringing together the representatives of different religious and ethnic backgrounds. All activities within the Turkish- American community was well known by Rev. Schneirla (to whom everyone referred to as Father Paul), because he was the priest of the church of which my sister-in-law Marie, and her family were parishioners. The church follows the Greek-Orthodox faith but its congregation is predominantly of Arabic speaking Syrian and Lebanese background. Since he had agreed to my proposal, I had contacted the Federation's President and after all the arrangements had been finalized, on Sunday November 24, 1985, in our home a historic meeting took place between Father Paul, his wife, and the following: the President of the Federation Dr. Ata Erim, Board members Mr. Erol Gürün, and Mr Ahmet Sandikçioğlu, their respective wives, my brother Terrence, his wife Marie, with Mary and I attempting to be the perfect hosts. Introductions, cordial and fruitful conversations, a delectable dinner, followed by a prepared statement by the host, after which we presented a plaque to each colleague as a remembrance of the harmonious meeting.

The following was the inscription on the plaque as composed by the author, "Sunday, November 24th, 1985; on this historic day men and women of good will gathered together and while extending their hands in friendship, broke bread and exerted their energies in building a temple of brotherly love."

The Federation then presented to Father Paul an inscribed book of the life of Mustafa Kemal Ataturk, the founder of the Turkish Republic from the ruins of the Ottoman Empire.

To say our efforts had resulted in a most successful meeting, beneficial and constructive for all parties concerned, would be an understatement. To endeavor to achieve brotherly harmony… who other than the Armenians would condemn my humble efforts? A hand extended in friendship is welcomed by another hand in the mutual search for understanding and harmony among peoples; I must repeat, who other than the Armenians would condemn my humble efforts?

The next phase of my lifelong labors on behalf of the nation which to this day, is despised by my Armenian co-religionists was and had to take place. More and more I had been approached by the Federation for me to join in their organization (without salary of course). President Dr. Erim, Mr. Kirlikovali, and others had urged me to work within this umbrella organization, and as the complimentary statements were gratifying to hear, it was fierce in their revelation that what I had to offer was needed by a community which would greatly benefit by our knowledge, experiences, and passion, which affected me deeply. It was impossible to decline, but I could not devote my time and energies to the Anadolu Club and the Federation at the same time. Our friends in the Anadolu Club, cognizant of that my efforts would be far more effective within the realm of the Federation, reluctantly released me from my pledge to them and supported my move to the Federation. President Dr. Ata Erim assigned me a title; I never had a title before, but in 1985, I became the Director of Public Affairs for the Federation of Turkish-American Associations, Inc. The organization's stationery had been printed, but the Public Affairs Director was overlooked.

Be that as it may, it certainly did not hinder my work or my enthusiasm in expressing the Turkish point of view on a multitude of topics. During my introduction to the many organizations affiliated with the Federation, I soon learned ours' was a reciprocal introduction. However, no one made me feel unwelcome, neither was there a hint of a suspicion of my motives, but many people were becoming aware of the fact that in their midst was an American of Armenian ancestry. I'm further certain that several, if not many, persons must have questioned Dr. Erim's reasons for his unusual decision. Dr. Erim's selection had been based upon his awareness of my years of work and my writings, and as an insightful person, he was certain of the honesty and sincerity of *this* Armenian. I'm pleased to say now after 19 years he has no regrets.

12. The first incident of noticeable discomfort, or uncertainty (a polite word for doubt), by several Turkish people took place on October 19, 1987, when Dr. Ata Erim and his wife Aynur drove Mary and me from their home in Islin, New Jersey, to the home of their friend Mr. Hakimoğlu, residing in the state of Pennsylvania. There was to be an election fund-raising campaign for Congressman Peter H. Kostmeyer of the State of Pennsylvania, who was running for reelection. Numerous Turkish-American friends had been invited to Mr. and Mrs. Hakimoğlu's home in Pennsylvania, where the gatherers would participate with their financial support. I had not questioned Dr. Erim as to why he wanted us to be there, especially since we would not contribute to the campaign. We were welcomed at the Hakimoğlu home, where about thirty people were shaking hands and speaking with candidate Kostmeyer. We greeted our host and since we knew no one, Mary and I found ourselves in a distant corner sipping our drinks. (Years later we learned that several people had criticized Dr. Erim for bringing his Armenian friends to that gathering.)

The time arrived when the Congressman was about to address his Turkish-American supporters. Typical of all politicians, Congressman Kostmeyer spoke the words which his audience wanted to hear. We were standing in the rear of the room with everyone's back to us. Then, the learned Congressman, in all his eloquence, made the following statement: "Friends, Armenian terrorism has taken the lives of so many innocent Turkish diplomats, and the United States condemns these acts. But let me tell you this: the United States has finally accepted and apologized to Japanese Americans for the injustice inflicted upon them during the Second World War. I believe if Turkey did the same and apologized to the Armenians for the genocide, this would bring an end to Armenian vengeance against the Turks."

At the conclusion of Kostmeyer's *brilliant* discourse, the Federation's President Dr. Erim, who had been standing next to the Hon. Recipient of Turkish financial support, spoke the following: "Congressman, if Turkey should apologize, it would then mean that indeed there was a reason for the apology. But we have a friend here who would like to respond to you, sir."

Kostmeyer's smile was still visible, while I controlled myself as I listened to his nonsensical statement. Dr. Erim gestured in my direction and those in front of us began to move to either side as I took a few steps forward. Dr. Erim, his face glowing with a proud smile, was the only person who knew just what was about to happen. In a calm and clear voice, while looking directly at the Congressman, our *Friend of Turks* declared the following: "Congressman Kostmeyer, to equate the Japanese situation in our country, to the plight of the Armenians of Ottoman Turkey, is totally inaccurate. If the Japanese-Americans had waged a twenty five year-long revolution in the United States, if the Japanese-Americans had killed thousands of American civilians and military personnel, and if these Japanese-Americans had threatened the sovereignty of the United States of America, then I doubt very much if our government would apologize to the Japanese community."

Then a bolt of electricity struck everyone in the room when the Congressman was also told: "Sir, I am born of an Armenian mother who had been an eyewitness to the terrible events during the war in Ottoman Turkey, and her words to me were: the Armenians did NOT suffer a genocide!"

The smile on Kostmeyer's face vanished and he appeared in dire need of oxygen. For a few moments there was a silence, then several people applauded, and those standing close to the Congressman began to move in our direction and revealed their amazement and expressions of appreciation.

When heads turned to the distinguished Congressman for his response, this is what they heard: "There is no question that Turkey is a valuable ally to the United States." *He was unable to respond to my statements.*

We no longer stood in the corner of the room, but were surrounded by many people, some with tears in their eyes (these emotional Turks!). An unknown gentleman came close to me and said, "May I ask you a question?"

I responded in Turkish, *"Tabii kardeşim* (of course my brother)."

His next question was, "May I kiss you?"

We embraced in Turkish fashion and kissed each other on the cheek. It was an event which I will remember all my life.

Dr. Ata Erim had touched the hearts of each person in the room, and his former critics were now asking him: "Where did you find this Edward?"

13. At this point it is necessary to remind the reader that only an infinitesimal number of events, meetings, and endeavors, are recorded in these pages.

As an example of the wide range of the events which revealed the immeasurable love for all things Turkish by the author, we would like to take you to November 1, 1987, when that evening a concert was given by Turkey's most beautiful and popular female vocalist in New York City. Ms. Emel Sayin, accompanied by her orchestra, warmed the hearts of over 500 people in the audience. As is the custom in Turkey, the performers while on stage, were given flowers (usually a single flower) by members of the audience as an expression of their love. That night there was one person who did something never done to honor a famous and beloved performer. Ms. Emel Sayin had sung several songs and while she enthralled her cheering audience with her vocal talents, her beauty, and her professional demeanor, and after many flowers had been given to her during her performance, one gentleman approached the stage from the front row of seats. When the star finally noticed her admirer, she saw he had extended to her an expression of his admiration: a small Turkish flag. She was noticeably filled with emotion, as she made her way to receive this unique expression of affection. With a warm smile on her beautiful face, she took the flag, kissed it and brought it to her forehead as a gesture of respect. It was another electrifying moment, as thunderous applause reacted to the emotional scene. Once again destiny played a part in my desire to express my love for Turkey, because even in the darkness of the audience, a Turkish newspaper reporter had to have seen the flag in my hand, so that he placed himself in a position where his camera would capture on film the beloved of millions, extending her hand to receive the small Turkish flag offered by this *friend of Turks.* The photograph, which had been published, became yet another one of our cherished moments.

14. On November 14th, 1987, my first formal public exhibition took place. As one of the Organization members of the Federation, the Turkish-American Youth Association had requested the author to present an exhibition of his material, and offer a lecture on the subject of Turkish-Armenian history. We of course obliged our young people and on the date just stated, Mary and I carried a large portion of my compilation of factual information to the Turkish Center in New York City, arranged the tables with documentation, books, published material, much of which from Armenian sources. The audience of close to two hundred people got the chance to review such viable material for the first-time, and learned a great deal of their own history, from the Ottoman period to the present times. All our efforts were well received, as expressions of appreciation touched us deeply.

15. On June 2, 1988, during a reception for the Prime Minister, His Excellency Turgut Özal, we were introduced to him and his wife for the second time (the first time had been in 1985). Our exchange was cordial and expressions of respect and affection were reciprocal.

At a dinner reception given in honor of President Kenan Evren, in New York City, we were introduced to his Excellency and he appeared pleased and interested with my brief introduction to our unique story. Of all the officials we have met, all have shared a common reaction: deep appreciation of our "Friend of Turks," and amazement. The date was July 1, 1988.

16. August of 1988 found the Tashjis on the Turkish Airlines plane en-route to Istanbul, Turkey, for our third joyous reunion with our multiple families and our beautiful *Anavatan*, Motherland. As during previous historic visits to Turkey, *kardeşim* (my brother) Dr. Oktay Cumhur Akkent, worked tirelessly in spite of his busy schedule, to arrange the following events which created widespread recognition of this humble American:

a. A press conference was held at the press and media buildings in Istanbul, where we could be prepared to answer (in Turkish) the many questions by which millions of Turks would become aware of the dedication and hard work of a unique Friend of Turks. I had known that Dr. Ata Erim was in Istanbul with his family, and as President of the Federation of Turkish-American Associations, I considered it appropriate to inform him of the press conference and to ask him to participate. He attended the conference and with about thirty members of the media present, Dr. Akkent and his second wife Özden, my wife Mary, and the renowned author Mr. Nejat Muallimoğlu (whom we had known in our Federation), also in attendance, I prepared several tables filled with my documents.

Dr. Erim spoke first presenting information about our Federation, and concluded with an extremely complementary introduction of his protégé and colleague. My verbal dissertation was very effective, as my ever increasing ad lib speeches were becoming less stressful and more successful.

The conference was covered in the Press.

b. An audience was arranged with the Governor of Istanbul, and Dr. Erim and I were welcomed by the Hon. Governor Cahit Bayar in his office in Istanbul. Again media coverage recorded our cordial and fruitful meeting.

c. A popular television interview program called *"Içimizden Biri"*, (Someone Within Us) wanted to interview, this time an American – *me,* with an incredible story to the nation. When the proposal was first made I felt more honored than skeptical. I felt this historic opportunity should not be wasted, and I should abstain from being worried about my ability to respond to questions in Turkish while millions would be watching. I was introduced to Mr. Mete Akyol, who interviewed me for a rare introductory conversation, and before I knew it … I was seated in the makeup-room with a young lady preparing my face for the television cameras.

Then it happened, the unnerving thought entered my mind: "What have I done? Me? Edward? Televisions, questions in Turkish, millions watching! I face public humiliation!" It was one thing singing a song as a teenager on stage, but this was to be a challenge of monumental proportions; my legitimacy and effectiveness could be permanently damaged. The questions were rehearsed; our first conversation presented some of my material, and the interview was to be taped rather then broadcast live. The finished product, however, did not have a single interruption during the half-hour interview. On the videotape given me, the continuity of our discourse is conclusively visible. Following the introduction, with each of us seated on opposite sides of the table, Mr. Akyol spent considerable time on how I learned the Turkish language so well, and made it clear that my comprehension left him incredulous. In response to his questions, I revealed the terrible war which caused my parents to immigrate to the United States; the influence of Turkish culture in our home; how I learned to speak Turkish and Armenian; my lifelong work in refuting the accusations against Turkey; my love for Turkish music; and so much more were described in a calm and persuasive manner.

Again my destiny played a role in this historic effort: totally unexpected, Mr Akyol referred to my love for Turkish music and asked if I could sing one of my mother's favorite songs. I was startled and certainly not anticipating such a request. But love is an insurmountable force and my desire to reveal my love for Turkey overcame my shyness about performing spontaneously and without music. Needing a moment to collect my bearing, I then began to sing an old love song, giving it my best effort. My host was very complimentary and went further by asking me to read a poem I had written (yes, in Turkish). As I read the verses which described my love for my ancestral homeland, the television camera focused on Mr. Akyol: it was apparent he had become emotional.

At its conclusion, Mr. Akyol began to applaud too, and said: "Mr Tashji, in the name of the people of this country, I congratulate and thank you for all your efforts on our behalf. You have given us a lifetime of service, all I could give you was half an hour; we honor you, sir. "

At this point I stood up, as he did, shook his hand and expressed my deep appreciation and repeated the inspiring words of the founder of the Turkish Republic, the immortal Mustafa Kemal Ataturk: *"Ne mutlu Tűrkűm diyene!* (Happy is he who calls himself a Turk.)" We embraced and kissed in Turkish fashion.

The television interview was a complete success, as revealed by Mr. Akyol, the executives, and the production staff. The effect upon the television audience when the interview was broadcast was overwhelmingly favorable, as stated to us by several sources. And another effort on behalf of love.

d. A short while later Dr. Erim informed me that he had been granted an audience with President Kenan Evren at his summer residence in Istanbul, and asked me if we would like to accompany him. We of course agreed, realizing we might not be able to meet with His Excellency, since the invitation was for Dr. Erim alone. As Mary and I were seated in the waiting room, Dr. Erim was escorted into the President's office. To be so close to the President and not to be able to meet with him again would be of major disappointment. But my destiny was not to be denied. Later we were told that during their conversation, the President learned of Dr. Erim's guests who were seated outside. "Why didn't you bring your guests in here?" asked the President.

"Your Excellency, the invitation was for one person only," responded Dr. Erim.

The President asked his aide to bring us into his office. (Turkish hospitality remains incomparable.)

When the aide told us the President would receive us, excitement raced through my body.

The office door opened, we stepped inside and observed the President and Dr. Erim standing nearby. As we entered, an expression of uncertainty appeared on the President's face, and he exclaimed, "But I know this man! When did I meet him?" He turned to Dr. Erim as if searching for that answer.

As we shook hands, Dr. Erim reminded the President it had been during a meeting at a New York hotel on July 1st, 1988. The President, with his warm and cordial demeanor, gave us one hour of his time and we had a lengthy and fruitful dialogue. We expressed our profound appreciation to the President for giving us so much of his time, and I assured him that my work, by the grace of God, would continue for years to come. But at the time the promise was made, I could not have conceived my future efforts would include an autobiography.

During our drive back, Dr. Erim commented that the brief meeting at a crowded hotel several weeks earlier, must have affected the

President so much that he recognized me today. I could only hope his comment was correct.

e. In September of 1988, we had a fruitful meeting with the then Foreign Minister the Honorable Mesut Yilmaz; he eventually became Prime Minister.

***

IX. Brief description of some of our activities, projects, meetings.

A. 1989: On June 2nd, New York Congressman Stephen Solarz had invited about twenty-four members of the Turkish-American community to be his guests in Washington D.C. Dr. Erim requested us to join him and his wife Aynur, in this historic event; my wife Mary and I were pleased to accept. The Congressman and his staff escorted our group on an extensive tour of the Capitol building including the Senate chamber and the House of Representatives. Later we were taken to the Congressman's home in Virginia to meet his family and to have a buffet luncheon. Our hosts were most cordial and eager to listen to the problems facing our community.

Dr. Erim introduced us to the Congressman and he remembered meeting us at a fund-raising reception at the Erim home in the State of New Jersey, several months earlier. As we conversed, I presented a brief commentary on the Turkish-Armenian issue, and as a group had encircled us, our host Congressman Solarz stated: "Edward, you are very knowledgeable on this subject about which the Congress knows very little. Would you be willing to address our subcommittee which is considering the Armenian resolution?"

This was the response of our *Friend of Turks,* "Congressman, would tomorrow at 9:00 a.m. be convenient for you, sir?"

This was followed by an uproarious laughter by all who had heard my polite "Challenge."

But as expected, the invitation for me to address the Subcommittee never arrived.

B. In June, author Nejat Muallimoğlu visited our home in Bayside, Queens, for the first time. He is not only an esteemed scholar of Turkish literature, he remains one of our most honored friends who for years has followed our humble efforts on behalf of the Turkish people. Years before he had startled us with the following comment, "Edward, Turkey should erect a statue in your honor in the center of Istanbul!" From such a distinguished gentleman, this is an expression of love which can never be forgotten. When he visited our home, he referred to it as an example of an Ottoman museum, a comment we have heard from many people.

C. During 1989 the ubiquitous Armenian Resolution once again came before the Congress of the United States. Armenian "Hate Merchants" continued their relentless pressures upon American politicians to pass a resolution which would have the government of the United States recognize the so-called "Armenian Genocide," an allegation totally void of all historical accuracy.

The Federation under the leadership of Dr. Erim asked me if I would prepare a sworn statement, in writing, expressing briefly my perspective as related to the Armenian allegations. My statement was to be published in booklet form and would be sent to each member of the United States Senate and House of Representatives. Of course I agreed, preparing my thoughts on paper without any form of coercion or pressure; also, in the office of an attorney and a notary, I took an oath to the veracity of my testimony. The booklet was titled: "Armenian Allegations: Fact vs. Fiction," and a copy was indeed sent to each member of the Congress. That year the resolution was defeated, but next year and a year after that, ceaselessly there will always be another Armenian Resolution accusing Turkey of "Genocide."

D. 1990, January 30th: An extraordinary meeting took place at the Plaza Hotel in New York City. Present were the following: His Excellency President Turgut Özal; his Excellency Nűzhet Kandemir, Turkey's Ambassador to Washington; the Hon. Volkan Bozkir, Consul General to New York; Dr. Erim, President of the Federation, and three Federation Directors, Mr. Erol Gurun, Mr. Erhan Atay, and Edward Tashji. During the fruitful and lengthy discussion Dr. Erim presented a copy of my sworn statement to the President. As everyone observed him in silence, the President read the entire booklet. He was deeply moved and expressed his appreciation to me.

E. On May 24th, we had very special guests in our home. Our dear friend Mr. Kemal Seçkin and his wife brought four honorable Turkish Veterans of the Korean War to our home. The gentlemen had arrived from Turkey to participate in our annual Turkish- American Day Parade in New York City. They were profoundly impressed with our work, our hospitality, and our "Ottoman home." They must have learned some facts from Mr. Seçkin, because they honored us by presenting us with a beautiful plaque. It was yet one more cherished moment for us.

F. September 1st, a historical meeting took place with the Mayor of New York City, the Hon. David Dinkins. He welcomed the following at his office in City Hall: President Dr. Ata Erim, Vice-President Mr. Mehmet Hasan, and Edward Tashji. A Turkish newspaper covered the cordial meeting with a story and a picture on its front page.

G. September 28th, Bishop Vsevolod, of the Ukrainian-Orthodox Church and his aide, had been invited as guests of our Federation, to the annual formal dinner at the Hilton Hotel in New York City, observing the celebration of the establishment of the Republic of Turkey. I had paid close attention to His Grace as a respected religious leader, and have maintained close contact with him to this day. The four hundred guests greeted His Grace Bishop Vsevolod, with a resounding applause as he was introduced, and at the conclusion of his magnificent speech touching on the friendship between the peoples of Ukraine and Turkey.

H. During November of this year, I had received from the Ellis Island Foundation, a Certificate of Honor for each of my parents, whose names and country of birth I had engraved on the great immigrant Wall of Honor at the historical site.

I. 1991: On February 16th, a conference was held at the Yale University and the topic of discussion was to be the definition of the term "Genocide: the Theory, the Reality." Being an institution of higher learning and dedicated to knowledge and the principles of human rights, the University Law School informed the Turkish Consul General the Hon. Volkan Bozkir, by mail, of their event and requested the participation of the Turkish community.

The Federation was informed and a group of about twenty attended the conference, with Professor Drew S. Days, moderating the event. Several speakers seated at a curved table were facing about 200 people in the auditorium. Among other topics, Nazi Germany, Cambodia, and of course Turkey were discussed. The latter was the topic of Prof. Richard Hovannissian, who had no difficulty reiterating the standard rhetoric of falsifying the Ottoman history. Of course in this citadel of higher learning, it did not occur to the brilliant scholars that it might be appropriate to have a Turkish historian to present the truth of the events of Ottoman Turkey, or Cyprus, Azerbaijan, East Turkistan, among other topics.

At the conclusion of the "scholarly" Turk-bashing, questions were invited from the audience. The Turkish point of view was effectively presented by our group, but Professor Hovannissian became obviously flustered when one individual stood up, identified himself as an ethnic Armenian, and proceeded to refute Hovannissian's allegations. A copy of our "Fact vs. Fiction" booklet was distributed with other material. Once again the blatant prejudices against the Turkish people became exposed, but one would think in a prestigious law school historical accuracy would have prevailed over blind hatred.

J. February 28th - March 3rd, a similar outrage took place at a unique symposium held at Tufts University, in the State of Massachusetts. There is a Briefing Book based upon the many lectures during the symposium, and because of my destiny, this valuable publication came into my possession. My wife's nephew, Mr. Denny Boyd, residing in Massachusetts, had been given the book by a non-Armenian friend. Aware of my position pertaining to all matters of Turkish concern, Denny asked if I would like to have the book, to which I emphatically responded in the affirmative. The book turned out to be precisely what I had expected it to be: another anti-Turkish publication. Isn't it comforting to have irrefutable evidence in your hands? As the Briefing Book reveals, the four-day scholarly symposium on the human rights violations around the world, included seventy five scholars, politicians, and media writers, referring to the topics of their expertise. Just as I had assumed, Turk-bashing was once again on the "Menu." There were a total of **15** pages of anti-Turkish presentations; a pitifully short ***4 lines*** on the persecution of ethnic Turks in Bulgaria, **1** (yes, you've read it correctly, a single one) page on the genocide of the American-Indian; NO mention of the slaughter of **2 million** Crimean Turks by the Russians, nor in East Turkistan, Cyprus, Azerbaijan, the Turks and Kurds at the hands of the Kurdish PKK, and other acts of barbarism around the world.

As the Briefing Book came into my possession months after the "scholarly" presentations, my four-page letter of protest submitted to the education director Mr. Sherman Teichman, at Tufts University, was dated December 10, 1991. No response was ever received to my letter which wanted to know why, out of **seventy five** spokespersons, NOT ONE Turkish historian was invited to the symposium.

An interesting news item appeared in the *Armenian Weekly,* dated January 4, 1992, with the heading: "Armenian history course at Tufts University." I mailed the article to the Director of Education, Mr. Teichman, together with my note commenting that his silence only confirmed my position, that the symposium was merely a subterfuge to conceal a specious agenda of Tufts University. My initial letter to Tufts had been published in full, in the January 15, 1992 issue of *The Turkish Times.*

K. May 27, at the Hilton Hotel in New York City, the Federation had sponsored the symposium presented by the World Turkish Youth Congress. Numerous speakers on separate panels discussed many topics of concern to the Turkish-American community, including education, unity, and our priorities in creating stronger bonds of friendship between the United States and the Republic of Turkey.

On the first panel one of the speakers was the Sr. V.P of Hill and Knowlton Public Affairs Worldwide Corporation. His speech was titled: "The Turkish-American community and the American legislative process."

I have found it necessary to comment here on this statement made by the vice-president of a major public-relations firm in the United States, because at the time I had to restrain myself from taking strong exception to a statement he had made. It is gratifying to know his firm no longer represents Turkey's interests in the United States. But as an instructive and constructive comment on my part for our Turkish Youth, I find myself obliged to reveal to our young people and their parents as well, that: You better know what you are talking about!

After I conclude my brief comments, I will offer the speech I had delivered during the second panel of the same program. It will be my second of three speeches recorded in my autobiography.

Mr. Hymel was introduced and as he brought the microphone closer, he proceeded to enlighten his Turkish audience with his *wisdom.* At one point he decided to turn away from his prepared statement, this proved to be a severe mistake. Spontaneously he related to his audience a brief exchange he once had with the Honorable Tip O'Neill, the former Speaker of the House of Representatives. The Speaker, according to Mr. Hymel, had inquired, "I don't know any Turks in this country, but they must be very few, how is it that they didn't immigrate in large numbers to the United States like many other people?"

Mr. Hymel recalled he had thought for awhile and then he answered the Speaker's question in this manner: "The Turks didn't come here in large numbers because the Turks did not experience persecution! *(Exclamation mark belongs to the author).*"

His words provoked my ire. How could he not be cognizant of his words? Even if I had revealed my outrage to him personally, it could not remedy the situation; but for years after, whenever the opportunity presented itself, I have offered the following statement as the only appropriate response to the speaker in question: "The Turks did not come to the United States in large numbers because they chose to remain in their devastated homeland, and began to build a new nation. With blood, sweat and tears, the Turks rolled up their sleeves and placed brick upon brick, to construct, to build a dynamic, secular republic under the leadership of the immortal Mustafa Kemal Ataturk."

THIS is what Mr. Gary Hymel should have said. Before I bring here the lines reserved for the next chapter, allow me to repeat my speech delivered on May 27, 1991:

"The Honorable Consul General Volkan Bozkir
Honorable Guests
Distinguished Ladies and Gentlemen:
At the very outset I wish to extend my deepest appreciation for this honor, in extending to me the opportunity and privilege of addressing this august assembly of distinguished ladies and gentleman. Were it within the realm of my humble efforts, I would have each of you on the edge of your seats in eager anticipation of the eloquent presentation of

this speaker. Alas, this is not to be; for this speaker is renowned neither for his oratory nor for his literary excellence. We shall however, strive to bring to your attention a very brief introduction to a living story the likes of which Turkish youth have never heard before. A lifelong effort on behalf of the Turkish people, my historic and ancestral brothers and sisters, cannot be told in the space of a few minutes. But as I address myself to the future of the Turkish people, the young Turkish-Americans, read between the lines if you can, and fill your hearts with the love and the pride which I have felt throughout my life … because my roots began in, and came from, the great land known as the Republic of Turkey!

The youth of every nation is the future and the aspiration of its people. The continuation with honor and pride, the language, the faith, the culture and history, of every ethnic group is the most significant priority of every civilized society worldwide. But you, my beloved Turkish brothers and sisters, are faced with challenges and obstacles unknown to other ethnic groups in the United States. To reverse the tide of anti-Turkish sentiment primarily in the American News Media is your greatest challenge. Each of you must be the ambassador of the Turkish people and its true history. Each of you must be the teacher of the humanity and compassion of the Turkish heart. Your task will be faced with much difficulty and frustration; you will be criticized and ridiculed; your voice will be a minority among the minorities. Because the history, the art, the culture, and civilization of the Turkish people continue to be an unknown to most Americans, it is *you* who will reveal the greatness of the Turkish Nation. There is no obstacle which you cannot overcome, just look at your own history: *You* are the children of the millions who shed their blood for the creation and sovereignty of the Turkish Republic. *You* are the proud sons and daughters of the immortal Mustafa Kemal Ataturk, and no power on earth will hinder your dedication and eventual success.

In the near future the American Congress will once again consider the passage of an infamous resolution which would, if passed, blame the Ottoman Government of "Genocide." As the devoted son of Armenian and Syrian-Orthodox parents, I do not require the so-called scholarship of Toynbee, of Gladstone, of Morgenthau, or of anyone else, to learn the history of my people. As eyewitness to the tragic events of 1915, our parents taught us that *all* the peoples of the land had suffered the ravages of war. Many other factors which history has not recorded have been instilled in my heart and mind by those who suffered and had no reason to distort the events of that period. To accept the accusation of "Genocide" against the Armenians by the Turks, is to believe in a total falsehood, and an absolute myth.

Ladies and Gentlemen, with your kind indulgence, I shall conclude my comments in my faltering Turkish, and on behalf of my wife and myself, extend to you my deep appreciation for your attention. May God's love fill your hearts forever."

As stated above, the remainder of my speech was presented in Turkish.

L. 1991 continues: June 25th was a historic day of monumental significance. Our years of working, maintaining our bonds of friendship with numerous chapters of American Veterans of the Korean Memorial Commission, has been and continues to be, among my priority endeavors. The Turkish-American community was greatly honored by being invited to participate in the Unveiling and Dedication ceremony, of the New York Korean War Veterans Memorial, which was to be preceded by a parade down the "Canyon of Heroes" on Broadway in New York City. We were few in numbers; about 15 people from our Federation, but the effect our group with Turkish and American flags, created upon hundreds of thousands of Americans, was literally an explosion of emotion. In front of our marching group was the banner of our Federation, behind it was a large American flag and a large Turkish flag, of equal size, held by the author. On either side of me were three dear friends, honored gentlemen, who had actually served with the Turkish Military Forces in the Korean War. It is with profound respect that I bring recognition to my three brothers: Mr. KEMAL SEÇKIN, MR. SÜLEYMAN KANA, and Mr. DOĞAN AK.

If there was one person in our group who did not shed some tears, I am not aware of it. Thousands upon many thousands of Americans, when seeing the Turkish flag, began cheering and shouting: *God bless Turkey! The Turks saved American lives! Long live Turkey!*

It was an electrifying moment. Yes, we brought love and respect to Turkey and the Turkish people. Our joy was supreme.

M. On July 25th, of this year, a lengthy article appeared in the *Bayside Times,* a community newspaper. The topic of the article was "Animal rights," yes, *animal rights.* My next sentence will respond to the obvious question in the reader's mind: What conceivable correlation could there possibly be between animal rights and my defense of the Turkish people?

Let me begin by first revealing the name of the animal lover which will tell you all you need to know: the letter is written by Mr. Garo Alexanian. If that does not reveal to you the obvious, then I will assist you further – after all, this is the purpose of my book; to inform you of facts which for some mysterious reason remain unknown to most Americans.

The article written by Mr. Alexanian, on the date and in the newspaper revealed above, begins as follows, "An Armenian born in Turkey who witnessed the persecution of his people abroad, Bayside resident Garo Alexanian, was not about to tolerate the victimization of animals in America..."

The remainder of the article refers to the writer's opinions on the subject of his composition: *animal rights.* This is an example of the Armenian psyche and the Armenian obsession with hatred, an evidence of the inherent structure of the Armenian character. An article on animal rights spewed hatred for the Turks, an anomaly which only the convoluted mentality can comprehend. But the example I have just presented for your consideration, has not yet convinced you, right? Before my final thoughts to the reader find their place toward the conclusion of this autobiography, the reader will be informed of many examples of the Armenian insatiable appetite for hatred. My intention has not been to convince anyone to accept my expressed position, but as the immeasurable facts are presented by the author, I do request what knowledge demands, namely, your unbiased consideration of the information presented in this work. One CONCLUDING item of this section remains: much of the facts which I have yet to present here, whether you are an Armenian, Turk, or neither, will be offered from no less than Armenian sources.

N. August 29th, brought the Turkish response to the article referred to above. On this date in the *Bayside Times,* the response to the article expressed an "emphatic protest," the correspondence which had been printed in its entirety, was written by a *friend of Turks.*

O. On October 28th, I received a letter from our most honored friend, His Grace Bishop Vsevolod, of the Ukrainian-Orthodox Church. His correspondence was one of many which I have kept in my files for years, but in this letter one sentence touched me so deeply that I considered it a distinct honor by repeating here: "You are truly to be congratulated on behalf of all people for your good work in promoting the harmonious co-existence of the brotherhood of Mankind." To receive these words from a true Servant of God has left me humbly grateful and joyous beyond my ability to express. Just recently I have learned that the Bishop has been elevated to Archbishop of his church and on behalf of the Federation, I extend our congratulations and prayerful best wishes to His Eminence Archbishop Vsevolod by mail.

P. 1992: This had been a busy year and therefore brevity is required.

January 3rd, as a result of our efforts with Archbishop Vsevolod and the Ukrainian community, when the Vice-president of the Crimean parliament, his Excellency Refat Çubaroğlu was visiting the United States, I had approached the Archbishop for a possible contact between his community and the Turkish-Crimean officials. As a man of peace, he arranged a personal interview with the Editor of the Ukrainian newspaper, the *Svoboda.* The Editor interviewed the V.P., who revealed the plight of hundreds of thousands of Turkish-Tatar-Crimeans, who continue to suffer as a result of Russian massacres of innocent civilians and the expulsion of the people from their ancestral homelands. The author was also interviewed giving information of the Federation of Turkish-American Associations, and our community endeavors.

Q. February 14th during a dinner reception given in honor of the Turkish Prime Minister, His Excellency Süleyman Demirel, I brought together and introduced two distinguished religious leaders: the ranking Imam of the Turkish Muslim community, and His Grace Bishop Vsevolod (at that time he was a Bishop). Photos were taken during their historic brotherly dialogue.

The Imam's name: Burhan Satar.

R. On March 3rd, at the United Nations, nine former republics of the

Soviet Union had gained their independence from Communist persecution, and in front of the United Nations building a flag raising ceremony took place.

Several Turkic countries, and Armenia, were among the nations whose flags were unfurled to join the other nations represented in the U.N. There where about two hundred Armenians and approximately thirty Turks gathered in separate groups.

At one point, and to this day I know not for what reason, I walked away from our group and entered the area where the Armenians had assembled. While standing in the midst of the "Enemy" and not speaking to anyone, an elderly "Gentleman" came close to me and said: "Are you the (expletive) Edward Tashji?"

He spoke in Turkish and loud enough for many people to hear. At first I assumed that the gentleman was Turkish and was merely joking with me, but I was proven wrong when this angry individual shouted at me in Turkish: "Why are you standing over there?" Pointing to where the Turks were standing, he continued, "You belong here with your own people!"

I felt the crowd around us very close to me, emotionally, as I replied in Turkish, "You asked me a question, let me respond! It is because our peoples have lived together as brothers for six centuries, that's why I stand with them!"

Someone began to pull me out of what could have been a terrible confrontation. The Turks never left my side and as a result they were able to pull me out and return me to civilization. No other incident occurred, but after the murder of so many innocent Turkish diplomats and other civilians, I could have been yet another target for assassination.

S. May 9. At the conference room at Harvard University, the Turkish-American Cultural Society of New England, had sponsored and arranged the 10th Anniversary Memorial Service in honor of the Hon. Turkish Consul Mr. Orhan R. Gűndűz, who was murdered by Armenian terrorists in Boston, Massachusetts, in 1982. The Federation was invited and a speech was requested by Edward Tashji.

Among the several speakers were the Honorable Volkan Bozkir, Turkey's Consul General, Dr. Ata Erim, President of the Federation, and the Director of Public Affairs, the author. My speech is presented here as my third and final public address to be included in this autobiography.

A speech delivered by Edward Tashji:
On May 9, 1992, in honor of the memory of the assassinated
Honorary Turkish Consul, Orhan R. Gűndűz
Delivered at: Harvard University.

"Distinguished guests:
Ladies and Gentlemen:

May I at the outset express my profound feelings of appreciation for this opportunity to reveal my comments publicly, as I also extend my deep gratitude for your kind attention.

We have gathered here this day coming from near and far with sad hearts, and with grief for a terrible loss. The young life of the late Hon. Orhan Gűndűz, who had faithfully served as the Honorary Consul in the Boston area, was taken from our midst in 1982, by a sub-human element, in an act of barbarism. No words of condolence could hope to convey the sadness of the Turkish people as one of her sons fell victim to the assassins. As we honor his memory, we also mourn the many other Turkish diplomats and private citizens whose lives were taken by the *hate merchants* who professed to be Christians. My friends, the tribute and the proper accolades which our brother, Orhan Gündüz, so rightfully deserves, will be expressed far more eloquently than by any effort on the part of this speaker. It could be said that this is not the appropriate forum for a political message; I concur. But is it not precisely as a result of political assassination that brings us here today? There is a unique reason for my grief to be filled with anger:

My dear friends, each of us shares the grievous pain of the entire Gűndűz family, yet no one in this room can feel the additional burden that is felt by this speaker.

Mine is a feeling of guilt by association; you see, I am born of Armenian and Syrian-Orthodox parents. It was their philosophy of pure love for all things Turkish coupled with a lifetime commitment to revealing the truth of the events of 1915 in Ottoman Turkey, which makes me ashamed of my co-religionists. I have grown weary of the pernicious and stereotypical attitudes towards the Turkish people which have festered in the minds of so-called intellectuals, politicians, and news editors. Even such an edifice similar to this institution of higher learning, has corrupted their scholarship with an anti-Turkish rhetoric. This manifestation will not deter us just as it did not preclude Orhan Gűndűz in his faithful service to his people. Rest assured dear brothers and sisters, our efforts will continue with our faith in God, our hand extended in friendship, our heart filled with love for all peoples. This was and continues to be the legacy of Mr. Orhan Gűndűz; this has been and will continue to be the legacy of the Turkish people for their beloved children!"

At the conclusion of the above statement, applause and shouts of *Bravo!* filled the room. It was an ovation which I could not have anticipated. Several diplomats and professors approached us with the numerous questions as I wondered silently: *Who is the student and who is the teacher?*

Later our group visited the cemetery where our brother had been laid to rest, and a Muslim prayer was recited by an Imam. We met with Ms.Gűndűz and her children, expressing our condolences.

T. July 31st, brought our Federation to the front door of NBC-TV studios in NYC. It was a peaceful protest against the sports-announcer Mr. Bob Costas. The manifestation of the blatant anti-Turkish posture of the American news media was once again revealed during the opening ceremonies of the Summer Olympic Games in this city of Barcelona, Spain. About 30 people from our Federation carried large posters and distributed printed material informing the public of our grievance against the stars and the management of NBC. Among the many millions of people worldwide, watching their television screens, it was only the Turkish people who became aware of the outrage.

The following is an exact description of what was seen on the television broadcast: The March of Nations revealed the entry of the respective teams of athletes from the participating countries, and as the flag of each nation was seen on the field, the name of the country was introduced over the public address system. During the colorful and exciting introduction of nations, I remember distinctly thinking to myself: *I hope this time there will be no commercial break when the Turkish team is introduced.* To explain: four years earlier, and during a similar procession, when Turkey was about to be introduced, a commercial appeared and Turkey was not shown. But this had happened many times, if a commercial appeared during introduction, the nations would not be seen and at the end of the commercial, the alphabetical sequence would continue. While I viewed the TV screen, now in 1992, I was determined not to be disturbed and if the telephone had rung, I would not have answered it. The nations continued to be introduced, then a commercial came on, and when the commercial ended I heard: "Tunisia!"

I had reason to believe this time there would be no problem.

The Tunisian team was shown and a moment later over the speaker I heard: "Türkiye!" (Turkey). While millions of people were waiting to see the Turkish flag, the television cameras were MOVED AWAY from the Turkish team and focused on the hundreds of athletes who had been assembled and were standing in place in the center of the field! The sports announcers continued to converse on several topics which had nothing to do with the nation that had just been introduced!

This dastardly behavior by a ‘respected’ professional sportscaster was the quintessential act of one consumed with delusions of his superiority. His name is Bob Costas. He has placed his venomous personal agenda before his fidelity to professional journalism. I turned off the TV and proceeded to write a letter of condemnation to NBC-TV News. Letters of protest from across the nation poured in to NBC, whose only response was a form letter sent to Turkish-Americans and our organizations.

Nevertheless, so it was that on this day our Federation proved that the act of moving the television camera away would not deter the Turkish-Americans from taking their proper place among the proud family of nations, by "knocking" on the door of NBC to say: WE ARE HERE, PROUD AND VISIBLE!

Lest the reader should ask: Why? Our response is: Bob Costas is an ethnic Greek who not only disgraced himself, but his people as well. In spite of the Bob Costases of the world, rational people must continue in search of harmonious relations between Greece and Turkey; our respective peoples have much in common.

U. On August 7th, the author had appeared on the radio program "Voice of Islam" which was hosted by his friend Mr. Ghazi Hankhan. I had been introduced to the listeners as an American-Christian, representing the Federation of Turkish-American Associations, who wanted to draw the attention of the Muslim community to an important project with which I had been involved for over five years. My appeal to the listeners was for them to write to the New York City Council and to the Department of Transportation, with the aim of having the suspension of alternate side of the street parking regulations, to include Muslim religious holidays. Several Muslim communities had for years labored to have this law passed, and within the Turkish community since 1987, the tireless efforts in this major project, had been conducted by a Christian "Friend of Turks." In 1992, it finally became law that on the feast of Ramadan and Kurban, both Muslim holidays, in the entire city of New York, for three days each, and the alternate side of the street parking rules would be SUSPENDED! My joy was beyond measure.

V. On October 22nd, the New Jersey State Senate was considering a resolution which would commemorate the 500th anniversary of the Jewish people being welcomed by Ottoman Turkey in 1492, as a result of the infamous Spanish Inquisition. In support of its passage, several representatives of our Federation as well as from the American Association of Jewish Friends of Turkey, made effective statements to the Senate Sub-committee. The author in his comments emphasized the total freedom the Christians had, and continue to enjoy to this day, the practice of their faith while maintaining their respective schools.

The resolution was unanimously adopted.

W. On October 23rd, we met with His Excellency President Rauf Denktaş, the President of the Turkish Republic of Northern Cyprus.

X. After years of effort, on November 6th, we finally had a private meeting with His Eminence Archbishop John Cardinal O'Connor, in his office in New York City. He was extremely warm to the Federation President, Mr. Erhan Atay, the Vice-president Mr. Onur Erim, and the author. His Eminence became emotional when I showed him my original Baltimore catechism which I had used as a student in Saint Francis Xavier Parochial school in New York City of over 50 years earlier. Recently we became heartbroken when Cardinal O'Connor passed away; we shall never forget him.

Y. 1993, on June 30th, the Federation had a private meeting with the

German Consul General in New York City. The Hon. Dr. Eberhard Koelsch and his aide welcomed the following at the German Consulate: President Mr. Mehmet Yar, Vice-president Dr. Şevket Karaduman, and the author whose letter to the Consul General was responsible for this historic meeting.

For several years within numerous German cities, groups of the racist neo-Nazi mutants had been attacking and killing residents from other countries. This psychopathic group had bombed the homes of many ethnic Turkish workers, and many innocent men, women, and children, lost their lives at the hands of these miscreants of Adolf Hitler. With our emphatic condemnations of these barbaric murders, the universal Turkish search for harmony, tolerance, and good will toward all nations, inspired the author to write and request a meeting with the German Consul General in the spirit of friendship which had, and continues to exist between Germany and Turkey. Statements of apology, sorrow and condolences, on the part of Dr. Koelsch could not eliminate the shadows of the few hate-monsters, but be that as it may, at the very least, our cordial and fruitful meeting proved to the world that ours' is a philosophy of peace and trust.

Z. August 21st, was the day when the Korean War Veterans of New Jersey, honored the Turkish-American community for its efforts in maintaining close relations with numerous veterans organizations. At a dinner reception held in New Jersey, several recipients were duly honored by the officers of the Chorwon Chapter, Mr. Joseph Poggy, and Mr. Thomas Jefferies presented us with the Department of the Army Commander's of Award Medal for Civilian Service. In our acceptance statement, I expressed on behalf of the entire Turkish-American community, our humble and most profound gratitude for the honor they had bestowed upon us.

As the reader has surely observed by now, I have used the entire alphabet in presenting what my chapter heading has described as "some" of our efforts. Only after reviewing my files, have I come to realize the full extent of our humble service to the Turkish people. The monumental physical, moral, and time (not to mention financial), support as described in the previous pages HAVE NOT revealed the totality of our years of work. As the following chapter will serve to present my fundamental position on Turkish-Armenian history, I have decided to omit much (but not all) of the remaining events which would further describe this most unique "Friend of Turks."

We shall continue with an "A" again for each entry but will add the numeral "1" to each letter. Of all our efforts, the most effective, the most successful, the most inspiring, and the most physically and emotionally exhausting events are yet to follow. These events became the culmination of my lifelong work.

A-1. October 15th, 1993 brought public recognition by another chapter of American veterans of the Korean War. The Central Long Island Chapter of the Korean War Veterans had invited Mary and the author to a dinner reception given in Long Island, N.Y., where an audience of over 300 guests witnessed this "Friend of Turks" receive a formal certificate of appreciation from the Chapter President Mr. Bob Morga, for our efforts in maintaining harmonious relations between the Turkish-American community and our American Veterans of the Korean War. Other recipients had also been honored, and our statement of deep gratitude on behalf of our community was received with many handshakes and a loud ovation. The certificate and a medal from the Department of the Army, remain on display in my den.

B-1. December 6th found several representatives of the Federation and our Jewish friends at the New Jersey State Senate Education Committee which was considering a resolution submitted by Assembly Speaker Congressman Garabed Haytayan. Because earlier attempts to teach in the New Jersey classrooms the subject of the mythical Armenian genocide had failed, the ubiquitous Armenian Resolution was again sponsored by Haytayan with a different bill number. Together with a change in the content of the bill, which was a subterfuge designed to conceal the personal agenda of Haytayan, other historical genocides had been included. Statements were allowed from concerned parties and during his presentation Haytayan displayed his interpretations of the events in Ottoman Turkey with the usual Armenian diatribe, with its usual gory deception. Numerous speakers from our side including Turkish and Jewish historians, presented factual information refuting the allegations which the senators had just heard. Our last speaker was the author who succeeded in concealing his anger at these politicians who sat in judgment of the Turkish Nation while knowing nothing of Turkish history. The effective statements of an ethnic Armenian who was opposed to the resolution may have made an impact on them, because at this hearing the resolution did not pass. Our comments drew the attention of the television crew as they approached us for a live interview. And thus, it was done!

C-1. 1994. On December 4th of this year, an event took place at the Turkish Center in New York City, which only the participants remember. The news media would not cover any event at the Turkish Center unless it involved a bloody confrontation. But this was an event of religious and ethnic harmony and love; no, it would not interest the media. But because of the date, in the Christmas greetings on behalf of the Federation, to President Clinton and Mayor Giuliani, the alert author referred to the following event as part of his holiday greetings. In their response letters to me a reference to the event was made above the signatures of President Clinton and Mayor Giuliani.

The American Association of Jewish Friends of Turkey had held a Memorial service in tribute to our beloved friend, the late Mr. Louis Levy. Mary and I had been invited to attend and we were honored to participate. President pro-tem Professor David F. Altebè had invited us to sit close to the speaker's table, for a specific reason which was revealed later. Among many of our friends in attendance were: Dr. Albert deVidas, Mr. Zachary J. Levy, Professor Altebè, Mr. Joseph Elias and other ladies and gentlemen who are members of the Sephardic community. In the center of the speakers' table a menorah had been placed as the date coincided with the celebration of the Holy Festival of Hanukkah. The service began with Hebrew prayers and during the assigned moment, each candle was lighted. Mr. Louis Levy had been the beloved founder of the organization and as each candle was touched with a small flame a profound emotion filled the room. After the fifth candle was lit there was a brief pause, and then Professor David Altabè spoke out by inviting me (as a Christian) to light the sixth candle. From the speakers' table I addressed the audience of two hundred people in the following manner: "As Christians, my wife Mary and I accept your kind honor, and in the name of the history shared by our respective peoples in the Turkish homeland, I now light the sixth candle."

One candle remained unlit and the author continued: "In that historic spirit of harmony, with your permission, I should like to invite our sister, and Turkish Muslim, Mrs. Esen Behen, who is here with us, to come forward and light the remaining candle."

I entered the audience and escorted Mrs. Behen to light the final candle. There we stood behind the glowing lights of the menorah, peoples of Jewish, Christian and Moslem faiths, bound by a mutual history and their sharing the desire for brotherhood. An event left unknown to a world that hungers for such a simple gesture of humanity.

D-1. 1996. On June 8th, a *New York Times* news item offered the following headline: "In Central Park." We are told that serious crime has decreased in our city, but the victims of thousands of criminal acts which surely challenge these "statistics." Also, this illustrious newspaper as a rule, does not report about such terrible assaults on innocent people, but this story had an unusual element, for reasons to be revealed, the author has included in this book.

The reader will remember the "Animal rights" story; well, here we have a similar display of the Armenian psyche and the blatant anti-Turkish posture of this newspaper. The name of the young woman, who had been brutalized in Central Park, shall not be mentioned here, but in the newspapers and on the television news reports, her full identity had been revealed. In the lengthy article which described the attack upon the young music teacher, its concluding paragraph revealed the ethnicity of the victim: She was described as an ethnic Armenian, and as if it was very pertinent to the assault upon her, her "passionate" study of the Armenian genocide had been brought to the attention of the public. The young victim had survived the vicious attack upon her, but like so many other Armenians she remains a victim of hate.

E-1. October 2nd brought into my hands an extraordinary letter from Turkey's Ambassador to the United States, his Excellency Nűzhet Kandemir. I am pleased to say we had had many meetings with him and his predecessors going back many years. I am also honored to reveal that the author has copious examples of letters to and from the Turkish Embassy in Washington D.C. But this particular correspondence had included an invitation for me to be his guest at the embassy. Subsequent letters and phone calls had resulted in the following:

On November 4, 1996, I flew to Washington D.C., and at the destination departure area, I spotted several people holding cards with the names of the arriving passengers printed on them. For the first time in my life, I observed one card which read: "Tashji - Taşçı," both in Turkish and English. I could not disregard the gentleman visually scanning the many arrivals. We greeted each other in Turkish, and he did not allow me to carry my suitcase nor my attaché case. I had been informed that before going to the Embassy, I would be taken to a hotel to check in and freshen up. No name shall be mentioned here; the hotel suite was luxurious with all the amenities everywhere. All of this was at the expense of the Embassy, including air travel and the dinners with officials as my host. My departure was to be the following day.

It seems the author has not mentioned his destiny during the many previous pages, but my inexplicable destiny did make an "appearance" once again as I had checked into the hotel. The reception desk in the small but elegant lobby had placed an arrangement of many small flags of the countries whose representatives may have visited the hotel. My attention was drawn to this display of flags, and then my mental question was answered: I could not see the flag of the Republic of Turkey because there was NO Turkish flag!

The receptionist observed my attention to the flags and the smile on his face surely indicated his gratitude for my apparent "approval." In a polite but firm voice, I inquired about the conspicuous absence of the Turkish flag to which he replied: "Because we never received one, sir."

To which my second question was: "Would you include a Turkish flag if one was given to you?"

"Of course we would, and it would be an honor for us!"

My brief statement to my driver was followed up by his deep appreciation and later I had been informed that within one hour, the driver returned to the lobby, presented a Turkish flag, and the flag joined the flags of other nations.

Arriving at the Turkish embassy, I was welcomed by Ms. Sina Baydur, Counselor to the Ambassador, a most charming young lady with whom I had had many phone conversations. The agenda for my brief visit was to begin with a meeting with embassy officials and representatives of public relations firms who were supposed to serve the interests of Turkey in the United States. My private meeting with his

Excellency Ambassador Nüzhet Kandemir was to take place on the next morning, after which I would fly back to New York. The conference room was large, informal, with comfortable chairs arranged around a long mahogany table. I was seated at the right of the First Secretary, Mr. Inan Özyildiz, who was seated at the head of the table. As he conducted the meeting, he asked each person, starting from his left, to introduce him/herself, and with my introduction I was urged to briefly describe our perspectives and efforts on the issue of Turkish-Armenian history. The many questions I was asked by the ladies and gentlemen, who were busy taking note of my comments, indicated their total lack of factual knowledge on the subject which caused much anti-Turkish sentiment in the United States, mainly the Armenian allegations and the distortion of Turkish history.

An hour and a half later the meeting ended with expressions of appreciation from the participants for the information which filled their notebooks. Before adjourning, Mr. Özyildiz mentioned the story of the flags at the hotel, adding, "You see how dedicated Mr Tashji is to the Turkish people; how many of us I wonder would have reacted to the missing Turkish flag?"

After farewell greetings, I was escorted to my hotel room and informed that at six p.m., I would be picked up in the lobby to be taken out for dinner.

The evening drew to a close with a mental review of the day's events, and concluded that it had been a fruitful effort.

The following morning, after breakfast, Ms. Baydur escorted me into the Ambassador's most impressive office. We greeted each other warmly and I was invited to present my thoughts, my suggestions, and even my complaints if I had any. In the room there was only one other person, Ms. Sina Baydur, and since it was a private meeting, I shall omit certain comments. What is of vital importance however is the fact that our exchange was cordial and constructive, and yes, I did have a complaint. I informed the ambassador in detail about the material in my possession which I had presented in the form of a public exhibition, at the Turkish Center, in New York City. For years I had informed many officials of the content of my exhibition which I had named "An American's Love for Turkey." Many books, some written in the Ottoman Turkish language, copies of my thousands of letters and published articles on the Armenian issue, columns of photographs, depicting our efforts as described on these pages, as well as the beautiful photographs of our "Ottoman" home, examples of our Turkish record collection unequaled in the United States (with many recordings close to 100 years old), also many facts refuting the Armenian allegations, numerous examples of stereotypical images of Turks, to which my letters of protest received letters of apologies (an important sample of my work NOT recorded in this bio).

During my polite complaint, I asked the ambassador the same question which I had asked of many people verbally and in writing: "I'm willing to donate my entire exhibition to Turkey, whose representatives have seen the material, but no one has stepped forward to receive it. What will become of my years of work, this priceless exhibition?"

The ambassador promised to expedite the transfer. Ambassador Nüzhet Kandemir was warm, friendly and very kind in his expressions of gratitude for our humble efforts on behalf of Turkey and the Turkish people. The visit to the Turkish embassy was brief, but I'm pleased to say it proved to be very successful and most gratifying to all parties concerned. The event remains vivid in my memories.

F - 1. November 15, 1997 was the date of my first of this series of articles which had been published in *The Turkish Times,* the weekly newspaper of the Assembly of Turkish-American Associations, located in Washington D.C. Each of my numerous articles had been published just as I had written them; not one word was ever deleted from my offerings. The paper, which had printed many of our individual letters for years before the series ever began, under the heading: *"I am called a Turk Dostu* - A Friend of the Turks," published my final article on January 29th 1999. My offerings always pertained to subjects of Turkish concern, with strong emphasis on the Armenian enigma. I remain grateful to the *Turkish Times* for the honor they have shown me.

G - 1. October 27th, 1997, is the date of the letter sent to the author by the Turkish Consul General, the Hon. Fuat Tanlay. His letter was mailed along with an official letter sent to the Consul, by the Ministry of Foreign Affairs of the Turkish Government; the document was dated October 24, 1997. The content of each correspondence pertained to the author's petition to the Turkish Authorities to be granted permission for his future burial in Turkish soil. After five years of countless letters and faxes, and following all legal requirements, our final resting place in the homeland of my parents had been granted.

H - 1. 1998: *A year of fulfillment!* Of supreme joy! A year of unexpected honors! It would require many pages to describe a most significant event which took place in 1998 and again in 1999.

I must strive to be concise in describing the historic events which included many officials and countless warm people whom I am unable to name. Once again I present to the reader the most magnificent example of the destiny which continues to guide my life and my humble efforts on behalf of the Turkish nation and her people. Within the following narrative I'm certain some names will be overlooked; this is not intentional but due to the fact certain names were not obtained or lost. In either case, I apologize for my omission. For many years and to many people in the United States and in Turkey, I had asked the same question and in later years each time I had repeated my question, the tone of impatience in my voice (or in my writings), had become noticeably increased.

The question had been: "What is to become of my priceless exhibition?"

On May 22nd, 1995, I had presented my exhibition for a one-day viewing at the Turkish Center in New York City, as one of the week-long events during our annual Turkish-American Week and Parade. My wife and I wrapped all of the material we could take, and labored for two hours just setting up the tables filled with many topics pertaining to Turkey and our efforts on her behalf. Among the many people who visited the exhibition which I had named "One American's Love for Turkey," and expressed their deep appreciation for the most unique compilation of material, were the following three Turkish Congressmen: The Honorable Rifat Yűzbaşioğlu, of the city of Niğde, the Honorable Dr. Gaffar Yakin, of the city of Afyon, and the Honorable Musa Eraici of the City of Konya.

Each gentleman, at the completion of my guided tour of the entire exhibition, said with emphasis that this should be presented IN Turkey. Alas, their promises to expedite such an event proved in vain, for among other reasons, during the subsequent election, none of the hon. gentlemen was re-elected to office. But nothing was to impede my destiny, and three years later fulfillment was to be achieved: An invitation to my wife Mary and the author, from the Ministry of Culture!

The culmination of many correspondences resulted in the following: On behalf of the Minister of Culture of the Republic of Turkey, in the capital city of Ankara, we were invited to present our exhibition for public viewing, to start with official openings ceremonies, beginning August 18th, 1998 and concluding on August 24, 1998.

Before continuing with the events of a most significant endeavor in the capital city of Ankara, it is incumbent upon the author to recognize some of the ladies and gentlemen who had been very helpful in the monumental task of preparing this incomparable collection of documents and material. Once again I apologize for any names I may have unintentionally omitted.

The Minister of Culture His Excellency Istemihan Talay; the Minister of Defense His Excellency Ismet Sezgin; the Honorable Ilhan Uğuroğlu, Director of Foreign Relations for the Ministry of Culture; Mr. Halil Hepdinç of Foreign Relations for the National Library of Ministry of Culture; the Honorable Fikret Unlu, State Minister; Mr. Ardican and Mr. Műmtaz Idil, Ministry officials; Ms. Belgin Karahan and Mrs. Fatoş (Gűr) Akinoğlu, both officials of the National Library of the Ministry of Culture; Mrs. Sevinç Yaman, Library official, our guide, hostess, appointment coordinator, and above all, our beloved sister; Dr. Cenk Büyükünal, who was nine years old when we first met him and his family back in 1960; and finally our beloved kardeş (brother), Dr. Cumhur Akkent. To these and many other people, we remain eternally grateful.

From the moment my wife and I arrived in Ankara (one week after our landing in Istanbul, where on the airport I had been interviewed by the press and television), we knew it was going to be the most exciting week of our lives. It began as we stood in line behind at least one hundred people, to have our passports stamped by an entry official. Since no one we knew would be there, we hoped that a representative of the National Library would at least be present to take us to our destination. It was going to be a long wait (so we thought) but within five minutes a distinguished gentleman approached us and asked: "Do you have a diplomatic passport?"

I thought to myself, *ME, diplomatic?*

After my polite response, "No, we don't," he requested we follow him. Again I thought: *have we done something wrong?*

We were taken to a counter with a sign that read: "Diplomatic passports only," in Turkish and English. Another worry: *did he not understand me?*

We stood before the official presenting our passports and a letter from the Ministry of Culture. As he proceeded to stamp our documents, with a warm smile, he said: *"Hoş geldiniz, beyefendi* (welcome, honored sir)."

Later on we were warmly welcomed by an official from the Minister of Culture. After our exchange of greetings, I revealed my concern for our luggage (consisting of 12 pieces), most of which contained the material for my exhibition. Within a few minutes a large dolly was wheeled near us, laden with each piece of luggage sporting a red ribbon which we had tied to the handles. We counted the pieces and sighed with relief. There was no shortage of personnel assisting us from the airport to the hotel, and then up to our suite. We were urged to take an hour to freshen up and agreed that we would go directly to the National Library.

There is much which for obvious reasons the author can not refer to in fully describing the events, the countless numbers of people we spoke with, and the extent of the success of my exhibition; but we shall strive to succinctly reveal the culmination of my life's work.

It was on August 18th, 1998, when my compilation of material was presented for public review, in Ankara, capital of Turkey, within my exhibition entitled:

"One American's Love for Turkey!"

With the exception of several albums of important photographs, the entire presentation of hundreds of items was *donated* to the National Library.

We were driven to the National Library, a most impressive modern building, and as we entered a huge reception area with a sunken sitting facility, within two minutes several ladies and gentlemen (whom I had mentioned in my expression of gratitude) who in various capacities worked for the National Library and the Ministry of Culture, approached us. In the forefront was a lovely petite young lady with a leather folder under her arm. (We've never seen her without that folder!) She was Mrs. Sevinç Yaman, and was assigned by the Ministry of Culture to be at our side, during our 10-day visit to Ankara. We did nothing and went nowhere without the prior knowledge of our *kardeş* (sister) Sevinç, because her folder continued the program of our meeting, press and television interviews, presence at the exhibition, and our delectable 3 daily meals. Not only was a car and driver assigned to us, but as we were driven through the crowded streets of Ankara, we continuously heard a police siren: But there was no vehicle in front or behind us.

Mary whispered, "It's coming from *this* car!"

We were speechless as we watched people and vehicles make way for the car in which we were passengers. We will never forget being driven with a loud siren and a rotating blue light to the left of the driver. We had two days to complete our set-up, and after greeting the group which had welcomed us, we entered a large exhibition room, well lighted and with a high ceiling. With the assistance of the library staff, the many display tables were brought together and arranged as requested by the author. Eventually eight pieces of our luggage and both of my briefcases were brought into the room and each item was opened on the floor. The massive work began by covering 15 long tables with large, red plastic table covers, brought from home. I had spent a lifetime gathering the information which the visitors had never seen before, and this had to be a perfect presentation. I had a large sign made with the name of the exhibition, placed on a tripod. Near the entrance on a large poster, was a blown-up statement of welcome in Turkish. As the visitors were departing, there was a similar blown-up message of appreciation by the author for their visit to the exhibition. People wanted to help us with the set up, but I politely declined, because only I knew where each of the *hundreds* of items needed to be placed. One by one, 76 large posters, documents, books, columns of letters and photographs, some examples of my priceless Turkish record collection, a section devoted to the Armenian issue, and much, much more, each item found its place in this historic exhibition.

But how would it be received? Would it be successful?

The reader should not overlook the fact that each word spoken with many officials and hundreds of visitors was in the Turkish language; this by an individual who taught himself to speak the world's most beautiful language. It was magnificent to see my wife Mary, communicate with so many people IN Turkish; I was very proud of her, indeed.

The opening day of the exhibition brought several unexpected surprises and challenges to the author: There was to be an official opening ceremony; the Minister of Culture would be present to cut a ceremonial ribbon at the entrance; print and television reporters would be there; I was expected to deliver a speech!

My wife gave me the moral support I needed; she knew this monumental endeavor would be a complete success. For an instant, I wished to be in my den in our home in Bayside, Queens, but there I was, about to face the greatest challenge of my life: *You say you are a "Friend of Turks," well then, PROVE IT!* This psychological challenge filled my heart and soul. *Oh God, please help me!* was my silent prayer.

The spacious reception area was filled with many members of the media, equipment strewn everywhere and soon at least two hundred visitors and Ministry officials were gathered. Mary and Sevinç were nearby when a silence came over the hum of the crowd: the Minister of Culture had arrived. Subordinates on either side of me urged me to walk forward to meet his Excellency Istemihan Talay. I was determined not to blemish this golden opportunity with any signs of emotionalism or uncertainty in my dialogue. We extended our hands and as we shook hands, with our smiles our reciprocal greetings were warmly expressed. I searched for Mary so that the Minister could meet my better half. The Minister was beginning to feel the pressure of the media, and he gestured to the podium which was waiting for two speakers. Because of the crowd we slowly approached the podium, and an official introduced the Minister of Culture. The minister took the microphone for the purpose of introducing the author to the gathered.

Once again I stood before an audience expressing my love for Turkey, but this time I decided to ad lib my way IN Turkish, in the company of Turkish officials. Standing erect, as clearly as I could speak, and having no major problem with my Turkish vocabulary, I introduced myself, thanked them for their participation, and proceeded to briefly describe the content of the exhibition they were about to view. I concluded with a poem which I had written specifically for this historical occasion. A resounding ovation brought a most welcome feeling of achievement.

But where was Mary? I had lost her in the rush of the news media who were everywhere, jockeying for just one more picture. I could not see my Mary for at least twenty minutes!

The Minister of Culture, his Excellency Istemihan Talay, standing at the podium, addressed the audience with expressions of gratitude and praise for the author and his lifelong work for Turkey. On behalf of his Government the Minister expressed his appreciation for the donation of my exhibition. With his statement concluded, the Minister moved to the entrance of the salon, in front of an extended red ribbon. He was given a pair of scissors to which he commented, "I hope the scissors are sharp, usually they can't cut a ribbon!"

The people who were near us burst into laughter. As we held opposite ends of the ribbon, the Minister cut the ribbon (with no difficulty) and this was followed by applause. At this point several aides began to separate the crowd to allow an official carrying an impressive large box covered with dark blue velvet, to approach. The box was then opened and a sigh of approval was heard by everyone close enough to see a magnificent work of art – it was an *Ibrik* set (an ornate vessel with a handle and spout). This handmade pitcher was made of porcelain from Kűtahya, Turkey, with hand-painted floral designs in vibrant blue, green, and red leaves and flowers, and golden trim. The separate deep round bowl in which the *ibrik* stands, is handmade as described. Each piece has the name of the artist, a date, as well as a registry number. The Minister presented this most beautiful gift to us as he reiterated his gratitude for our exhibition. This splendid example of Turkish Art remains on display in the living room of our unique Ottoman-Turkish home. I don't believe it would be an exaggeration on my part, as I am convinced this gift is surely an example of gifts that are presented to heads of state and diplomatic officials we are humbly grateful.

The unexpected was to continue. We were requested to give the Minister of Culture a guided tour of the entire exhibition. The first table showcased documents from the Ottoman period, dating back to 1920, 1921, and earlier, also passports of my parents, together with a document written in the Ottoman-Turkish script, drew an immediate reaction from the Minister. His amazement and endless questions continued for over one hour, as we went from table to table, from topic to topic, and at its conclusion, came the most satisfying and most rewarding achievement of this "Friend of Turks."

This will be described in Chapter XI of this work. There is a simple yet most profound message to the entire world. The Minister recorded his personal comments into a guest book which was a magnificent suggestion of Sevinç Yaman. Slowly we made our way into the reception area where food and beverages were served. The Minister of Culture, followed by his entourage, stopped at the main entrance, extended his hand, and said thank you and goodbye.

I learned later that my "missing" wife had been pushed aside by the swarm of aggressive media members; nonetheless Mary had managed to take priceless photographs recording this historic event. Countless people asking countless questions, revealed countless expressions of deep love, gratitude, and appreciation, for the monumental compilation of material they had just reviewed. The first day of the exhibition was supremely successful, but very exhausting as well. The eventual conclusion was indeed most welcome, and with the security personnel in place, we exited and were driven to our hotel to rest and later meet Sevinç for dinner. I had apologized to Sevinç many times for keeping her away from her husband and child, but each time she smiled and reminded us of her position with the Ministry of Culture

It would not be possible to reveal the huge number of events which produced profound statements of affection from young and old, offered to two Americans whose work on behalf of Turkey was beyond comprehension. But the author cannot conclude our week in Ankara without referring to three most important events: 1.The folder held by our sister Sevinç, among other meetings and interviews, included our visit to *Anitkabir,* the magnificent Mausoleum of the Founder of the Turkish Republic, the immortal Mustafa Kemal Atatűrk! 2. We had been invited by the Turkish Veterans Association to visit their offices and join them for luncheon at the restaurant. It was a distinct honor to meet with these magnificent gentlemen, and our luncheon filled us with emotion as we were surrounded by these *defenders of the homeland.* As we departed, the author kissed the cheeks of fifteen veterans with expressions of brotherly affection, as is the Turkish fashion. Finally, Mary, Sevinç, and I hurried to our car where the driver had the engine running.

The author throughout this work has often referred to his destiny, and this is once again manifested by the next unexpected challenge. Permit me to introduce this awesome event with a question to the reader: What would your reaction be if you were invited to appear on a LIVE TELEVISION interview, broadcast FOUR HOURS, in a language NOT your own!?

Turkey's most popular television interview program in 1998 was called: *Cevizkabuğu* (walnut shell), which was hosted by the gentleman with whom we were about to meet. We were informed an invitation had been extended to us to appear on this most prestigious program, but that the host wished to meet us first. Our guide Sevinç, Mary, and I were taken to the office of Mr. Cevizoglu, a tall, impressive looking gentleman who for a Turk, did not smile much. Our cordial exchanges continued for forty five minutes, as I responded to each of his many questions. As we spoke in the company of my moral support (Mary) and several production people, I assured our host that I had no problem with the length of the live program, IN Turkish, of course. At the conclusion the host must have been favorably impressed with what he saw and heard, that he revealed his looking forward to the interview; and the date was set.

We must summarize a four-hour interview program. Starting time was to be at 9:00 p.m.; and as we drove to the television studio, I thought to myself: *WHAT have I done? Millions of people will be watching!* This was live television; if I failed I could be humiliated! I was in a state of panic but revealed it to no one; besides in my breast pocket was a cross from our Syrian-Orthodox church. I was seated in a chair in front of a large lighted mirror, and a charming young lady applied the make-up. Mary and Sevinç were taken to another floor to view the program from there. We sat at the table facing each other seated on comfortable chairs, and the small microphone was clipped on to our lapels. With everything prepared, I heard the voice, counting from 10 backwards, and then the introduction began. In response to many questions I gave my name, background, a brief history of our family's story, and my childhood in our home filled with the affection for and the traditions of, Turkey. The inception of my interest and my work on behalf of Turkey, and examples of our work were discussed; my position on the Armenian issue and the ubiquitous Armenian-Resolutions and anti-Turkish posture in the United States was the prime topic of discussion. I was completely at ease, aware of the honor shown me by this interview, and fully cognizant of my subject, with no hesitation for the next statement. As the program progressed I became more confident.

Then came the inquiry, "Would you be willing to take questions from our viewers?"

"They would honor me sir, I welcome their questions and criticism, if any," was my response.

The questions were received by telephone in another room, and every few minutes I would see a hand beyond the view of the cameras, placing slips of paper near the host. Few of the questions were read as most were verbally given after the host revealed the name of each caller. The calls and messages continued without a pause, the slips multiplied.

I had been totally unaware of time and did not look at my watch even once. Without any exaggeration, almost each and every caller began with deep affection for the author and profound gratitude for his work. Yes, there is an "Almost," because a female caller speaking on the air, identified herself as an ethnic Armenian and citizen of Turkey, but refused to give her name. The host was incredulous and asked if I would respond to a caller who would not identify herself.

"Of course, she's my sister!" I replied.

But there was to be no question. The lady did not believe the author was an ethnic Armenian and that I had specious reasons for my position. My immediate reaction was to speak in Armenian, but I hesitated, not wanting to neglect the host. My extensive response did not convince the nameless caller and as I concluded, the host called for a brief intermission; I could not believe that the two hours had flown by so quickly.

I was asked if I needed anything, to which I replied, "No, thank you," for the glass of water near me was all I needed.

The door opened and my moral support entered; with a mild rebuke in her voice, Mary asked: "WHY did you not speak in Armenian?"

A brief exchange followed and Mr. Cevizoğlu added, "When wc rcsumc, plcasc spcak in Armcnian."

The live interview continued with the host referring to the caller who doubted my ethnicity and requested a reply in the Armenian language. In Armenian I said, “Dear Lady, I am the son of an Armenian mother and I have never denied my Armenian ancestry.”

After translating my brief response into Turkish, the program continued. Calls from other Armenians were very favorable, but the huge number of calls coming in created a problem in communication. The host announced that in the history of this program, no other interview had ever received such a monumental reaction from every area in the country. Upon conclusion, the host expressed his deep appreciation for our visit to his program and praised our efforts on behalf of harmony among all peoples. In my concluding remarks, I thanked my host, the television staff, and the viewing audience for the love and honor shown to me.

When the doors opened, numerous people approached us with tears in their eyes. Expressions of *"Şahane! Tebrikler!* (Marvelous, congratulations!)," filled the room. With Mary and Sevinç on either side of me, we revealed our appreciation and affection to each person and at 1.45 AM we returned to our hotel.

While en route, I repeatedly asked, "How was it? Was I understood? Were my responses factually informative?"

It could be said that they were biased, but my wife and Sevinç agreed: "Spectacular!"

Their complimentary assurances, as comforting as they were, could not convince me that my interview had been favorably received by the public.

On that morning there was to be little sleep; we woke up early for breakfast and rush to the Library. We met Sevinç in the lobby, our driver was waiting outside, and once again with the car siren blaring and blue lights revolving, we made our way through the crowded streets of Ankara, filled with extreme anxiety about yesterday's interview.

We were on time as we arrived at the National Library, which had remained closed until our arrival. As we approached the building we noticed a gathering outside. What could this mean?

As we stepped out of the car, the crowd of at least forty people began to move toward us. We noticed that several women began to cry, some to applaud, and expressions of appreciation and love were repeated by so many, all of whom had viewed the television program. I was overwhelmed by this display of affection. Several people came to us with gifts as an expression of their love. It was beyond my ability to reveal my most profound gratitude to so many people, all of whom were strangers. All these people, whom I did not know and most probably would never meet again, had gathered here as a display of brotherhood. Eventually everyone entered the exhibition salon, and the journey of history, a lifetime of work, search for brotherhood, was to begin for each visitor.

The remainder of the day was similar to the remainder of the week: media interviews, meeting hundreds of visitors, and responding to countless questions. The final day arrived and as we removed several albums of photographs, I wondered about how I was to leave my valuable exhibition and just walk away. As the finale drew near and I stood at the entrance, I looked back over my shoulder and for the last time observed my "One American's Love for Turkey," exhibit and struggled not to become emotional.

Many of the staff and officials were waiting in the reception area for our farewell greetings. It was indeed very difficult to say goodbye to so many who had been so cordial and helpful. With this final task completed, we returned to the hotel to prepare for our flight back to Istanbul. At the airport, to see us off was a young man to whom we are deeply in debt for his many assistances and his love for us, our *"kardesim"* (brother) Mr. Halil Ekmekçi, an exceptional human being. To say goodbye to Sevinç Yaman was the most painful of all. Yes it was a tearful separation and time demanded we enter the passengers ' lounge.

We left Ankara with memories that will remain in our hearts for the rest of our lives, as he had reason to believe our effort was indeed successful.

The previous sentence remains factual as stated but one item must not be overlooked pertaining to the exhibition: We had been informed by Sevinç, that the Minister of Defense would visit my exhibition. Our very important visitor appeared with his escorts, and we were introduced to the Hon. Mr. Ismet Sezgin, the Minister of National Defense of the Turkish Republic. As we had done for the Minister of Culture, the author gave the Minister a tour of the entire exhibit as he continually asked questions about hundreds of items. He had honored us with his visit, his warm compliments, and by his full-page hand-written message in our guest book. He invited us to visit him at his office the following day; it became a most memorable visit. In the building of the Ministry of National Defense, we were escorted into his very impressive office. Sevinç, Mary, and I were deeply touched by his warmth and hospitality. Just prior to our departure, Defense Minister Sezgin presented the author a bronze and copper medallion representing the Ministry of National Defense; I was honored beyond words. Photographs were taken and entered in our exhibition album, which is a recorded document of our historic exhibition.

Our return to Istanbul was brief, as we visited the home of our sister, Mrs. Ayhan Büyükünal. We had been invited by our dear friends Dr. Necip and Gűler Koylu, residing in the city of Isparta, a two-hour flight from Istanbul. This wonderful couple did so much for us, as did their entire family. As their guests we were flown to Isparta and after staying at their home, they drove us in their car to Turkey's most beautiful resort, Antalya, on the edge of the blue Mediterranean Sea. Again as their guests we flew back to Istanbul and prepared for our return to the United States. For the love they have given us, we remain eternally grateful to the entire family of Dr. Necip and Güler Koylu.

Back in Istanbul, our beloved brother, Dr. Oktay Cumhur Akkent had informed us that he arranged an audience with the Metropolitan (Archbishop) of the Syrian-Orthodox Church in Istanbul. This was a magnificent development, one of so many which had been brought about as a result of the tireless efforts of our beloved brother Dr. Oktay Cumhur Akkent.

(A note to the reader: this section has lasted much longer than I had expected, but the events of 1998 had been of significant importance which needed to be made public. Our next meeting without question, fits in this category, and therefore the following will bring an end to detailing efforts of the year 1998.)

Dr. Akkent and I went to the Sűryani (Syrian-Orthodox) Church for our meeting with his Eminence Metropolitan Yusuf Çetin.

In a large, spacious conference room with large chairs situated on either side, three larger chairs were placed at the head of the room behind an ornate desk, with beautiful Turkish carpets on the floor. From the ceiling hung two huge chandeliers which illuminated the already sun-drenched room. On the walls hung Ataturk's photos, the present Patriarch, and former Church officials. In addition to the above as we entered the room we observed a large Turkish flag placed to the right of the seated Archbishop, who was kind enough to stand up as we approached him. I kissed his hand in the Turkish fashion and was invited by an aide to sit at the left of His Eminence, with Dr. Akkent seated to my left. There were about eight members of the Church directors seated on opposite sides of the room facing us. The Metropolitan began to speak with polite expressions of welcome, as tea and small cakes were served from silver trays. Our entire dialogue was in Turkish as the usual questions were posed on how I learned the Turkish language. Everything was very formal and cordial, but the atmosphere was to change. Dr. Akkent, always eager to extol our efforts, began with references to our first meeting back to 1960. He described my work as if he had been my publicist; but he always spoke that way, because he loved his people and his nation, and shared my philosophy to the letter. The Metropolitan spoke of the problems of his church and community, namely, their difficulty in teaching the Aramaic language to their youth. He was emphatic about the freedom and comfort enjoyed by the community, and revealed the love and loyalty of his people for their country, Turkey. Eventually the author began to speak, first with appreciation for being received by the Metropolitan, and then proceeded to briefly describe our work. How was I to know there was an Armenian present?

Since my comments revealed during the meeting are extensively in Chapter X of this work, there is no need to make known here my expressed views, but as I spoke I could clearly see signs of distress on the face of the gentleman seated to the left of the Metropolitan. When I concluded, the only negative comments came from the gentleman who only then was identified by name (an Armenian name), and angrily he criticized me for using the phrase *Turk düşmanliği* (enmity toward the Turks) BY THE ARMENIANS!

To be precise, what he said was: "There is no hatred for Turks by the Armenians!"

Without being contentious I replied, "My brother, either I did not express myself correctly, or you did not comprehend my statement." The meeting came to a conclusion with handshakes and friendly farewell greetings.

We returned to our home in Bayside, N.Y., in early September with much valuable information for our family, friends, and for the Federation of Turkish-American Associations, Inc. Together with many photographs in newspaper articles and interviews, the response from everyone was unanimous, a major achievement deserving of the highest praise. To say the author was overjoyed by the complements of so many, would be an understatement, but expressions of supreme love and praise were to come from totally unexpected sources. I cannot conclude the magnificent events of 1998, without offering the reader the following:

In the month of September 1998, a letter arrived at our Federation addressed to the author. The letter had been dated August 22, 1998, written by a gentleman I was not familiar with. His name was Mr. Mehmet Ali Baysal, a resident of Kűçűk Çekmece, Istanbul, Turkey, and in his 1-page typed letter he revealed his age as 86. His letter had been prompted by an article about the author, and his eloquent words of praise revealed the depth of his love and respect for this friend of Turks. To translate even one sentence of his profound statements, would suggest an element of conceit on the part of the author. If the reader thinks this writer had not been overcome by deep emotion, you then would be grossly mistaken. Mr. Baysal, who had requested pictures, had been a complete stranger. My grateful response was immediate, typed on stationery which had a red and white colored Turkish flag imprinted on the top center of the page. Since then our correspondences have continued and we have phoned him several times offering him and his family our love and profound gratitude.

Two months later, again at the Federation office, the author found an envelope addressed to him and mailed from Amman, Jordan. The author of the handwritten letter was a female Turkish student who had gone to Jordan with their parents, and continued her studies in Amman. In her letter dated October 28, 1998, she identified herself as Elâ Uluatam and her age as 13. Once again emotion overcame my senses, as our office staff feared some "Bad news." Her letter, similar in content to the Baysal correspondence, was filled with the pure love from the heart of a 13 year-old child. In addition, she had enclosed a letter which she had written to the Minister of Culture, in Ankara, Turkey, informing them that while her family was on vacation in Ankara, she had visited our exhibition and had been overwhelmed by the volume of historical information and the efforts of one humble American on behalf of the Turkish people and nation.

This unbelievable year would end with the author's name included in a crossword puzzle in Turkey's leading newspaper!

How is it possible to bring to these pages the supreme joy felt by the author who has in his possession the written statements of two strangers from distant lands, who are philosophically compatible in their quest for human harmony? One of them a 13 year-old child, the other an 86 year-old gentleman, who have been profoundly affected by an individual whom neither had met, because they shared his lifelong passion to eradicate hatred and the infestation of prejudice into the minds of young children.

Is this what the author has done? Has he touched the hearts of these writers so much that each of them, by their expressions of love, were compelled to reach out to him in similar fashion? The author remains humble and eternally grateful to Ms. Elâ Uluatam and Mr. Mehmet Ali. God bless their loving hearts.

I- 1. 1999. Our work continues with additional unexpected major developments which must have confounded friends for the stamina and dedication of this person who during this year was 67 years old, and whose destiny could not be denied!

January 27, 1999. The date of the historical meeting with the Archbishop of our Syrian-Orthodox Church. As a result of written requests by the author, His Eminence Mor Cyril Karim, agreed to receive the Federation's representatives in his office at the Archdiocese in Lodi, New Jersey. The President, Dr. Ata Erim, Executive Director Egemen Bağiş, the author, and his wife Mary, were warmly received by the Archbishop and several members of the Church Board of Directors. The dialogue was most cordial and fruitful with several complimentary statements by the Archbishop intended for the author for his work within the Turkish community. No one in the room, other than Mary, could have been aware of my joy for this friendly meeting, and for the mutual expressions of brotherhood by two Honorable entities: one

Christian, and the other Muslim. As is the custom of our mutual communities, we were served cakes and tea by our hosts who displayed their sincere pleasure about our visit. The atmosphere had been formal but the hour-long exchange was filled with warm, mutually friendly, and humorous comments. The only prerequisite was a desire by people of good will, to meet, offer friendship, and receive friendship in return. Our departure was as cordial as our arrival, and expressions of gratitude were exchanged by everyone present. The meeting did not receive the attention of the news media, but I was convinced each person that night fell asleep with satisfaction in their hearts knowing the meeting had been fruitful.

Unfortunately, a similar scenario as described above, taking place within the Armenian Community is inconceivable. With one final reciprocal gesture, gifts were exchanged: Dr. Erim presented his Eminence Archbishop Karim, a centennial album of the life of the immortal Mustafa Kemal Atatűrk, the architect of the modern Turkish Republic. His Eminence presented each of us with a compact disc recording of traditional hymns of the Syrian-Orthodox Church of Antioch, performed by the Archdiocesan Choral Society, all young children of our church. Not only is the Biblical city of Antioch today's modern city of Antakya, in Turkey, but the music for the hymns, the instruments played, as well as each *"taksim"* (an introductionary instrumental), were all in the Turkish mode. The lyrics were sung in the Aramaic-Syriac language. It is magnificent.

February 1999 brought us amazing news from our *sister* Sevinç Yaman in Ankara: the Minister of Culture was inviting us again to present my exhibition, this time in the major city of Istanbul, Turkey! Mary's joy was supreme: SHOPPING! The author was overwhelmed with mixed emotions: surely this was a monumental honor, not only to be invited again so soon after the first exhibition in August of 1998, but the place for the exhibition was to be at the Atatűrk Cultural Center in Istanbul! Time has always been my most harmful adversary, even though most of my material had been left in Ankara, and all of it was to be brought to Istanbul, my greatest fear was: *Will I have enough time to prepare?* Since the layout and the preparations in Ankara had been known, surely the setup in Istanbul would be much easier. This is what I had assumed. During the weeks before our arrival in Istanbul, had I known of the anguish which was to confront us, honor or not, I would have declined the invitation

March 10th through March 16, 1999: these were the dates of the duration of my "One American's Love for Turkey" exhibition. Everything had been prepared for us; round-trip airline tickets, hotel reservations, and even *sister* Sevinç was going to be flown to Istanbul to assist us as she had done in Ankara.

Then it happened, there it was, written on the fax sent to us: We were to arrive in Istanbul on March 9, 1999! Surely there was a mistake. Frantic, I called Ankara. No, it was NOT a mistake! We were expected to arrive one day before the opening!

My happiness was ripped apart by this impossible development. Our preparations here, together with the material we would be taking with us, had been gathered and ready for our flight. It was obvious someone had prepared our itinerary, but how would we be able to set up 20 tables? The tables! Would the tables be there in place?! Distress filled my heart, how could I conceal my worry from so many people? My worst fears were about to be realized...

Our arrival at the airport was again an emotional upheaval; none of our "FAMILIES" were present to meet us – not a familiar face anywhere among the crowd. However, our passports were stamped without delay, and as Mary and I walked down the sloping surface to the main arrival area, we were filled with consternation, because the time was about 2 P.M in Istanbul, and the opening was scheduled for TOMORROW MORNING!

Our apprehension disappeared in an instant as we spotted a face from heaven – Sevinç Yaman! We embraced each other with joyous, tearful kisses, and before we could speak we found ourselves surrounded by television cameras and media people of at least twenty men and women. In the perimeter of the circle around us, hundreds of people had stopped to observe the arriving couple. Flashing cameras, many questions, reporters extending their microphones into my face – this was the challenge of the moment.

Mary took charge of the luggage and several workers were eager to gather our pieces on to a large dolly. I knew these people had been waiting for us and surely it was my duty to offer the information which they sought. Without any trace of the turmoil within my body, in a calm and audible voice I described the purpose of our visit, at the invitation of the Ministry of Culture, and informed them of our exhibition and our lifelong work on behalf of Turkey and her people. Eventually Sevinç again came to our "rescue" and as we slowly moved away, we thanked everyone for their attention to us. With our luggage in one car and we in the other with Sevinç, we made our way to our hotel.

We had no time to unpack, so we freshened up and returned to the lobby where Sevinç, her folder in hand, was awaiting us.

The Atatűrk Cultural Center was a most impressive modern building, with a sunken park in front of it. To the left of the building facing the thoroughfare, a huge banner had been hung; it had the name of the author and information about the exhibit printed on it. As we entered through sliding doors, we observed that the interior was massive, modern, with a wide carpeted staircase leading to the second floor. Officials of the Ministry of Culture and the Cultural Center were there to welcome us as we took our first steps inside. Following the pleasantries, I had only two questions: Where was the area for the exhibition and where were the tables?

A very polite gentleman gestured toward an area which was to the left of the entrance on the street level. Very spacious, yes; a very high ceiling, yes; bright sunlight, yes; and the TABLES? WHERE were the tables? Not ONE table was in place!

"The tables are being brought here," I was told.

The time was now 4.30 PM; it would not be humanly possible to set up twenty tables when there was not even a single one in place! I could no longer conceal my distress. Officials whom we had met for the first time, each eager to assist us, were now aware of my feelings. But I was never impolite and made every effort not to add to their worry. Mary feared a heart attack as I verbally vented out my outrage. This was my presentation, my life's work, and every expectation was that far more people would visit this week-long exhibition than in Ankara. I continually paced the floor, talking to myself, not believing this utterly chaotic turn of events.

A truck appeared outside and workmen began to carry in large, heavy furniture-type tables, all of which were dusty and each table HAD NO LEGS! Tools were brought in and the work to attach the legs began. I pleaded: "I had asked for 6-ft long, light weight aluminum tables with FOLDING legs; there MUST be tables here in the building used for other exhibitions!"

A feverish search began while the work continued in front of us. Nothing could ease my distress; anger would be more appropriate a description. A worker approached us and in a breathless voice announced, "We found the tables here…." The rest of his statement as welcome as it was at the time, is not needed here. One by one the aluminum tables were arranged as per my request. Alas, the two wooden tables which now stood with the legs attached, had to be taken apart! Even now, the author wonders if anyone could find an element of humor in the above stated comedy of errors.

At long last, at 6 PM the tables were in place and the set-up began. The material from Ankara and the items we had brought with us were all placed on the floor, covered each table with the red table cloths from home, and from table to table we began the massive effort in preparing the exhibition. Sevinç remained with us and the three of us labored for over three hours. Several people had suggested we complete the preparation the following morning, but I exclaimed, "I will not leave here tonight until it is finished!"

At 9.30 PM it was finished to my satisfaction, but we were exhausted. After our flight to go directly to the Center and endure what has been briefly described above, had been a most arduous experience. Sevinç mentioned dinner at the hotel, after which she returned to her room and Mary and I to our room for a few hours of sleep. Now my thoughts returned to the realization that my work was again to be reviewed by hundreds of people and the media. What would be the reaction of the people? With the events of the day fresh in my mind, Mary's positive predictions could not dispel my anxiety, my pessimism, in short my dire fear that the exhibition would be a failure.

As disastrous as the beginning had been and in spite of my vision of total disaster, from the opening ceremonies to the moment of the closing, my exhibition was received with sublime esteem. A representative of the Minister of Culture was present at the ribbon cutting ceremony. There were hundreds of people, many members of the news media, and two immense, beautiful floral arrangements had been sent. After a statement and introduction from the official, the author resorting to every ounce of energy left in his exhausted body, addressed the people with deep appreciation for their participation and continued just as he had done a few months earlier at the National Library in Ankara, Turkey.

Not wanting to consume as much space as I have in describing my first exhibition, I have to be brief here, while paying recognition to numerous special and beloved people.

During the week-long exhibition, the author was interviewed by T.R.T (Turkish Radio and Television) on Radio Ankara, revealing the significance of the exhibition and my work on behalf of Turkey.

Among the many hundreds of visitors, the following had been included: the Bűyűkűnal family: Ayhan, Tűrkân, Dr. Cenk, and Dr. Evin; the Kőksal family: Dr. Osman, Şadan, Bahar, and Ceylan and their families; our dear friend Halil Ekmekçi; a young lady who had said she was the wife of Mr. Kemal Kutlu (in the Army at the time) with whom we had been close friends in New York; and our most honored friend Mr. Mehmet Ali Baysal, his wife, and their family. We embraced each other as every one was tearful. To embrace the gentleman who had written such beautiful letters to the author, was an honor which will live in my heart for all time, and I pray for the day to embrace this saintly man once again!

One day, a lady approached us with at least fifteen young children behind her. She explained that she was their teacher and she decided to bring some of her students (aged 12 to 13 years old), to study the exhibition. We were deeply honored by their company, and while the children surrounded us, pictures were taken. One day, my attention was drawn to a young man who had been spending much time at each of the many tables. After he read the material on the very last display (which the reader will find included in Chapter XI), the young visitor approached me and spoke the following, "I am a proud Turk and a university graduate, and I have learned MORE here in the last hour about my history than I did during four years of college education!"

It was beyond my ability to express my appreciation for his words, but my love for this stranger was indeed evident in my eyes. Our Guest Book was filled with hundreds of hand-written messages from our visitors, all of which were filled with love and gratitude. To the families listed above, we must add Dr. Necip and Güler Koylu, and Dr. Oktay Cumhur, and Özden Akkent; we were deeply grateful for their participation.

Each day hundreds of people had visited the exhibition, much to our pleasure, and countless people of all ages would approach us and reveal their appreciation for the years of work which was presented by the displayed material. One afternoon we had to leave the exhibit in order to meet with Turkey's former Ambassador to the United States, His Excellency Ambassador Nüzhet Kandemir. During his tenure in the United States we had many contacts including my invitation to the Embassy in Washington D.C. As a result of correspondences, the ambassador had made an appointment with the author to meet in the lobby of Istanbul's most exclusive hotel. At the designated day and hour, Sevinç, Mary, and I, arrived at our destination and met with the ambassador in a warm exchange. He invited us for tea in the luxurious dining room, with his aide joining us. Tea, coffee (Turkish in each case, of course), and pastries were ordered as we discussed our mutual concerns. Each of us was deeply honored by the ambassador's warm hospitality and we expressed these feelings as we prepared to depart over an hour later. We returned to the exhibit where many people were viewing the material the likes of which they had never seen before. Our days were few, the closing drew near, and Mary had no time for shopping. However, one afternoon, as I remained with the exhibit, our driver took Mary to several places and she could shop to her heart's content.

We had gone to the offices of Turkish Airlines with the hope of extending our stay in Istanbul, but all flights had been booked for weeks to come. March the 16th, 1999, was two days away. This night there was to be a major social function at the Ataturk Cultural Center and Sevinç had discovered that the Minister of Culture would be in attendance. As we waited outside, Sevinç rushed searching for the Minister to request a few minutes of his time to greet us. He agreed and once again Sevinç rushed down the stairs in order to take us back upstairs to meet with his Excellency Istemihan Talay. Even though it was a few minutes, we indeed met with the Minister who told us that he had viewed the exhibition before attending the reception.

Many people attended the exhibition in its final day. The countless expressions of love by so many people filled us with a supreme joy. Then, the last visitor departed and I stood at the entrance observing my life's work. We gathered several albums to return home, and for the second time I slowly walked away from my treasure of information. There was no time to visit our "families" as the following day we had to depart. At the Airport, Sevinç was waiting, this time she had no folder under her arm. It was very painful to say goodbye to her, our beloved "sister" who had done so much for us. Yes, we embraced, we kissed and we cried (these Turks are so emotional!).

As we flew back to America, Mary and I relived the memorable events of the past week. Our distress of the first day, of course vanished as the exhibition resulted in an overwhelming success. But the earlier distress of the author manifested itself into serious problems, first on the plane and second, after we arrived home. We were about two hours from New York when the author had one of his frequent nose-bleeds. As had happened for years, the amount of heavy bleeding was most stressful and whatever we did it would not stop. Mary asked for ice and tissues, mounds of tissue – nothing helped. The next attempt took place in the restroom; putting pressure against the right nostril with one hand, and with the other trying to clean the sink area of my splattered blood, all this while trying to maintain my balance because the plane was still flying!

The plane incident finally ended, but it returned in the baggage claim area. At home, the author's condition worsened; first a severe case of influenza developed into acute pneumonia. Who could even think of a successful exhibition under these conditions? The only other thing which needs to be mentioned is that eventually the author recovered and continued his activities.

March 21, 1999. On this date, our beloved "sister" Gőnül Akin, while in her home in Ankara, Turkey, was completing her crossword puzzle, and toward the end of it, there it was a clue to the author's name! She filled in the letters and mailed the puzzle to me. To have our name included in the crossword puzzle of Turkey's leading newspaper, for the second time, was indeed a totally unexpected delight.

June 23rd 1999. The State of New Jersey, Channel 10, phoned the Federation and requested an interview with an individual who would present the Turkish perspective of the Armenian issue. *The Turkish perspective!* While for years the media had remained indifferent to the Turkish perspective, here we had a news program which would broadcast the Turkish point of view. The author was approached and of course he welcomed the challenge. Since the Federation office was being renovated, it was decided to use the offices of the World Turkish Congress, located in the same Turkish Center building across from the United Nations.

Mary and I escorted the interviewer, Ms. Juri Tatsuma and her camera-man, to the office and preparations began. Before the taping Ms. Tatsuma asked several questions in order to prepare herself. The interview lasted for over half an hour, subject to their editing, of course. Though it had not been a network news program, hundreds of thousands of Americans heard some facts which they had not heard before and for that much, our effort was successful.

J -1. February 23, 2000, was the date when the author received a phone call at this home, from the White House. A teleconference with the White House and Federation Representatives had been arranged to discuss the Cyprus Problem. As one of the speakers selected, I was directed by the White House aide to be at my telephone the following day at the designated hour. This day had been 16 days after my hospitalization due to my collapsing from severe anemia.

February 24, 2000, during the afternoon, the phone rang and for forty five minutes our colleagues defended the Turkish position pertaining to the Cyprus conflict. Our efforts on behalf of the Turkish people did not only pertain to the Armenian issue. Cyprus, Azerbaijan, Bosnia-Herzegovina, Crimean-Turks, and other Turkic peoples had been included in our work with our Federation. The teleconference did not change the position of the United States, but at least the Turkish point of view was heard.

February 28, 2000, found us in Richmond, VA, where the State's Senate Education Committee would consider yet another Armenian Resolution. Selected parties from the public had been invited to participate, and the Federation rented a large van; Mary, six of our Federation colleagues, and the author undertook the seven-hour journey to the capital of the State of Virginia. When we had arrived and entered the Committee room, the session had already been in progress. Our associates from the Washington-based Turkish-American Assembly had been seated and the author was brought to the front row of spectators. The Senators debated numerous items on their agenda. Fortunately, the Armenian Bill was at the end of the agenda. Had it been debated before our arrival, the Turkish presentation would have lost an important speaker. (Do you still question my destiny?)

The room was filled with Armenians; in total we were about fifteen ladies and gentlemen, the Armenians numbered over two hundred people; three speakers from each side were allowed to present their respective positions within a period of five minutes. The Armenians spoke first, resorting to their usual tirades and distortions of the factual events of 1915 in Ottoman Turkey. The Armenians in the room knew there would be three Turkish speakers opposed to the Resolution, but not one of them could have anticipated that one of the Turkish speakers would be an ethnic Armenian! It was decided the author would speak last. (There is a saying about keeping the best for the last.) Our speakers were calm in their effective presentations, and each remained within the five-minute limitation. The third speaker was introduced, and as he had done many times in the past, he was determined to keep speaking until he was asked to conclude. The third speaker of course was the author, as he stood at the podium and adjusted the microphone so as to be certain everyone could hear him; he then looked at each of the honorable senators, who were seated in a crescent form facing him. The author identified himself and his affiliation with the Turkish-American Federation, but for the moment he did not refer to his ethnic background. His very first words were spoken as he raised a copy of the Senate resolution and declared: "Gentlemen, this resolution is an abomination!" He proceeded to make effective comments pertaining to the Armenian treason and warfare against the Ottoman authorities, together with other facts, which will be presented in the following chapter. "I know well of what I speak, because I am the son of an Armenian mother and a Syrian-Orthodox father!"

A moment of stunned silence pierced the room, followed by several moans and groans were heard from the Armenian spectators. The Chairman called for order, and the speaker being very careful in his demeanor and choice of words, gave the senators a brief education on Turkish-Armenian history. It was a subject about which each of them lacked even an infinitesimal knowledge. As had been stated, the speaker had no intention of stopping, but as anticipated, the Chairman requested him to conclude. Thanking the senators for their attention, the speaker moved back and returned to an area where his people were standing. Now each of the senators presented their views on the Resolution, fully aware of the presence of their Armenian constituents, whose money and years of pressure demanded their "YES."

Several of the senators at least verbally indicated they would need to study further the pertinent history before they could cast their vote. But this was a mere subterfuge intended to placate the Turkish side, at least temporarily, because a few weeks later we learned that the Resolution had passed, and as a result, the schools in Virginia could teach their students the mythical Armenian Genocide. Once again, American pusillanimous politicians surrendered to the Armenian Hate Merchants, and jeopardized the friendship between the United States and the Republic of Turkey!

The room began to empty and our people surrounded Mary and the author as we slowly made our way into the waiting hall. Eyes filled with hate were directed to one person: the author.

I heard a female voice order in Armenian, "Spit in his face!"

Later, I was told that a man raised his arm to strike me, but Mary pushed his arm away. I was told later, another female speaking in Armenian had declared: "He is the son of a prostitute!"

Had I heard these words, there would have been chaos….

Because the Republic of Turkey was among the nations which supported the United States during the Korean War conflict, the Federation has been invited to join thousands of American veterans, during their march down Broadway to Battery Park for the historic unveiling of the memorial monument dedicated to the sacred memory of the thousands of young American men and women (and those of our allies) who lost their lives in that hell known as the Korean War. The bonds of friendship among numerous chapters of the Veterans of the Korean War, and the Turkish-American community, had been initiated by the efforts of the author years earlier, and for us to participate in the Grand Parade and the monument dedication, was indeed an exceptional honor. With our large American and Turkish flags, following the banner of the Federation, together with about twenty of our people (I had hoped for at least a hundred), we took our place in the line of march. There was no way we could have anticipated the reaction of thousands of people viewing and cheering the marching veterans. As we marched, among the people lining the sidewalks, we heard countless cheers and voices shouting in unison: "God bless Turkey! God bless the Turks! The

Turks are the best!"

We were overwhelmed by the ovation of the masses who were cheering at the sight of our Turkish flags, a full block away of where the throngs of people had assembled. We waved our gratitude and appreciation to the thousands of Americans whose sons, fathers, and brothers remembered well the bravery of the Turkish soldier in Korea. Gen. Douglas McArthur epitomized the Turkish Military Forces with these immortal words: "The Turks were the bravest of the brave!"

Ever since that unforgettable day, when Americans and Turks, though complete strangers, embraced each other, symbolic of the trust and friendship between our respective peoples. Since 1991, the A.F. Kivlehan Chapter of our American Veterans of the Korean War, have each year invited the Turkish-American Federation to participate in their annual memorial service. To each of the veterans and their President, Mr. Joseph Calabria, we pledge our eternal respect and our brotherly love to each of you and your families. The people of the United States and peace-loving nations worldwide owe you a debt of gratitude.

We should add here, that when possible, some of the veteran chapters have joined the Turkish-American community in its annual Turkish-American Day Parade, in New York City. In the year 2001, during the month of May, the Federation organized our 20th Annual Parade, displaying our pride in our culture and history, and loyalty to the United States.

Let us return to the June 24th, 2000 memorial ceremonies. The significance of this event had been the 50th Anniversary of the Korean War, with well over 300 people attending, including the public and the veterans from the Kivlehan Chapter. Among numerous foreign diplomats and city officials, the Turkish Council General the Hon. Ambassador Mehmet Ezen was also in attendance. The Federation's wreath drew much attention as it was in the form and colors of a huge American flag. We were deeply grateful to our friends, Mr. Rüstem Ateş, for bringing the magnificent wreath, President Joseph Calabria, as always performed his duties as MC, in a flawless manner. The invocations were read by a priest and a rabbi, but when the *hoca* a (Muslim clergyman), Mr. Çetin Demirtaş, arrived from the Fatih *Camii* (Mosque), I approached Joseph to see if our *hoca* could recite a short Muslim prayer.

Even though it was not included in the program, Joseph as a

most kind gentleman, said, "No problem! Get him ready, he'll be next." He will never realize how deeply his gesture touched our hearts, as over 300 hundred people, Christians and Jews, all stood up, as our Turkish-Muslim cleric recited a prayer. After a moment of silence, speeches were delivered by numerous representatives, and the author speaking on behalf of the Turkish-American community, read from his prepared statement. Our speech was received with a resounding ovation. The presentation of the Honor Guard, flags, and wreaths were placed at the base of the Universal Soldier Memorial monument.

The entire event was worthy of the highest praise. Other than the flags of the United States, South Korea, and the United Nations, the only other flag was presented was the Turkish flag!

October 16th, 2000, found us in the office of the United States Senator Charles Schumer, in his office in New York City; it surely was a historic meeting. The President, Mr. Egemen Bağiş, the author's wife Mary, a Turkish businessman, and the author had a cordial dialogue with the Senator. Always being prepared, the author presented the senator with some of his material pertinent to the Armenian allegations against the Turkish people. This meeting was to be an introduction before a reception given in honor or the senator at the Turkish owned Marmara Hotel, in New York City.

October 25th, 2000. About fifty Turkish-Americans welcomed Senator Charles Schumer and his aides in a room with a magnificent view of New York City at night time.

When the guest of honor arrived, everyone moved closer to greet him, only one individual took several steps backward – the author. When the senator shook hands with Mary, the first thing he said was, "Where is your husband?"

Amazing that he should remember. This was not the first time we had met and shook hands with an American politician, the author had never been moved by the experience, simply because, today the elected official smiles and says what his Turkish audience wishes to hear, and tomorrow he/she makes a speech on the mythical "Armenian Genocide." Even though the Turks are generations-late in playing the political game, we must do our part in formulating a constructive dialogue with politicians who have no knowledge of Turkish history. So it had been during our second meeting with Senator Schumer, who had been gracious and friendly to the group who listened to his statements. Questions were asked as several people urged the author to ask a question of our guest. The senator's response to our questions was similar to the following, "There was much I did not know of the history of the Turkish-Armenian issue, but I've learned a great deal from our good friend." With these kind words, he gestured toward the author, and everyone applauded; all was "well in the world!" In conclusion, a powerful United States senator had come to realize an active Turkish-American community will no longer remain silent in disseminating the truth of Turkish history and culture.

November 11th, 2000, was for the Turkish-American community another historic day. The United War Veterans Council of New York, requested by mail from our Federation, our participation in the Veterans Day Parade on Fifth Avenue, New York City. This was for us a major development and we had informed the Council we would be honored to join the thousands of American veterans. A new member association of the Federation generously sponsored a float to be used by the Federation during the parade. Our group numbered about seventy adults and young students, and our float received an overwhelming response from many thousands of spectators. We had distributed hundreds of small Turkish flags, which the veterans and the public had requested from us. It reminded us of the parade in 1991, to Battery Park. As honored as we were to be included in the parade, paying tribute to American veterans, by the ovations and expressions of the American public and veterans, their respect and affections for the Turks were warmly revealed.

We have come to the conclusion of this lengthy chapter. In reviewing our work, I've used letters of the entire alphabet, one and a half times, and yet much has been omitted; the next chapter brings the author to the area of his life's work. It's an area which he had wished he never had to enter. The author is irrevocably convinced of the historic accuracy included in the following pages. Personal gain or publicity have not been my motivation, I seek harmony among peoples who share a common culture and history.

(At this point in time the continuity of my work is interrupted by terrible news which we have just received by telephone from Istanbul. In addition to my references to "Kardeşim" (my brother), Dr. Oktay Cumhur Akkent, there were still comments to be made about this great Turkish gentleman in the following chapters of this book. But I am heartbroken to learn that my brother has just passed away! His demise has crushed my wife and me to an extent where my composition cannot, at this time, continue. I recognize my obligation to the reader and such, I shall return soon; I must phone his wife, our beloved Özden, in Istanbul.)

X. My basic philosophy and espoused position about the Turkish Nation and the Armenian Allegations against Turkey.

After many years of work, ad lib comments, speeches and interviews, one would assume this chapter would be easy to complete, but it is not, for two reasons:

First, because the author is diametrically opposed to the position of his co-religionists on the subject of Turkish-Armenian history and relations.

Second, because the mission to which the author has dedicated himself, namely the continuation of Turkish-Armenian Brotherhood, has no similar effort made by a single individual of the author's ethnicity. One major factor deserves to be repeated here: My mission does not exclude the Süryani people, due to the fact the Syrian-Orthodox community harbors no animosity toward the Turkish people, whereas my other half, the Armenians (outside of Turkey), not only hate the Turkish people, but perpetuate this illogical hatred by inflicting their animosity into the hearts and minds of innocent children. Keep in mind that the author is born of an Armenian mother and a Süryani (Syrian-Orthodox) father, and it is his Armenian co-religionists whom he condemns for their philosophy of hate against the people with whom they share over six centuries of historical and cultural harmony. We are cognizant of the Armenian vehement reaction toward the author, as well as the bewildering admiration of the Turkish-Americans and the Turkish nation. As regrettable is the former, and as far more desirous is the latter, of paramount significance to the author is the fact that the author himself believes in the logic and justice of his position. If I may use the first person singular, I see no logical purpose in teaching hatred to young children for events about which historians maintain different perspectives. While scholars engage in intellectual debates, our politicians in the desire to placate their wealthy Armenian constituency, totally lacking any historical knowledge, portray themselves as prosecutors, judge and jury and convict the Turkish nation for crimes which they did not commit!

Because for many generations in our country there had been no Turkish response, it became a popular and expected practice to blame the Turks for killing innocent Christians. For years the Turks were even blamed for the drug addiction in the United States! Why Americans were and continued to be slaves to drug consumption is never questioned. American Military bases on Turkish soil, Turkish support in the Korean and Gulf Wars, and when it serves the interests of the United States, then Turkey is our ally, but *Armenian money* surpasses all that the Turkish nation has given us!

In our espoused position on behalf of the Turkish Nation, if friend or foe, believes the author finds the Turkish Nation, whether be Ottoman Turkey or the Republic of Turkey, as being without fault during the 1915 period, then this misunderstanding must be corrected. Since the Armenian allegations against Turkey go back to 1915, then we must also go back and refer to the history of Ottoman Turkey. It would be absurd to even suggest that the Ottomans made no mistakes during the period in question. It is however, also grossly absurd to believe the Ottoman Turkish Government of Ottoman Military leaders during the First World War period had planned and carried out a 'genocide' of the Armenian people. The last sentence sums up the avowed position of the author and as a result, he had been verbally and physically assaulted and considered a pariah, deserving the contempt of every Armenian. The Armenians in the United States could forgive this writer even if he were to publicly curse God, attributing his blasphemy to a mental disorder. But for his speaking on behalf of the Turkish-Armenian brotherhood, he will remain unforgivable!

How can the Armenians justify this insane manifestation of multi-generational hatred while at the same time, they profess to be Christians? The God they claim to worship has said: "Love thy Enemy," and "Blessed are the Peace Makers, for they shall be called the Children of God!"

They fill their churches as faithful adherents of their Christian faith while at the same time the sanctity of their churches, and the holiest symbol of Christianity, the Holy Cross, are used as an entity of hatred. These quintessential hypocrites, these Armenian "hate merchants," continue to blaspheme the God of All Mankind.

Before we return to the events of Ottoman Turkey, let us review the author's position on four subjects where he believes the Turks committed disastrous blunders. (And you thought the author could not criticize the Turks.)

1 – The Ottoman authorities, under the edict of the Sultan, joined Germany and the Central Powers during the First World War, against the Allies. This decision, made while the Ottoman Empire was disintegrating, would have eliminated the Turkish homeland had it not been for the immortal Mustafa Kemal Atatűrk.

2 – The relocation of the Armenians caused a human catastrophe, which gave the Armenian *Hate Merchants* the opportunity to create an "event" which never occurred.

3 – With the establishment of the modern and secular Republic of Turkey, the educational system did not sufficiently educate the public of the many factors pertinent to the Armenian issue prior and during the First World War.

4 – In the United States, the Turkish-American community increased in numbers and began to establish viable, active, and organized social and religious entities throughout every sector; however, for many generations, it remained ineffective with regards to the Armenian allegations and anti-Turkish activities.

Now that we have stated our "criticisms," the author will present his "defense" of the Turks. (Did you think the author would conduct himself like American politicians and the news media, by just condemning the Turks and negating all relevant circumstances? We will address the Armenian allegations, yet to follow.)

1 a. Similar to many other empires throughout world history which have survived only in the pages of history books, so the once powerful Ottoman Empire had declined and was replaced by the modern, democratic and secularized Republic under the leadership of Mustafa Kemal Ataturk. The Ottoman sultans ruled its ever expanding empire for over six centuries, starting around 1300 A.D. Many regions of Asia, Europe, and Africa had been under the influence of Ottoman Turks, until Kemal Ataturk and the Young Turks movement disposed the Sultan and the control of the Sultanate was terminated with the founding of the Turkish Republic on October 29th, 1923. Not only did Turkey suffer as a result of joining the Germans but widespread internal revolution had threatened the very existence of the Turkish homeland.

2 a. Armenian treason against the land were they had prospered for over six centuries convinced the Turks the Armenian minority became its enemy before and during a world war, and therefore felt compelled to relocate the Armenians from the eastern regions of the country, where they could no longer support the Russian armies. (This will be discussed in later pages.) The Armenians suffered terribly as a result of their own treachery, but they alone did not suffer; all the peoples of the land suffered the ravages of war. Turks killed Armenians and Armenians killed Turks; neighbors became enemies and vengeance created more vengeance. The evidence will irrefutably prove that it was not 'genocide.' The word itself came into existence in 1945, to describe the murder of the Jews by Nazi Germany.

A single word which signified to the world the suffering of the Jews of Europe, and the Armenians appropriated the term which did not pertain to them, and exploited the word in their accusations against the Turks. To this day, the Armenians use the word as a badge of honor "to gain the support of Americans."

5 - The author surely is not in a position to criticize the educational system of the newly established Turkish Republic, but even as an outsider, it becomes obvious that the years of Armenian treason and revolutionary activities had not been taught sufficiently, if at all. Many years of conversations with Turks over the age of forty, confirms my position. Those under the age of forty were not even aware of the Armenian issue until Armenian terrorism conducted against Turkish diplomats made the front page in the United States, starting in 1973.

The obvious question of WHY? should be considered. Even a limited study of the Turkish character shows a total absence of hatred against any ethnic group. Not wanting to create an anti-Armenian attitude in the New Republic, the events of the First World War, were revealed WITHOUT reference to twenty *years* of Armenian revolution! But there were other reasons as well: Ataturk's monumental reforms and Westernization policies were the educational priorities. The entire nation went to school to learn the Latin alphabet which replaced the Arabic script. They had to learn to write and read from the left to the right, instead of from the right to the left. Could you imagine such a similar situation in the United States? Social and religious reforms took place, re-elections, equality between men and women, competition in a free market, technological advances, and so much more, had to be learned on the fly. The Turks found no logical reason to teach the conflict between the Turks and the Armenians. Philosophically, it could be said, it had been a constructive and compassionate decision.

Ironically, however, during these years when hatred was renounced in Turkey, at the same time in the United States, and continuing for many generations, Armenian children were "taught" a falsified history of the Armenians of Ottoman Turkey. A steady diet of anti-Turkish sentiment within the Armenian Church and social organizations has created a new generation of "hate merchants" who are destined to pass on the legacy of hate to yet another generation of Armenian Youth. It should be understood, the Armenians of today's Turkey, including the Armenian Patriarch, *condemn the position of the Armenians in our country.* In our private meeting with the beloved late Armenian Patriarch, in Istanbul of 1968, His Eminence Snork Kalutsyan blessed the author for his efforts. A most precious meeting which I can never forget.

6 - In retrospect, as we consider the ineffectiveness of the Turkish-American community, in its reaction to the well-organized and highly financed activities of the many Armenian groups throughout the United States – all of which had an anti-Turkish agenda – we must consider the three factors just mentioned: organization, financial resources, and number of groups.

During the early years, the 1940s and onward, the Turkish community totally lacked the conditions which were necessary to respond to the Armenian distortions and allegations. As it had been, when the Armenians had first arrived in this country, finding work, a place to live, putting food on the table for their families, and adjusting to the American way of life, were the priorities of the Turkish families coming to the United States. With the establishment of the Federation of Turkish-American Associations, Inc. (in New York in 1956), and years later, the Assembly of the Turkish-American Associations (in Washington, D.C.), the birth of the active Turkish-American community took place. It had been a slow, arduous endeavor, but the Turkish spirit of hard work, dedication, and unity has brought the Turks to their rightful place as a fruitful and honorable ethnic entity in the United States. From the New England states to California, proud Turkish-Americans with their socio-religious organizations, continue to demonstrate their solemn faith in God, coupled with their profound allegiance to the United States of America.

Now that the author has concluded with his "defense" of the Turks, let us now return to Ottoman Turkey and review the Armenian allegations which remain prominent to this very day. For the edification of the reader, the following pages will present as accurately as possible, the Armenian allegations as though they were written here by an Armenian, who hates the author more than he hates the Turkish people. Though this work is an autobiography, the author, without bias, will present the Armenian position in a manner which the Armenian CAN NOT dispute. Is the author fair or is he not? Each topic will begin with the word: ALLEGATION, to which the author's perspective will begin with the word "RESPONSE."

At the conclusion of the allegations and responses, the author will present for your consideration, NOT his comments, and NOT the position of the Turkish historians, or representatives of its government and organizations in our country, but actual quotations from Armenian sources! Since the sources will be *Armenian,* who then will suggest the statements come from Turkish "misrepresentations"? The spoken or written words of the Armenians THEMSELVES will refute THEIR ACCUSATIONS!

1 – ALLEGATION: The Turks have conquered the ancestral Armenian homelands and as a result many cities and regions of today's eastern Turkey, are in reality Turkish-occupied Armenian lands. The Armenians demand the RETURN of these lands.

RESPONSE: An independent Armenian Nation, which had been the successor of two earlier Armenian kingdoms, beginning in 189 B.C, had been governed by a single ruler, Tigran (95-56 B.C.). Tigranus, who had been called "King of Kings", brought to Armenia an independent Kingdom, which lasted only four centuries, due to the wars between the Romans and Parthinians. Thereafter the Armenians were ruled by the Romans, the Assyrians, the Persians, the Byzantines, and the Arabs, among other empires, centuries BEFORE the Seljuk Turks came to the region and to Anatolia. With the arrival of the Turks, Armenian culture, religion and language, flourished to the present times. The habitation of the Armenians in Ottoman Turkey was not located only in the Eastern regions of the country, but they had resided in every sector of their homeland. As an example, the author's mother had been born in Balikesir, on the Western border of the country. Her relatives had resided in Manisa, Tekirdağ, Bursa, and Istanbul. Travel to every part of Turkey had never been restricted.

2 – ALLEGATION: The Armenians of Ottoman Turkey, though loyal, and defenseless Christian subjects of the Ottoman government, were for centuries mercilessly persecuted, who could not speak their Armenian language, and maintain their Christian faith. Subsequently, because the Armenians refused to convert to Islam, they were made to suffer 'genocide.'

RESPONSE: Within the above allegation there are five words which are fundamental in the Armenian version of events, which to this day, are repeatedly emphasized in order to secure the support of the politician and writers: loyal, defenseless, Christian, persecuted, and genocide. Each word is a "catch term" meant to gain the sympathy of an impartial person, be he/she a politician, scholar, an editor, or a student. The facts reveal the Armenians of Ottoman Turkey were neither *loyal,* nor *defenseless.* For over twenty five years, the Armenians carried out rebellion in the land where they had prospered in freedom for over six centuries. Revolutionary organizations and paramilitary forces supported by the Russians and the promises of the British were responsible for the deaths of untold tens of thousands Turkish civilians and soldiers.

Though the author does not support that every ethnic Armenian had engaged in rebellion against Ottoman Turkey, the fact is that Armenian political revolutionary groups had been established, and they conducted their treasonous activities for over twenty-five years. The Armenakan, Ramgavar, Hunchak, and Dashnaksagan groups have been mentioned, but the latter revolutionary organization needs to be described further. Written phonetically in English: the Dashnaksagan Party had been – and continues to be in the United States – composed of an extremist fanatical segment of the Armenian people. Under its official name in the United States THE ARMENIAN REVOLUTIONARY FEDERATION not only harbors a ceaseless hatred of Turks, they remain separated from the mainstream Armenian community as well as the Armenian Church, because of a bitter animosity between the Armenians themselves.

The bitter discord among the Armenian political parties in Ottoman Turkey had been transplanted into the United States when in

1933, during a Christmas morning Mass, the Armenian Archbishop Tourian was assassinated *in church* – by those Dashnaksagan fanatics. Thereafter, the Dashnaks (the short form of their name), established their own church, their own clergy, and even their own *Catholicos* (the highest rank within the Armenian Church). As a result of this illegal act that divided the community, which continues to be split to the present times, families are torn apart, and even their cemeteries remain separated. The Mother Church, with its spiritual leader found in the city of Etchmiadzin, Armenia, and the Dashnak "Church" in spite of many attempts for reconciliation, remain divided. The only area of church and community "harmony" is in their illogical hateful position toward the Turkish people. But even this manifestation of hate has not eliminated the animosity within the Armenian community.

With reference to the Armenians, being denied the freedom to practice their religion, or to speak the Armenian language, the following facts will expose yet another fraud, which the anti-Turkish revisionists disseminate to the "uniformed." As to the "denial" of religious freedom, if we are to believe the Armenian distortion, why don't the Jews of Turkey declare they had been forced to convert to Islam? The same question please, to the Syrian-Orthodox and the Greek-Orthodox communities!

Let's face it, if, as the Armenians would like us to believe, the Turks forced non-Muslims to accept the Muslim faith, then WHY would they force the Armenians, and not the other three groups? Each religious community practiced its respective faith according to its ancient beliefs and practices. As evidence of the continuation of the centuries of religious freedom, to this day, the Greek-Orthodox Patriarch, the Armenian Patriarch, the Syrian-Orthodox Metropolitan, and the Jewish synagogues are all to be found in the city of Istanbul, functioning in the dogma and language of each faith, totally in freedom, peace, and harmony with each other and the Muslim majority.

The assertion that to speak the Armenian language had been forbidden by the Ottoman Government is to be added to the long list of Armenian mythology. The subject of language usage in Ottoman Turkey can best be described by the following exchange between the author and his beloved mother, Izabel, "Mom, often you have said that the Armenians in Balikesir were never forbidden to speak the Armenian language, either in private or in public. If this was true, why then did your entire family speak Turkish, only?"

"My son, you were born in the United States and the language of this country is English, that's why you speak the language of this land. But suppose one day you decided to learn another language, what would you do?"

"I would go to school."

"Exactly, it was the same in our Turkey, every Armenian who went to Armenian schools learned to speak and write in Armenian. We had Armenian newspapers, which only the Armenians read." My mother in later years learned to speak Armenian without the benefit of schooling. As it had been in Ottoman Turkey, so it is to the present times: Armenian, Greek, Arabic, Kurdish, French, English, among other languages as well as Turkish are all freely spoken.

3 – ALLEGATION: The book written by United States Ambassador Henry Morgenthau, describes in graphic details, the cruelty of the Turks toward the Armenians and it confirms to the world the occurrence of a 'genocide.'

RESPONSE: The title of the book is: *Ambassador Morgenthau's Story,* published in 1918. In the space of this response, the author will offer just a few of the many facts which will seriously challenge the credibility of the book and the author. The first problem with Morgenthau's book is that he did <u>not write it!</u> Henry Morgenthau had been a New York real estate developer, who had assisted Woodrow Wilson's 1912 presidential campaign. When Wilson was elected President, he rewarded his friend with an appointment as ambassador to Ottoman Turkey. But contrary to ambassadorial objectives for good relations between respective nations, Morgenthau's mission to Ottoman Turkey had a specious plan. This was to create in the minds of the American public a terrible image of the Turks by their purported ill-treatment of the Christians. The American administration had been called upon by the Allies in Europe to enter the World War against Germany. As has been described earlier, the Ottomans had joined the Germans during the First World War. The Mission of the Turcophobe Morgenthau was to convince the American public opinion of Turkish brutality, and thereby secure support for Wilson's decision to take America into the First World War.

The anti-Turkish scheme began to function without delay by Ambassador Henry Morgenthau's arrival in 1913, into the Ottoman capital city of Constantinople (the Christian code for Istanbul; while "officially" the name was changed in 1930, this had already been changed back in the 15th Century, as soon as the city was conquered. No one called Istanbul "Constantinople" within the Ottoman Empire. The only ones who stuck with that name were Westerners who couldn't accept that the city was "taken" from them.)

Other than English, Morgenthau did not speak any of the numerous languages throughout the country of his visit; therefore he was in need of assistance. His office secured the services of two aides, BOTH of whom were *Armenian!* One of them was named Hagop S. Andonian, who became the personal secretary of the Ambassador, from whose pen Morgenthau's *book* was created. The life and work of Henry Morgenthau are preserved in a monumental collection of papers found in the Library of Congress, recorded on microfilm. A second major compilation of Morgenthau's papers are to be found in the Franklin Delano Roosevelt Presidential Library in Hyde Park, New York. Prof. Heath Lowry, after extensive research upon countless material, published a book in 1999, titled: *The Story behind Ambassador Morgenthau's Story*. The documented papers of Morgenthau clearly reveal that during his tenure which ended in 1916, he had sent many letters to his family and associates in the United States. He also kept a diary of daily events and meetings. The following is a quotation from one of Morgenthau's letters, dated May 11th, 1915: "… so I have instructed Andonian to take my diary and copy it with some *elaborations of his own.* Of course this relieves me of all *responsibility, for any errors*." (Italics added by the author.)

At the conclusion of the quotation, the index states: "Henry Morgenthau, to children, letter of May 11th, 1915."

During the three years that Morgenthau was in the Capital, he never left the city, and nowhere in his *book* was this mentioned. The evidence points to his personal secretary, Hagop Andonian who prepared the written material as though they were the composition of Ambassador Morgenthau. The front pages of the *New York Times* gave much coverage to the sufferings of the Armenians, but failed to report the Armenian slaughter of thousands of Turks. But Turkey was the enemy, why should we care about the Turkish losses?! Was America ever concerned about German, Japanese, Korean, or Vietnamese, civilian or military dead? Of course not. But the situation in Ottoman Turkey had been UNLIKE the other conflicts. (To be discussed in the next ALLEGATION.) The "elaborations" of Hagop Andonian were compiled and eventually submitted to Burton J. Hendrick, an American historian/journalist, who TWO YEARS after Morgenthau left Turkey, wrote the book with the title of Morgenthau's "book," with Morgenthau shown as the "author!" The Western press and historians believed the distortions in the book which Morgenthau DID NOT write. The accusations against the Turks therefore took hold on the thinking of many governments and the news media.

The distortion of events in Ottoman Turkey was accepted as historical facts, but my book seeks the truth and justice.

4 – ALLEGATION: Morgenthau's "Book" proved the genocide took place, but to the present times, only Turkey denies that such an event occurred, and refuses to admit, refuses to apologize, and refuses to pay compensation, to the Armenians.

RESPONSE: In the previous response we have briefly touched on the forgeries of Hagop Andonian and the explicit fraud of Morgenthau's "book." In each reference to Hagop Andonian, this author has made a point of mentioning Andonian's first name because there is *another* Andonian, whose name was *Aram* Andonian. Morgenthau and the *two* Andonians performed their "duties" to the fullest satisfaction of the Armenian hate machine. Aram Andonian's "contribution" to the Armenian cause was his book of blatant forgeries and outright fabrications. Published in London in 1920, Aram Andonian's creation was titled: "The Memories of Naim Bey: The Turkish official documents relating to the deportations and massacres of Armenians."

During the same year the book was printed in French, in Paris, and in Armenian, in Boston, Mass., where to this day there is a large Armenian community. The book purportedly contains copies of "official Ottoman documents," given by an Ottoman official "... named, Naim Bey," TO Aram Andonian; the so-called "documents," "letters," and "telegrams" "confirmed" the Armenian "Genocide." Aram Andonian's book of fraud, deception, and total disregard for historical accuracy had been the third and possibly most damaging assault upon the image of the Turkish people in the Western world.

Within the scope of this work, it would be impossible to enumerate the colossal forgeries of the book, hereafter referred to as the "Memories of Naim Bey." But in 1983 a 270-page book printed in English and authored by two Turkish scholars who present copies of original Ottoman copies and the forged "translations" by Andonian. The book, titled "The Talat Pasha Telegrams, Historical Fact or Armenian Fiction?" also reveals many irrefutable blunders committed by the forger Aram Andonian. For the purpose of this work, the author will present some facts which will expose the fraud which Turkey's enemies, to the present day, had presented to the world as "historical documents!"

The forger Andonian created his book of "official Ottoman documents," in order to convince the West of the Ottoman Turkish "premeditated extermination" of the Armenian people. A scholarly review of Andonian's book, described here as the "Memories of Naim Bey," requires knowledge of the Ottoman Turkish language, in which the actual documents had been written. Among the many blunders of the forger Aram Andonian, might we present the following four examples which will prove Andonian was an ardent forger, and that he was not even proficient in his criminal activities:

1 – Aram Andonian, in his book of forgeries, refers to an "Ottoman official, Naim Bey," with the problem (for the forger) that in the extensively researched Ottoman archives, the name "Naim Bey" is *nowhere* to be found! If we are to believe in the Armenian mythology as describing this person as an "Ottoman official," then we must assume again "Naim Bey" was "an official" in charge of pencil sharpening. This author feels compelled to inject the question: If indeed there had been an Ottoman "official," named Naim Bey, for what conceivable reason would he <u>give</u> "official documents" to the potential propagandist?

2 – Are we not to take for granted the necessity and importance of recorded dates on any correspondence, and especially government documents? Andonian was so consumed with publishing the so-called "documents," that (as impossible as it is to believe) he overlooked the differences between the Muslim and Western calendars. As a result, the forger Aram Andonian, in his rush to complete his book of forgeries, gives the documents the dates which did not correspond to the actual period in question.

3 – As stated, the Andonian book was printed in English, French, and of course, Armenian. Included in the many "official correspondences," there was a copy of a so-called "telegram," sent by Talat Pasha, who had been the Minister of the Interior, in which he purportedly orders the annihilation "of the Armenians." In this and countless other documents, there are many differences in the translation of the English and French printings. In addition, the words, spelling, and grammatical construction of the written Ottoman language, indicate the documents, letters, could not have been written by educated Ottoman officials. That the forgeries have been prepared by Aram Andonian and his circle of supporters, it is conclusively proven by his most revealing and damaging blunder, not only did he blunder, he also revealed his stupidity.

4 – In official documents and correspondences during the Ottoman period, it had been common practice to include at the top of the page the following supplication:

BISMILLAHIRRAHMANIRRAHIM (in the name God, the compassionate, and the merciful).

For obvious reasons an abbreviation would be used: BESMELE. In the book of the forger Andonian the supplication does not follow the formal and thus normal, format. In addition, in numerous "official letters" the name of Allah (God) is incorrectly written! It strains human logic to believe that any Ottoman official could have been guilty of such monumental grammatical error.

One final irrefutable fact needs to be mentioned here: On March the 15th, 1921, in Berlin, Germany, the Minister of the Interior Talat Pasha was assassinated by the miscreant, Soghomon Tehlirian. This brutal act had been committed with premeditation and the design of the Dashnak Committee, as were the other assassinations of Ottoman officials. During the trial of Tehlirian, of June 2-3, 1921, in Berlin, Talat Pasha's widow (who was also shot by the assailant) was not permitted to testify, for reasons which only German "Justice" could comprehend.

Most of the witnesses who were allowed to testify were Armenians, key witnesses and each testified to the "humanity" of the defendant who had been compelled to commit murder, because of physical and psychological "disorders." The so-called Andonian "documents" WERE NOT allowed to be presented as evidence for the obvious reasons, even a layman's review would have revealed that the "documents" were forgeries. At its conclusion the jury acquitted the assassin, and the murderer thus remained a free man. To this very day, Tehlirian and other Armenian assassins are considered by so-called "Christian" Armenians as "national heroes." In 1960, Tehlirian died of natural causes after a life of wealth and comfort for his "contributions" to civilization.

THE FOLLOWING ARE STATEMENTS FROM ARMENIAN SOURCES:
A FEW QUOTATIONS TAKEN FROM A BOOK ENTITLED 'THE ARMENIAN REVOLUTIONARY MOVEMENT," by Louise Nalbandian. Published: 1963 (italics by this author.)

Page 55: "… Under (Grigor) Ardzruni's editorship, the pages of the Mushak (newspaper) were filled with *revolutionary propaganda.* During a critical period of the Russo-Turkish War, as the Russian armies were *marching into Turkey*, he wrote: "If Turkey vanishes from the face of the earth as a nation, the Armenians of Turkey must try every means to *join* Russia."

Page 67: "The centers of *revolutionary* activity in Turkish Armenia were Zeitun, Van, and Erzerum. The Zeitun *Rebellion* of *1862* was the *beginning of extensive uprisings* directed against the Ottoman Government…."

Page 74: "… The results of the *victory* at Zeitun *encouraged revolts* in other cities in the Ottoman Empire…."

Page 90 "… The Armenakan Party was the first Armenian political party in the nineteenth century to engage in *revolutionary* activities. It was organized at Van, in *1885*…."

Page 97: "… Under the heading: "The Program of the Armenakan Party…: 5. by inculcating in the people the spirit of self-defense-training them in the use of *arms* and military discipline, *supplying them with arms and money,* and organizing guerilla forces…"

Page 101: "…Certain episodes indicate the Armenakans did not stop at mere action, but also *incited trouble and committed terrorist acts…"*

Page 150: "…The Russian-Armenian Revolutionary societies, both in the *pre* and *post*-Russo-Turkish War period (1868-1890), contributed to the Armenian *Revolutionary* Movement. All encouraged more nationalistic feeling, advocated *rebellion* in Turkish Armenia, and brought about a closer bond between Russian and Turkish Armenians..." "...The Armenian *Revolutionary* Federation of the Dashnaktsuthiun..." formed "during the summer of *1890* ... was the result of the merger of various Armenian groups, primarily *in Russia*, into a single political party..."

Page 156: "...Under the banner of the Federation of Armenian *Revolutionaries* the Party declared a 'people's *war* against the *Turkish Government...*"

A STATEMENT ATTRIBUTED TO ADOLF HITLER WAS NEVER MADE! THE TITLE HEADING OF AN ARTICLE AUTHORED BY AN ARMENIAN READS: 'HISTORIAN OF ARMENIAN DESCENT SAYS FREQUENTLY USED HITLER QUOTE IS NOTHING BUT A FORGERY."

Published in *the Armenian Reporter,*
Dated: August 2, 1984.

"...Dr. Robert John, a historian and political analyst of Armenian descent from New York City, declared here that a commonly used quotation of an alleged statement by Adolf Hitler concerning the Armenian massacres was a forgery and should not be used. Dr. John demonstrated how he had traced the original document in the Military Branch of the National Archives of the U.S.A ..." "...The quotation 'Our strength is in our quickness and brutality...' 'I have sent to the East only my Death's Heads units, with the order to kill without pity or mercy all men, women, and children... Who talks nowadays of the extermination of the Armenians?"

"Dr. John showed slides of this document, undated and *unsigned,* with some words cut out of the last page. The statement was supposed to have been made at a meeting of the top German staff of the Obersalzberg on August 22, 1939. The document was released to the international press covering the Nuremberg War Crimes ... 250 copies were given to press correspondents, but only 5 copies were given to 17 defense counsels ... Much later in the trial the German defense lawyers were able to introduce the most complete account of the address, taken down by German Admiral Hermann Boehm, which runs 12 pages in translation. There is *no mention of the Armenians* or the *rest of the quotation ..."*

THE FOLLOWING IS TAKEN FROM AN A.R.F. PAMPHLET:
(KNOWN AS *THE ARMENIAN REVOLUTIONARY FEDERATION.)*

Published in New York City,
Date: Not provided

" ... A Few Words about the Armenian *Revolutionary* Federation – Its History: Struggle for National Liberation. Founded in 1890, as a confederation of various *action groups* struggling for Armenian national and human rights, the Armenian *Revolutionary* Federation (ARF), known as Dashnaksoutian, carried on this struggle with all available means: political action, *propaganda* and at times, *armed struggle..."*

THE FOLLOWING IS TAKEN FROM A LENGHTY NEWSPAPER ARTICLE: TITLE HEADING 'ARMENIA'S ENEMIES NOT FORGOTTEN IN GLENDALE.'

Published in *the L.A. Times*
Date: February, 1990

"Edna Petrosyan is only 6 years old, but she knows all about Armenia's enemies ... the child of an Armenian neighbor upstairs is having a birthday party, and Edna wants to go ... the mother brings Edna close to her lap, puts an arm around her shoulder, and softly asks in Armenian: "What's that number you write down whenever I draw a cross?" Edna mumbles: "1915." "Now recite that poem I taught you," Tello Petrosyan instructs her daughter.

The child steps out of her mother's embrace, raises her head, puts her hands in her pockets and, with the face grave beyond her years, begins: "It's better that I be a dog or a cat than a Turkish barbarian..."

The poem promises that "When the Armenian wind blows, it will not leave a single Turk standing in Armenian land."

A PUBLISHED ARTICLE FROM AN ARMENIAN NEWSPAPER.
"COMMENTARY – FRIENDS, THERE ARE NO FRIENDS."

Printed in: *The Armenian Reporter*
By: Ara Baliozian
Dated: May 28th, 1994.

"True friendship among Armenians is a rare thing, indeed…" -- "Hatred and envy: they seem to come naturally to us." – "We are all familiar with the old saying: Armenians are their own worst enemies." – "For those among us, who may not be familiar with some of its many variances, here is a handful:"

"Anonymous: 'To have an Armenian friend is to have an enemy.' – 'Derenik Demirjian (1877-1956): Every Armenian has another Armenian whom he considers his mortal enemy.'

"Rafi: (1835-1888): 'An Armenian's worst enemies are not *odars* but Armenians.' (This author's note: *Odars* is the Armenian word for 'strangers.')

"Shahan Shahnour (1904-1974): 'For my generation of Armenians, the enemy is not the Turks, but us.'

"Siamanto (1878-1915): 'Our perpetual enemy – the enemy that will eventually destroy us – is not the Turk, but our own complacent superficiality.'

"Antranik Zaroukian (1912-1989): 'What kind of people are we? Instead of compassion, mutual contempt … instead of common sense, fanaticism.' … 'I could go on and on … divisiveness has a long history among us. Our past is filled with countless instances of betrayal and treachery…'

"In his "Human, All too Human," Nietzsche (this author's note: Frederick Nietzsche, 1844-1900, was a German philosopher), quotes a philosopher's famous last words: 'Friends, there are no friends!' Nietzsche does not identify the philosopher's name or nationality, but I can't help suspecting that he was an Armenian."

* * *

THE AUTHOR'S PERSPECTIVE OF THE ABOVE FIVE ARMENIAN QUOTATIONS:

1 – Nalbandian's book titled "The Armenian Revolutionary Movement," is the work of an Armenian author; if it had been authored by a Turkish writer, then the Armenians would have claimed: "It's propaganda!" Anything that is from a Turkish source is labeled as "Turkish Distortion of History," by the Armenians, but every word from the Armenians is considered as the gospel truth. Since this author has presented five questions from Armenian *sources,* should we therefore not assume that this author has presented at least "some of the gospel truth?" The title of the book speaks for itself, but if twenty five years of rebellion had taken place in the United States of America, what would have been the reaction of the people and the government of our country? But as long as the Turkish people and homeland were the victims of Armenian revolution, there was no condemnation of Armenian treason, and as a result, an Armenian resolution appears everywhere.

2 – One of Hitler's generals had said "If you repeat a lie often enough, the people will believe it." Is there an American politician who knows that Hitler NEVER referred to the Armenians in the context they attribute to him? But there are many members of Congress and State legislators who have repeated the "statement" supplied to them by their Armenian lobby. One Armenian historian has researched the so-called "quotation" and has informed the Armenians in his column that it is a mere forgery! One more Armenian fraud is exposed by an Armenian, his name: Dr. Robert John.

3 – The A.R.F. pamphlet describes in glowing terms the "greatness" of the Armenian *Revolutionary* Movement, which to the present times, the organization each year celebrates its founding in Ottoman Turkey in 1890! 25 YEARS BEFORE the events of 1915.

4 – The quintessence of the Armenian obsession with hatred is the spoken words of an innocent *6 year old child!* The cruel words which a little girl is forced to memorize reveals NOT HER HATRED, but the infectious hateful philosophy of her mother. An innocent child, the creation of God, is destined to a life of hate against a people and a nation with whom she shares 6 *centuries* of cultural and historical harmony. As if this outrage was not terrible enough, the mother by her blasphemous behavior, has equated the sign of the Holy Cross with the year of 1915, in the child's heart. This the most heinous of sins to implant the legacy of hatred into a heart filled with love!

5 – This author during his years of work on the subject matter of this book has made countless negative comments about the Armenians outside of the Republic of Turkey, for the willful distortion of Turkish history and for their total obsession with hatred. But when compared to the above quoted article, written by Mr. Ara Baliozian, my condemnation of the Armenians are extremely mild. Having the full page article written and published in ENGLISH, defies all comprehension. Is it possible that the Armenian sources of the quoted statements were unaware of the horrendous implication for their own people? "True friendship among Armenians is a rare thing, indeed." – "Hatred and envy: they seem to come naturally to us." – "Our past is filled with countless instances of betrayal and treachery." These and the remaining quotations explicitly reveal the nature of many Armenians BY Armenians! Yet their "gains" in the political arena in this and other countries, have enabled the Armenians to be considered as "victims" of Turkish "atrocities," while disregarding over ONE MILLION Turks killed by Armenian Revolutionaries in Ottoman Turkey.

IRREFUTABLE EVIDENCE OF ARMENIANS CONSUMED WITH HATRED:

Other than the five Armenian quotations presented above, we shall offer the reader the following six examples of deception, fraud, inculcation, and even murder, all of which reveals the inherent characteristic of hatred within the Armenian community. This remains the legacy instilled in the hearts of Armenian children:

1 – We have shown in this work the division and bitter animosity within the Armenian community in this and other countries, which has extended to the Armenian churches and its clergy. The extent of the separation between the MOTHER CHURCH and the Dashnaksagan "Church," that being its respective communities, and church hierarchy, is shown by an article published in "The Armenian Church," issue of September 1975. A two-page article written by a Mr. Hagop Nersoyan begins with this title: "On Armenian Church Unity – Is it a Must?" In a church publication that such a question could even be asked suggests there is a serious problem within the Armenian psyche. As incomprehensible as it is to believe, Nersoyan attempts to show the "advantage" of division within the one and same people and church. During the period of the article, there used to be a religious program broadcast every Sunday on television, as it is to this day, the media provides time for the Armenian perspective during the month of April of each year. Referring to the broadcast of the Armenian version of the events of Ottoman Turkey during the 1915 period, Nersoyan writes, in part, the following: "…we certainly did much more and received much more attention from the American public because of our separateness. For one thing, CBS gave us two half-hour programs on two successive Sundays, instead of one. In this way we could cover both the significance and the history of the Massacres in two perfectly harmonious programs *ours'* and *theirs.'* The CBS shows are just one example. Had we been a united diocese, we would have had only one show. One may cite several other examples of increased activity due to precisely to our being two distinct organizations." Since most of the material presented in this volume has been in the possession of the author for many years, it comes as no surprise to me that the above quotation could appear in the publication of the Diocese of the Armenian Church of America. However, this author is anxious to consider the perspective of the reader, be he/she of Turkish origin, or not. Does the reader begin a mental evaluation of the Armenian people when an Armenian asks the question: "Armenian Church Unity – Is it a Must?"

A family, a community, or a nation which lacks the uniform character of purpose and the fundamental harmony with other human beings and nature, can not continue as a viable entity. Because of the division among the Armenians, Nersoyan is pleased because the Armenians had the opportunity to vilify the Turkish people twice*!* With the evidence presented here, from *Armenian* sources, any person of rational thought surely is perplexed by the suggestion that *unity* within a community should not be considered as a priority. But there are other examples of this manifestation of Armenian obsession with hatred, which the author presents here with saddened heart:

2 – In 1933, the division and mutual hatred *within* the Armenian community had begun, and continues to this time. While the Armenian Archbishop Tourian was celebrating Mass on Christmas Morning, and his procession moved slowly by the crowded pews, he was assassinated by the members of the Dashnaksagan fanatical organization. The

Archbishop had been knifed to death by his own people, during Mass, in front of God.

3 – Among the many fraudulent examples of Armenian "evidence" against the Turks, is a picture which depicts a pyramid of human skulls with the following caption: "Dedicated to the Memory of the 1,500,000 martyred Armenians who were massacred by the Turks in 1915."

This picture had been used in Armenian publications and distributed to politicians and universities as "evidence" of their allegations against the Turkish people. The picture is factual but it has NOTHING to do with the Armenians! In reality, the picture is a copy of an original painting which can be seen at the present time, hanging on a wall of the Tretyakov Gallery in Moscow. It had been painted by the Russian artist Vassili Vershehgan in the year of 1871. The artist, who had titled his painting: "The Apotheosis of War," died in 1904! (The date needs to be repeated: HE DIED IN 1904!) Is there one American politician or one news editor who knows that the painting just referred to has ABSOLUTELY NO association with the Armenian people? Not likely. Though the picture caption does not say the "skulls" are of dead Armenians, the intended accusation of the Turks is blatantly obvious. But anyone who has a reverence for historical accuracy surely will be able to recognize this example of Armenian fraud.

4 – The term "Armenian Hate Merchants," was first used many years ago, by the author who has never intentionally vilified his people. The Armenians, by their own actions, and with their own statements have verified the implication in my harsh but true terminology. Consider the following: in the suburbs of Boston, Mass., is a summer camp called Camp *Haiastan* (the latter is the Armenian word for Armenia), and an article printed in the July 17th, 1993 issue of *The Armenian Weekly*), describes some of the activities at the summer camp. One large black and white photograph shows a group of Armenian teenagers holding posters of which only one is readable: *Turkey Must Pay!* A caption reads: "Campers learn a little about activism during a mock demonstration in the cabin circle." The young people are being taught how to perform anti-Turkish demonstrations, but the use of the word "activism," is proven to be a subterfuge. When we look at a second photo with the caption "The Lisbon Five," the article says in part: "On July 27th 1983, five Armenians now known as the Lisbon Five took over the Turkish Embassy of Lisbon. These brave Armenians' purpose was to attract the attention to the unjust acts of 1915. The Lisbon Five were about to get caught, when the building blew up. All five Armenians perished. Last Saturday, July 10th, we at Camp Haiastan had our reenactment of what happened…" Beneath the article is another large photo showing six young Armenian boys and girls, with one boy seated in an office chair, his mouth gagged, and his arms supposedly tied behind his back. Behind him, on his back, is a young girl holding a large water gun aimed at the head of the seated male teenager. The depiction is a reenactment of the attack on the Turkish Embassy. Four of the six teenagers are smiling, which suggests they are still novice "hate merchants," but since the article is dated in 1993, we must assume they have "graduated" to the level of their demonic practitioners. Activism used to perpetrate hatred must not and will not be accepted!

5 – January the 27th, 1973 is the date which has no significance to the people of United States, but to the Turkish-Americans and the people of the Republic of Turkey, it is the date of the Armenian barbarism against innocent Turks. This was to be the date of the beginning of Armenian attacks upon Turkish facilities worldwide, and the murder of innocent Turks and non-Turks who had the misfortune of being in the vicinity of explosives set off by Armenian assassins. The first murder took place in Santa Barbara, California, on the above date, when Gourgan Yanikyan, an elderly Armenian and United States citizen, shot to death the Turkish Council General Mehmet Baydar and his Vice-Council Bahadar Demir. Neither victim was even born during the events of 1915!

During the 1970s and the 1980s, the media in the United States and throughout the world, for the first time, began to use the *term: Armenian Terrorism* as a result of Armenian fanaticism. ASALA, an acronym for the Armenian Secret Army for the Liberation of Armenia, had begun a campaign of murder and bombings of Turkish establishments and airport locations. ASALA was an extension of the Dashnaksagan fanatical group, the latter of which continues its philosophy of hate to the present time. During its years of terror inflicted upon people who had not been involved in the tragic events of 1915, over fifty innocent Turkish diplomats and family members, together with over thirty innocent non-Turks lost their lives to those who take pride in their "Christianity!" In addition, the untold thousands of people who were injured because they were in public areas remember well the results of the Armenian fanaticism. Many cities in Europe, Middle East, Canada, the United States, and other countries were witness to the maniacal actions of Armenian terrorists. As it had been in Ottoman Turkey, the ugly "Frankenstein Monster" of hate resurfaced in the United States. During these despicable acts of murder against innocent people, what was the reaction of the Turkish people in the United States and the Turkish homeland? How many Armenians were killed by the Turks, in retaliation? How many Armenian churches were bombed? The answer is NONE! Not only wasn't there a single act of vengeance, but the incumbent Prime Minister, the late Turgut Özal, urged his people NOT to use the terms: "Armenian terrorism," but to refer to the murders as "terrorism!" And we Christians speak of "turning the other cheek."

I remain in awe of the compassion, the humanity, and the kindness of the Turkish heart.

With so much negative reaction from the news media, one of the final acts of terrorism took place in Melbourne, Australia, in November of 1986. But the ingrained Armenian hatred for the Turkish people was to continue in their communities, their churches and in their influence upon the media and politicians.

6 – There are countless examples of the Armenian insatiable appetite for the hatred of Turks, some of which have been revealed in this work, but before we present other infamous examples, let us consider an event which took place as far back as 1962.

Because the following tragic event involved the author, the depiction presented here is in its totality a factual occurrence: Early in 1962 an Armenian neighbor residing near our home in Bayside, Queens, New York, had been friendly with my mother, as were our families. Knowing of our participation in a young mid-eastern band, she had suggested we perform for a bazaar dance, given by the Armenian Church which was and still is, one block away from our home. She had suggested we perform for the church function, gratis, as an introduction to the church community which was known to be an affluent parish, with the expectation of playing at their future functions. The suggestion was acceptable to me, as it was to the members of our group of young friends with whom we had performed for many years.

After contacting the church with our proposal, an appointment was made for this author to meet with the priest and members of the

Board of Directors. During our discussion in the church office, Rev. Vartan Megherian and church representatives were pleased with my proposal and requested I forward to them an informative letter about our band with names and any pertinent facts which they would print in their church publication. Our purpose for the function had been to perform gratis, the music of our people, as we had done for hundreds of audiences. We were young, to play our music was for us a supreme joy, but we were familiar with *this* community whom we were to entertain. This meant that there would absolutely be no REFERENCE to a single song sung in Turkish! As a group, we had resigned ourselves to such an incomprehensible situation, and in my letter of introduction to the church, the word Turkish did not appear. My letter presented the names of the musicians, our instruments, and other information about our program. Our letter was printed in the October 1962 issue of the church paper, with the following headline: "Mid-Easterns to play for Bazaar Dance," and distributed to the church membership.

Of the five names, one name was recognized as being the name of a Turkish gentleman. The "honorable" church directors became incredulous and outraged: *How could they permit a Turk to enter an Armenian Church reception hall?*

Meetings were held to discuss the acceptability of this individual! His name was Mr. Tarik Bulut, my beloved "kardeş" (brother), for whom the author has revealed profound respect and deep love in the early pages of this volume. I was incensed! I was furious! I was angry with disgust!

(For the first time in this autobiography, I begin with the first person singular): I connected my tape recorder to the telephone receiver and spoke to Mr. "K" (I will not request permission to use his name), who had been a senior church director and spoke the following: "I will not permit my brother, Mr. Tarik Bulut, to be exposed to ignorant Armenian hate merchants! Not knowing anything about Tarik's humanity, his talents, his compassion, his scholarship, his love for his family and all peoples, your Armenians refuse him because of his Turkish origin! I withdraw my promise to perform at your function!"

Mr. "K" attempted sincerely to ease my anger and said Tarik could perform, to which I replied, "Never!" I was neither vulgar nor abusive, but my statements revealed my outrage, and I was truly ashamed of "my people."

The most difficult aspect of the above events was yet to follow: what was I to say to Tarik? HOW could I tell him how ashamed I was of the people who claimed to worship Jesus Christ? As long as I live, I will never forget the response of my brother, Tarik, after I informed him of my conversation with Mr. "K".

Mr. Tarik Bulut spoke to me the following words: "Ed, I don't want to cause a problem between you and your church, please go on with your performance and I will attend as a guest and listen to your music. Had I known these things were to happen, I would have urged you to enter my name as: Bulut-yan." (Almost every Armenian surname ends with the letters *ian* or *yan*). THIS IS THE HUMANITY OF MY BROTHER, TARIK; THIS IS THE COMPASSION OF THE TURKISH HEART.

One very important fact will conclude the above narrative: Several months later, the same church was having its annual picnic, and my friend and fellow musician Mr. Harry Esehak, suggested to me that we attend the picnic and listen to some music. We went, and as usual there had been a large turnout. The musicians were all American-born Armenians and they performed well. At one point, this author noticed three Armenian priests walking together, with their hands folded behind their backs. Just then, over the loudspeakers, the audience heard the musicians play three successive Turkish songs, and each song was sung in Turkish! Each vocal was performed for the people to dance to, and a large number of people were dancing, the floor was covered with dollar bills as is our custom. Hundreds of people responded with joyous ovation! Turkish vocals played and sung in Turkish! In the convoluted minds of the Armenian hate merchants, their blatant hypocrisy defies all logic as their legacy of hatred remains manifestly present.

A legacy for their children for generations to come!

7 – A family reunion serves as the next example of the Armenian obsession with hatred as distinction must be made here of the author's family and the family of the author's wife, on their respective positions pertaining to my efforts on the subject of Turkish-Armenian history. On the author's side, his brother, his sister-in-law, four nieces, and their children, though never active in the Turkish-American community, had never displayed any negative attitude of our work, and in fact have occasionally praised the author for his efforts. But the situation in the home of the author's wife had been and continues to be dramatically different. However, my wife Mary's mother who had experienced the war in Ottoman Turkey had never instilled any anti-Turkish sentiments in the hearts of her five children. Mary's interest in, and knowledge of the events of the historical relations between Turks and Armenians, began to take form after her marriage to the author. Based upon her own intellect, and review of the facts, she had formulated her opinions without any influence from the author. But in the home of her maternal aunt, the seeds of hate had been planted many generations earlier. And as a result, anti-Turkish comments had been often heard by Mary, her two brothers, her two sisters, and her cousins.

As the years passed, my work had attained unbelievable proportions, and the displeasure of Mary's family had become quite evident. Whenever our families visited each other, I made every effort not to "upset" the in-laws, and avoided the subject completely. But Mary was determined not to conceal her deep pride in our work and proceeded to describe the recognition and honors given to the author. No serious confrontations ever took place, but the following scene will once again reveal to the reader the result of the Armenian legacy of hate:

It had taken place during our summer visit of the year 2000, to the home of Mary's brother, George Kachajian, and his wife, Anne, in Belmont, Mass. Many childhood friends of Mary, and her family, had attended the splendid cookout. One of the guests was Mary's cousin to whom I shall refer to as Cousin "A," the daughter of "Dashnaksagan" parents (both deceased). The author would have welcomed a challenge from Cousin "A," but I was determined not to be confrontational with her as she was well aware of my feelings. Every other sentence she spoke, she included religious comments, pertaining to Jesus Christ and Christianity, her words did not express the obvious animosity in her eyes as she focused her gaze upon the gold star and crescent medallion worn by the author every day of his life. Her pretense of being a faithful Christian was revealed when she could no longer refrain from spewing her hatred of the Turkish people.

After several hours of family conversation had concluded, cousin "A" could no longer control herself and while in the presence of the author and other family members she made an abrupt reference to the Armenian "genocide" about which NO ONE had been speaking.

The response from the author which she was waiting for was not forthcoming; he left her fuming and frustrated in her failed attempt to create an ugly scene. But dear cousin "A" did make a final attempt to prove she was a proud creation of the Dashnaksagan group, by referring to the Turkish people in this manner, "I can't even speak of them by name!"

Her last attempt also failed, but the author will refer again to Cousin "A" in the last section of this chapter, in which it will be revealed that she was responsible for supplying historical information that was to be of monumental significance to the author. Thank you, cousin!

(Dear reader, the manuscript of this autobiography has once again been brought to a sudden stop as a result of tragic news which has crushed my heart. During the above composition I received a phone call from kardeşim (my brother) Tarik Bulut, who informed me that his beloved wife, Frances, has passed away. My wife and I are devastated beyond words for the loss of our sister, Frances, who was a magnificent human being, wife, and mother. We grieve, and in time this work must continue....)

8 – The political influence and pressures upon state officials by the Armenian community in the State of California has been well known for years. In the City of San Francisco stands a 103-foot cross placed on the top of a hill. The Mount Davidson Cross stood (and still does), on public land, had been the subject of a lawsuit, citing separation of church and state laws. The courts agreed with the plaintiffs and gave the city the choice of selling the cross and its land or to take down the structure. By auction the site was purchased by Armenian groups for $26,000. Turkish-Americans from every area of our country protested this obvious attempt by the Armenians to perpetuate their allegations against the Turkish people. Should we not suggest that much more money was given to politicians other than the sale price?! The cross, similar to other Armenian institutions, served as a symbol of hatred against a nation of God-fearing people. Not only have they distorted historical events, the Armenians have (and will continue) to commit blasphemy against the God they profess to worship: their sacred churches, their Christian faith, the cross, are symbols of hate.

9 – Among the many other examples of the Armenian predisposition for hatred, we conclude this section with example #9. How the Armenian people who live outside of the Republic of Turkey, can justify their overwhelming hatred of the Turkish people, while at the same time proclaim their Christian faith, is the convoluted paradox which only the Armenian mentality can comprehend. Euphemistically speaking, we would say: "I hate spinach!" or "I hate liver!" but in reality what we wish to convey is our dislike of a certain food, a fashion, and so on. But in the avowed position of the Armenians, namely, "I hate the Turks!" there is NO euphemism, and the philosophy of hate continues to infect the minds and hearts of their innocent children. The children of our Almighty God, come in to our troubled world free of sin, free of immorality, and yes, FREE OF THE CAPACITY TO HATE. They are TAUGHT HOW to hate. In other words, they are taught WHOM to hate, by those who had been taught by their elders. This illogical cycle of hatred and vengeance has become the genetic cancer in the hearts of young people whose lives are wasted in the realm of eternal hatred. And this legacy of hate awaits the next generation of Armenian youth!

The above introduction welcomes the reader to Emerson, N.J, where we can see an Armenian old age home. On the grounds of this facility, near the front and main entrance, a monument to hatred has been erected and has remained there for many years. Engraved on the stone of hate, the following inscription is to be seen: "In memory of the 2,000,000 Christian Armenians massacred by the Turks, 1915-1918."

In front of this creation of Armenian "hate merchants," a picture shows an elderly resident who had been brought to her *knees,* and with both of her arms outstretched, the woman gazes skyward! I urge the reader to read the last sentence over and over again, and ask yourself the question this author has asked repeatedly: "What kind of people are they?"

In the words of one Armenian: "Instead of common sense, fanaticism." Another has said: "Hatred and envy – they seem to come naturally to us." As though this monstrous manifestation of hate was not sufficient, groups of young Armenian children are brought and assembled in front of the monument of hate and pictures are taken to be distributed to politicians, universities and the media, in their eternal attempt to defame the honor and history of the Turkish people. All peoples of rational and constructive conviction must condemn the Armenians for the repulsive commitment to hatred of a people with whom they share six centuries of harmony and brotherhood. The message of the cross has always been forgiveness and LOVE!

ADDITIONAL FACTS WHICH REFUTE THE ARMENIAN ALLEGATIONS.

When Turkish historians describe the events of 1915 in Ottoman Turkey as being a period of global warfare which had devastated ALL the peoples of the country, and by definition, the Armenian suffering WAS NOT due to a premeditated design for "genocide," then those who have researched Ottoman history are accused of being in denial. In this work, the author has not quoted the statement of a single Turkish scholar, politician, or spokesperson, and this is due to an intentional effort to thwart any denial allegation. As the reader has seen, the author has presented quotations from *Armenian* sources, and as a result, any suggestion of "Turkish propaganda," is therefore void and ineffectual.

The following which will confirm the fraudulent allegations of the Armenians are from NEITHER Turkish, nor Armenian sources:

1 – At the conclusion of the war, the Ottoman rulers had been stripped of their authority, and while the young Turks, under the leadership of the immortal Mustafa Kemal Ataturk, began to build a new nation, the *victorious* powers of France and Great Britain had arrested over 140 Ottoman officials and high ranking military officers, and held them in prison at Valetta, Malta. The indictments included war crimes and cruelty against the civilian population of Ottoman Turkey. The officials were held in prison for over two years, while the British and French prosecutors searched for evidence against them. As well, their ally, the United States had been requested to join the investigation with the hope of finding the evidence which would prove the charges.

Keep in mind: the Ottoman officials were being prosecuted by their former enemy, and were interned the entire time, as the British sought incriminating evidence; and after two years, EACH OF THE OFFICIALS WERE SET FREE on October 25th, 1921, because of "insufficient evidence!"

War? Yes. Premeditated *genocide?* No.

2 – Upon the emergence of a democratic, secular Republic of Turkey, the United States assigned its first American Ambassador to the Turkish Republic. Ambassador Admiral Mark Bristol and his staff, unlike Morgenthau, had visited many regions of Turkey to inquire and gather information about the allegations in the American press which supported the unsubstantiated accusations of the traitorous Armenians. Ambassador Bristol learned on the scene of Armenian atrocities against Muslim Turkish men, women, and children. In one of his letters to his associates in the United States, he writes: "The Armenian allegations made my blood boil."

American politicians and the "impartial" American news media eagerly referred to the "Morgenthau story," which he did not write, while at the same time negating the historical significance of the writings of Ambassador Admiral Marc Bristol, who wrote extensively of the Armenian fabrications against the Turkish nation. To publicize the Bristol letters would surely expose the Armenian myth which has perpetuated a fraud upon world public opinion for over 86 years!

War? – Yes. Premeditated genocide? – NO!

3 - In May of 1985, the *New York Times*, a paper known for its anti-Turkish posture for many years, published a half-page open letter addressed to "Attention Members of the United States House of Representatives." House joint resolution 192, had been debated in the Congress, considering a resolution to establish a National Day of Remembrance of Man's Inhumanity to Man.

The open letter was followed by the names of sixty nine signatories who were American academicians, whose expertise included Ottoman, Turkish, and Middle Eastern studies and history. We offer here some quotations from the lengthy letter:

"... we respectfully take exception to that position of the text which singles out for special recognition: *the one and a half million people of Armenian ancestry who were the victims of genocide perpetrated in Turkey, between 1915 and 1923.*"

"...our reservation focuses upon the use of the words *Turkey* and *Genocide,* and may be summarized as follows ..."

"...the history of the Armenian Ottomans is much debated among scholars, many of whom do not agree with the *historical assumptions* embodied in the wording of H.J. Res. 192. By passing the resolution Congress will be attempting to determine by *legislation* which side of a *historical* question is correct. Such a resolution, based on historically *questionable assumptions,* can only damage the *credibility* of the *American legislative process*…."

(Italics by this author.)

Sixty nine American scholars, NOT politicians, had placed their names and their affiliated universities with the honor of their scholarship before members of our Congress whose priorities are focused upon placating their constituency. The above scholars are to be commended for their courage in disseminating historical accuracy, in spite of these accusations and threats of the hate-merchants.

War? Yes. Premeditated genocide? NO!

4 – Included in the Armenian declaration of allegations against the Turkish people has been the continuing analogy of the genocide of the Jewish people by Nazi Germany and the condition of the Armenians during a world conflagration in Ottoman Turkey.

The Armenians to this day claim that the Jewish genocide would not have taken place if the alleged Armenian "genocide" did not occur in Turkey. Aside from this autobiography who is prepared better to respond to the Armenian allegation than a survivor of the Holocaust itself?

Recently the Foreign Minister of Israel, Mr. Shimon Peres, who had been a Nobel Peace Prize recipient, in 1944, during a press interview, said in part the following: "… we reject attempts to create a similarity between the Holocaust and the Armenian allegations." "…nothing similar to the Holocaust occurred. It is a tragedy what the Armenians went through, but not *Genocide."*

As was to be expected, the highly financed Armenian lobby proceeded to condemn the Israeli Foreign Minister, and in response to the Armenian-American newspaper *Asbarez,* the Israeli Consulate released the following statement: "This issue should be dealt with by historians, not politicians. We do not support the comparison of the Armenian tragedies to the Jewish Holocaust. Israel will not take a historical and political stance on the issue."

The preceding as well as the other facts presented in this section, are irrefutable and based upon historical accuracy, from the perspective of the author (but of course the reader knew that), why then are the news media and the majority of American politicians so eager to support the Armenian lobby, when so many facts have proven the fallacy of the Armenian allegations?

To anyone who has followed Turkish-Armenian history and relations, with the fervor, the passion, and the dedication of this author, the response to the above question is as simple as it is obvious. While the author is not a historian, nor a scholar (though many would take exception to the latter), he has LIVED the history of this work through the lives of his parents, and as a result of his life-long witness to the character of the Turkish and Armenian peoples. The response: during my youth the Armenians were unknown and their anti-Turkish agenda took form in their own communities. After generations of increasing in numbers and activities, to defame the honor and history of the Turkish Nation, the media and our politicians joined the Armenian parade to condemn the Turks for crimes which never occurred! During this onslaught, there was no Turkish response, and as a result today, the media have no space for the Turkish perspective, and politicians have no time to meet with Turkish-Americans! If this response does not convince the reader, write your paper about this book and wait ….

CENTURIES OF HARMONY AND BROTHERHOOD OFTEN OVERLOOKED

In any review of the history of the Turkish, Armenian and Syrian-Orthodox (Suryani) peoples, the singular ingredient which invariably remains omnipresent, is the assertion that these communities had been engaged in continuous political and religious conflicts, which had resulted in mutual hatred and ceaseless killings of each other. The assertion is not only historically false, it has been and continues to be as illogical as it is potentially destructive. The harmony and brotherhood as shared by the above peoples, to whom we should include the Greek, Jewish, and Kurdish, communities shared the joys and sorrows of the same homeland. No greater evidence of this historical fact can equal the significance of the total freedoms enjoyed by these peoples in their religion, their languages, their press, and their daily lives as Turkish citizens in the Turkish nation, before and after the establishment of the Turkish Republic in 1923.

Earlier, the author had "introduced" Cousin "A" as an example of Armenian animus, to the reader, and as promised I have included her in this section on harmony and brotherhood.

The apparent incongruity of this presentation will be clarified by the following narration, which serves as another example of Divine guidance upon me:

Several years earlier, during a family reunion of Mary's family, in the Boston, Mass., area, Cousin "A" had been present, and as we greeted each other, she removed from her purse a photograph which she wanted to give to Mary. Mary was very grateful for the photograph for it included a photo of her mother, and her maternal aunt (which would be the mother of Cousin "A"). This of course explained how the photograph had been in her possession, because it had been given to her by her mother, and the following information had also been given by her mother: The photograph reveals seven young Armenian women in a group tableaux taken in the town of Harput, Ottoman Turkey, around the year of 1910!

The family photograph was to become an invaluable source of historical information, but had it not been for the astute curiosity of the author, this scene from Ottoman Turkey, would never have been given the recognition it deserves.

As each of us studied the photograph, the author noticed that one of the seven young ladies was seated and had both of her hands placed upon an open book. The author asked Cousin "A" if she knew anything about the woman with the book on her lap.

Then, "Yes, I do. My mother had told me about her …"

At this point, dear reader, please note that one of the ladies in the picture was Mary's mother, and another was her aunt.

Cousin "A" concluded by saying, "The lady with the book was *blind* and she was reading an Armenian book written in Braille."

The author displayed no visible sign of jubilation, lest Cousin "A" realize what a blunder she had just committed.

I calmly thanked her for giving us the family photograph and slowly took it from her and handed it to Mary for safe-keeping. Cousin "A" could not have realized the major significance of a simple photograph, coupled with the information given her by her mother. But this author, did. To summarize: In a small town of Ottoman Turkey, around the year of 1910, the Armenians had been in possession of books written in Armenian Braille! Is this an example of persecution, or of total FREEDOM?

I wondered silently, if the Turks around 1910, even had books printed in *Turkish* Braille.

Yet the Armenians had literature printed in Armenian Braille which of course exemplified their desire for education. Keep in mind, also, the information given to the author was by a lady who was the daughter of Dashnaksagan parents, who took their hatred to their graves. If, as the Armenians continued to allege, the Armenians of Ottoman Turkey had been persecuted by the Turks, how then were they able to publish in Armenian Braille? We repeat, the schools, churches, press, language, and community activities functioned in total freedom. And so on to this day, my government and the American media continue their groundless accusations against the history and the honor of a staunch ally of the United States of America!

My country speaks of equality for all people; we are supposed to be the champion of human rights, we profess to maintain the fundamental freedoms of our Constitution, yet the blatant double standard in the issues concerning Turkey, is a disgrace. The Turks of Cyprus, the Turks of Azerbaijan, the Turks of the Crimea, among others, continue to wait for the support of the United States, gives the enemies of our NATO Ally – our Korean War Ally – our First Gulf War Ally – and our Ally who keeps our American Air Bases on her soil! Yet the ubiquitous Armenian Resolution remains a priority for politicians eager to satisfy the Armenian Lobby.

Let us return to the heading of this section:

Another historical testament to the freedoms enjoyed by the Armenians of Ottoman Turkey had been presented to the author and his wife in 1968, during a private audience with the Armenian Patriarch, the late and beloved Snork Kalustyan!

Our historic private meeting with His Eminence Patriarch Snork Kalustyan had taken place in the Armenian Patriarchate in Istanbul, Turkey, while my wife Mary and our beloved brother, Dr. Oktay Akkent, was present. While we spoke in English, his Eminence had informed us that he was aware of the anti-Turkish activities on the part of the Armenians in the United States. He instructed me to carry his message to the Armenian community in America: "Stop the harmful actions, as we are free in this our country, the Republic of Turkey." He blessed us for our effort on behalf of the Turkish-Armenian Brotherhood. As the Patriarch gave us a tour of the facilities and a beautiful Armenian church, in his office he pointed out a framed "firman," (an Imperial edict of the Ottoman Sultan), granting total freedom to the Armenians in their religious and community functions. His warm blessings and kind utterances filled our hearts and minds with profound respect, deep love and unforgettable memories. He remains in our hearts as does his successor, His Eminence Patriarch Mesrob II.

While the Armenians outside of Turkey have convinced the uninformed that persecution had filled their centuries of existence during the Ottoman period, history has recorded countless Armenians who had achieved the highest levels of the Ottoman governments: Senators, Members of the Grand National Assembly, Ministers of Education, of Finance, of Health, Foreign Affairs, Communications, Postal Service, Agriculture, among others, were held by "Armenians." The Balyan name to this day remains supreme in Ottoman Turkish architecture. The world-famous brass symbols used in rock bands and symphonic orchestras, worldwide, began with the famous Zilchiyan family of Ottoman Turkey! The names and the positions attained by the Armenians, as recorded, remain indisputable, and the denial and the fraud of the Armenians WILL NOT erase these FACTS.

On September 15th 1994, this author prepared a single page which presents living proof of the brotherhood of the Turkish and Armenian peoples. It is a page which no historian has prepared and yet this writer offers as his final example of the inseparability of these peoples. On one page I have listed the names of 47 Armenian, Sűryani, Jewish, and Greek, composers, artists, and musicians, who have contributed their talents to classical and contemporary Turkish music. The first group include artists of the Ottoman period; the second those born in Turkey and brought their artistry to this country; and the third, like the author, those born in the United States, and yet all of them have PERFORMED Turkish music. In music, in songs, in poetry, OUR PEOPLES ARE ONE!

Before the concluding chapter, the author will address himself to the Youth of our people.

XI. My concluding statements to Armenian and Turkish Youth.

The Author's final comments to the Armenian Youth:

If you have read the pages of this autobiography, you surely are convinced of one of the following three possibilities:

1 – The author, beyond question, is a megalomaniac, who has been consumed by hatred for his people and his faith.

2 – The author has worked long and tirelessly hoping to achieve an unattainable concept; he is delusional.

3 – The author is worthy of the highest praise for his determination, his dedication, and his life-long labors with the aspiration of achieving even a semblance of compassion, on brotherhood, in the midst of uncontrollable human hatred. Which of the three perspectives will describe your response to the author? If you wish, after reading the final chapter, to communicate with the author, you may do so by writing to the following address:

Edward Tashji, P.O Box 20152, D.H.C.C New York, NY, 10017. Or, fax: 212-687-3026. The author will attempt to respond to every correspondence, favorable or not, upon receipt of a signed letter with a return address.

My dear Armenian brother and sister, of the above perspectives the author most assuredly would wish that the latter would be your choice, but because the author is NOT delusional, he is inclined to believe your position will continue to be vehemently negative; but your feelings for this author should not be of prime concern to you. YOU are the main topic; YOU will live your life filled with hate or rational intellect; YOU will instill in the hearts and minds of your children, the gift of God's love, or the cancer of hate. No matter how severe your feelings for the author might be, after reading these many pages, can you really believe that I have displayed hatred for my people and my faith? Have I not described the infinite talents and achievements of our Armenian people? Have I not referred to the suffering of our people? If you recognize the suffering of ONLY the Armenians, while negating the anguish of ALL the peoples of Ottoman Turkey, then you have closed your mind to the terrible deeds committed by Armenian Revolutionaries. There were dreadful acts committed by the Turks, as well, it was a horrible war, and war destroys all lives. The beautiful tree of harmony, between our respective peoples, was grievously damaged by mutual hatred and one by one our branches were severed, but the tree of brotherhood DID NOT die! By mutual compassion and a desire for peace our tree was restored and continues to grow, offering its fruits of brotherhood and harmony among our peoples.

You may achieve position and wealth in your life, but if hatred remains in your heart, you will never realize true happiness. Your parents do not wish you ill, but the legacy of hate which they have inherited will pass on to you and you will be destined to pass on the perpetual cycle of hatred to your children. For how long will this illogical manifestation of hatred continue? Think of the world wars which have devastated millions of people; by its very nature, in any war, there can be no victor, only vanquished. Whether on the field of battle or in our relations with our fellow human beings, hate can only create more hate which will eventually cause other conflagrations. History has proven, yesterday's enemies can, and *have* become tomorrow's friends. There is no suggestion that to attain compassion and harmony while our hearts continue to grieve, will be easy. But YOU and YOU alone, no matter how difficult, MUST sever the bonds of hatred against a people with whom you share over six centuries of cultural assimilation. Not for the benefit of this author, not for the benefit of your parents, but for YOUR benefit. You might be criticized, but when you embrace your Turkish brother or sister, you will experience the infinite love of Him who has said: "Blessed are the peace-makers for they shall be called the Children of God!"

At this position in this autography, you have learned of the events in the humble life of the author, and the overwhelming response of the Turkish people and Government. In the final comments of the author to his Armenian brothers and sisters, the following is offered as the most rewarding development of his life:

As has been described, our first visit to Turkey took place in August of 1968, and our meetings with high ranking officials and media interviews were given wide coverage by the Turkish and Armenian Press. During the month of April, 1969, the author received a handwritten letter from Lebanon, which was sent to his home address. The brief letter was dated April 4th, 1969, and written by a person who signed his name as Boghos Mardirian, who described himself as a student of the Armenian Evangelical Secondary School, in Ainjar, Bekkaa, Lebanon. As you would expect, the brief letter was negative with the following conclusion: "…in reality you are a foolish person, shame on you!" Signed: Boghos Mardirian.

Needless to say, I was not pleased by the correspondence of this total stranger, recognizing his "ailment." I responded to his statements with a 3-page letter written by an "ağabey" (older brother), rather than an adversary. But what could be said to a "student of hatred?"

My letter to Mardirian was polite and emphasized my search for brotherhood and the futility of the specious agenda of his "educators." I had suggested we become pen-pals, while revealing the historical harmony between the Armenian and Turkish peoples.

A second correspondence by Mr. Mardirian arrived, dated May, 1969, in response to my "brotherly" letter, his second letter to me was far worse than his first. With my name at the top of the page, a statement begins: "We, the students of the upper-class of the Armenian Evangelical Secondary School…" and this ending: "We advise you to understand the evil spirit and nature of the Turks, and to keep silence. Below the statement are added the signatures of 46 young students, who 'fully agree' with Mr. Boghos Mardirian…"

Being exposed to the maniacal behavior of Armenian "hate merchants," all my life, why would this letter affect me any differently? But it did! Two words continued to pierce my heart: *Evangelical*, and *Students.* Was this the message of their Christian faith? As students, they are taught to hate, is this the purpose of their "education?" I became outraged at the teachers more than the students, because they were the creators of the next generation of Armenian Hate Merchants! They are not educators, they are not Christians! In my second letter to Mardirian, I expressed these comments, among other, which condemned their so-called teachers, for their mission of hatred.

Five years were to pass when another letter from Lebanon arrived at the home of the author. The hand writing was familiar, and signed by the same Boghos Mardirian; this was indeed unexpected. Dated June 10th, 1974, the letter reads as follows:

"Dear Mr. Tashji,

I have dishonored you personally and do not know how to ask for forgiveness. Be sure you have taught an Armenian not to hate. I hope you'll consider this a very personal letter and shall not disappoint me. Honestly, (signed) Boghos Mardinian."

The hand written letter brought to me a supreme joy which words can not describe, and as tears filled my eyes, I read the letter over and over again. Among the many honors which have been presented to the author, as described in this work, none have affected me as much as a letter from a young man I have never met, and possibly will never meet (personally). If I achieved nothing else in my life, that I had something to do with changing the heart of ONE young person from hatred, is my greatest "reward."

I call upon the Armenian Youth to emulate Mr. Boghos Mardirian and free yourself of hate, and reach out to your Turkish brother and sister, they await your embrace!

* * *

The Author's Final Comments to Turkish Youth

There would be no useful purpose in repeating here the initial comments as presented to the Armenian Youth, by this author at the beginning of this chapter. However, my concluding statements are directed to your attention as well, because the author would welcome your perspectives pertaining to the work and philosophy of this unique "Friend of Turks."

It could be suggested that comments from Turkish readers would certainly express a pre-dominantly favorable response, the assumption might appear to be correct, but if there are to be negative opinions from the community for which I have worked, it would not be the first time. As much as has been described in these pages, there are countless other events, meetings, and endeavors, which have not been recorded here. Because of our tireless work, much if not most of our efforts have resulted in successful conclusions. This has received the gratitude and deep affection of the Turkish people. But in rare instances, my wife and I have been perplexed by the behavior of former close friends who no longer even greet us. According to other friends, this phenomenon is attributed to a subconscious manifestation of envy. The convoluted theory follows this form: This person (referring to the author) is an American; non-Turkish, non-Muslim; who has taught himself to speak and write in Turkish; has become an ardent advocate, and an eloquent spokesman, and a fearless defender of the Turkish people; and in addition, he is an ethnic Armenian!

How can this be? Is money or egotism the unknown factor in this inexplicable situation? The response to these questions will be offered in the following, concluding chapter. Therefore the author will anticipate at least some negative reviews from our Turkish readers. But as I have advised the Armenian youth, the same advice is directed to my beloved Turkish brothers and sisters: Only your conclusions and your attitudes should be your guide in formulating your knowledge of Turkish-Armenian history. Regrettably, Armenian Youth has a major "advantage," over Turkish Youth, and that is: being able to disseminate to an ill-formed American public, media, and government, their own position on the history of the Turkish-Armenian relations. The fact that their espoused position is based upon fraud, forgeries, and distortions, will not affect an audience which is so eager to blame the Turks for anything they can think of. But what of YOUR position? Are you in a position to refute the Armenian allegations? If you are accused or engaged in a debate, will you be able to present historical facts which will *prove* the Armenians are wrong? I am convinced you are poorly prepared to defend your history and ancestors.

Yes, the author believes that Armenian Youth has a major “advantage” over Turkish Youth, because of many existing factors, proven by the following:

The comments of a six-year old daughter of an Armenian family in Glendale, California, which has been described in this work, is the quintessential example of the dilemma which Turkish Youth faces. Words mean something, they can comfort and they can hurt; they can speak the truth, and express falsehoods. Words have been put into the minds of innocent Armenian children, and the inescapable result is: fallacy has become “historical accuracy.”

For many years, Turkish youth have revealed to this author: “I was never taught to hate the Armenian people, or *any* people!”

Can we argue with the philosophy of such magnanimous humanity? I regret to say, we must, for the absence of hate by itself, can not eradicate hatred toward our fellow human beings. The author does not espouse the hatred which fills the heart of a six-year old child, but the fact is, while Turkish youth have been taught compassion, they have been left mentally “crippled,” by their lack of the in-dept facts of Turkish-Armenian history. If Turkish youth do not possess even a minimum knowledge of the events which took place in Ottoman Turkey, with particular attention to the Armenian issue, then the anti-Turkish tirades of the Armenians will remain unanswered and as a result in the minds of the uninformed the Turks will be destined to face every vile accusation. The anti-Turkish American news media, the speeches of politicians, placating a wealthy constituency, and the stereo-typical images of Turks, and the Muslim faith, will all remain prevalent in Western society. If YOU remain indifferent, uninvolved, and mute, then you surrender the honor of your people and your homeland to those groups which seek to weaken the stability of the Republic of Turkey and defame the Turkish people worldwide.

My beloved brothers and sisters, look at your history. And as it is, in the pages of the history of all the nations of our world, we will find events of political conflict and human suffering. The history of the United States is filled with man's brutality towards other peoples, while at the same time, volumes would be needed to describe the glory of America, our humanity, our freedoms, our technology, our art, and our welcome to all the peoples of our earth.

The genius of Man has brought us to walk upon the surface of the moon, and yet, Mankind is unable to live in harmony with his own kind. Indeed, history is filled with tragic events, but how did the Turkish people survive the ashes of the Ottoman period, and build a dynamic and free nation?

Who else but YOU (Turkish Youth) knows (certainly should know!) the history of the Turkish people? This author has no right, nor is it his intention to describe (even briefly) the intolerable suffering of young people during the period of the First World War, and their subsequent establishment of the democratic, secular, and progressive, Republic of Turkey. The military forces of the invading enemy had penetrated the Turkish homeland, and as the people of "Anadolu," (Anatolia) faced annihilation, the existence of Turkish sovereignty was on the verge of total collapse. Turkey was left alone with her meager resources and shattered defenses, and to compound her imminent disintegration, twenty five years of Armenian rebellion pierced the heart of the Turkish people.

But the aim of Armenian treachery and the military ambitions of the enemy forces WERE NOT TO BE! A name, an inspiration, an indestructible force appeared on the battle field and ignited a spirit of determination and fearless courage in the hearts of this people to preserve the Turkish Anavatan (Motherland): MUSTAFA KEMAL ATATURK.

YOU, Turkish youth, have read your history and are aware of the loss of millions of Turkish lives to preserve their land and independence. During that epic struggle, not only for your parents, grandparents, and great grand-parents, achieved victory over a far more powerful enemy, but also established a modern, dynamic nation and the Republic of Turkey stands today in history, as a proud, productive, and democratic member of the world family of great nations. Yes, indeed, YOU, the Turkish Youth, know all these facts and much more, therefore, with the realization of the sacrifice and dedication of your ancestors, how can you permit a few Hate Merchants, in this and other countries, to continue in their distortion of Turkish history?

Compared to the suffering of the Turkish people and their eventual victory, how can you remain indifferent as the Armenian onslaught continues? Because of their (Armenian) influence upon American politicians and news media, the ubiquitous "Armenian Resolution," like scorpions, continues to be seen in the chambers of Congress and State Legislatures. SO WHAT? Point is, can you refute the Armenian allegations against your people? Are you prepared to intelligently debate the Armenians with the facts that are vital to prove that the Turks continue to be unjustly condemned?

Turkish Youth, if you are now angry with the author for his admonition, then so be it, it doesn't matter what you think of me, because I don't seek your commendation or your condemnation. Your priority must be the topic of this book and as a son or daughter of the immortal ATATURK, your participation in the needs of the Turkish community, worldwide, will make known the facts of Turkish humanity and profound pride in your culture and history.

In addition, reserve your energy, your intellect, your involvement, your love, for the honor of the Turkish people and the Turkish homeland. Maintain your efforts on behalf of the Turkish-American friendship, and likewise wherever ethnic Turks reside throughout the world. Maintain your beautiful Turkish language and sacred Muslim faith; maintain your forceful dialogue with friend or foe, in revealing the facts of the Turkish-Armenian history, or any subject pertaining to the Turkish people.

As an American, who from early childhood on has been blessed with a pure love for ALL things Turkish, I have taken the liberty of advising Turkish youth, I may have even displayed by the previous pages a tone of impatience on my part. If this author has created that impression, he requests your forgiveness, and for you to recognize my frustration toward the Turkish people of my older generation, for not preparing you to deal with the extent of Armenian hatred for your people in the United States.

The enormous philosophical differences between the Turkish and the Armenian peoples, can not be dismissed as insignificant, because it is here that the legacy of these ancient inseparable peoples becomes visible:

A young Turkish professional says: "I was never taught to hate Armenians or any people!"

But a six-year old Armenian child has spoken these words: "Rather I be a dog or a cat, than a Turkish barbarian!"

The seeds of hate have been planted, and from it ONLY hatred will come into God's earth. The heart, the mind, and the soul of the author have been blessed with the seeds of concession and love, and I dwell in my life free of all hatred.

As I bring my final thoughts to Turkish Youth, to a conclusion, I am certain you will live your lives void of animosity because you are the fruit of love planted in the Turkish heart. Now, during the final phase of my life, filled with memories of sorrow and happiness, I wish for you and your loved ones, God's infinite blessings throughout your lives.

My beloved Turkish brothers and sisters, I would welcome your comments, and as I sincerely thank you for reading my humble offering, please remember this "Turk Dostu," Friend of Turks, and receive each page herein as my embrace of each of you, as I conclude with eternal love. *I kiss your eyes, I kiss your cheeks!*

XII: My Concluding Statements to the Reader of this Autobiography.

The author has taken the reader on a journey covering the span of over one hundred years, beginning in Ottoman Turkey and extending to the year of 2001, in the United States of America. If this author was a celebrity or a person of wealth in this country, it is fair to assume that this work would have received a far greater literary review and public recognition. But this author, most assuredly, is neither a celebrity (possibly with the exception of the Republic of Turkey – he said, in all humility), nor an individual of material wealth. At this writing, we are not even certain this long effort will even be published, and if it should not come to print, the copies of my manuscript will be given to some of the beloved names I listed in the acknowledgement of this book. Each of them has given the author and his family the deep brotherly love which has given us the support and the encouragement for our work to continue. Their names and love remain in our hearts:

Dr. Selahattin Bűyűkűnal, Dr. Oktay Akkent, Dr. Cenk Bűyűkűnal, Dr. Osman Koksal, Dr. Naci Barut, Mr. Tarik Bulut, Dr. Zeki Uygur, Mr. Ergun Kirlikovali, Mr. Halil Ekmekçi, Mr. Mehmet Ali Baysal, Mrs. Gönűl Akin, Bishop Vsevolod, Dr. Ata Erim, and of course my beloved Mary, to whom I shall refer before the conclusion of this autobiography.

Each of the above, together with many others, has known for years the sincere motivation of the author and his pure love for the Armenian, Syrian-Orthodox, and Turkish peoples. It would be a gross omission on my part if I did not, even briefly, refer to a distinguished gentleman and beloved "brother," his name, Nejat Muallimoğlu, to whom I referred in Chapter IX, letter b.

Mr. Muallimoğlu has for many years been a renowned author, poet, artist, linguist, teacher, and translator, in his Turkish homeland. In his colossal masterpiece, entitled "Hitabet" (the art of speech making, elocution, or discourse), published in 1998, Mr Muallimoğlu has prepared an 1,106-page scholarly work on the techniques of conversation and public speaking. He has translated the statements of many of the world's recognized scientists, writers, poets, philosophers, heads of states, and the words of the founders of the world's religions. As difficult as it is, to comprehend, this Turkish scholar, Mr. Muallimoğlu, has devoted no less than *eight pages* of his book, to this writer, his work, and two of his many speeches. When I received his autographed book, I read those precious pages, I became emotional and continue to feel that *I am not worthy of such an honor from a person who is held in such high esteem.*

Throughout this work, the writer has continuously referred to himself in the third person singular, words such as: 'The author," "This writer," "he," "him," "his," and other references, have been deliberately used with the intention of de-emphasizing the reader's attention towards the – yes – the author. Rather than stressing the first person singular, this book aspires to convey a story, a philosophy, from which the reader will hopefully come to recognize the humble efforts of a humble American and his life-long efforts on behalf of the search for brotherhood.

But the long history of Mankind, is filled with countless examples of the humanitarian labors of men and women of all races, creeds, and nationalities who have, with their deeds, intellect, their artistry, and leadership have given to the peoples of our world the hope of a better future.

Therefore, from this point forward, the reader will come to know me, in the first person, singular – after all, this is an autobiography, is it not?

My concluding comments are offered as a summarization of some of the many factors which have caused me to be condemned by the Armenian people in the United States, while being embraced with brotherly love from the Turkish people worldwide. If the reader believes that I have been highly honored by the Turkish people because of my emphatic opposition to my own people (that being the Armenians *outside* of the Turkish homeland, and NOT the Sűryani, or the Syrian-Orthodox people), then you must return to the dedication of this book and read these pages again. My position continues to be what it has been throughout my adult life: the Armenian allegations against the Turkish nation, pertaining to the events of the 1915 period in Ottoman

Turkey, are in their totality, void of historical accuracy. It has been to this often repeated thesis, that the Turkish people have displayed such affection for this unique Armenian who has presented his position publicly. It is the Armenian distortion of historical events, and their obsession with hatred, to which I remain emphatically opposed. That the Armenians of Ottoman Turkey had suffered terribly (during the raging fires of the First World War), is beyond dispute. But what of the other religious and ethnic communities who had also endured the horror of worldwide conflagration? To this day – 86 years later – the Armenians and the many politicians, whom they have influenced, claim the Turks had perpetrated "genocide" against the Armenians. The Armenian selectivity of historical accuracy blatantly negates the TWENTY FIVE YEARS of rebellion against the nation wherefore over 6 centuries they shared the fruits of Turkish-Armenian history, which continues to the present times.

I have grown weary with the Armenian failure to free itself of the maniacal manifestation of hatred, against not only the Turkish people, but with the same fury, their hatred for their own kind. This Armenian failure is by design, as it has been described in this work; Armenian writers have emphasized the "advantages" of the division within the Armenian community. This defies all comprehension! To understand this convoluted Armenian philosophy, an individual must be an Armenian "Hate Merchant!" This phrase has been used for many years, NOT by a Turkish writer or spokesman, but by ME. This extremely offensive phrase does not please me, but I will not apologize for inventing and using the words in relation to the Armenians *outside* the Republic of Turkey! It is due to necessity which has caused me to describe my people in my writings and speeches.

But now another word has caused me to be criticized by my beloved wife, Mary. During the preparation of my manuscript and after each page was typed, I have read my entire composition to her. In the totality of this work, one word (one *single* word) has caused her to protest, and she has suggested that my usage of the word could diminish the quality of my autobiography. But once again necessity has prompted me to keep this word in place, and not wanting to upset her any further, I will not enter the word here. However, I feel in appreciation for your reading my book, I should give you a clue as to where, among thousands of words, you will find that "terrible" word: In the previous chapter, which is Chapter XI, in my final comments to Turkish Youth; yes there you will find the metaphorical reference to an INSECT (better said, *arachnid).* Yes, an arachnid has been named in describing the abominable Armenian Resolution. Such is my disdain for our pusillanimous politicians, who have no knowledge of Turkish history, and reward their wealthy Armenian supporters with continuous anti-Turkish resolutions.

To compound the Armenian hypocrisy, world-wide with the Armenian people under their dual "leadership" (keep in mind the Dashnaksagan group created their own church *Catholicos),* are celebrating the 1700th Anniversary of the establishment of the Armenian Christian Church. This is truly a blessed event deserving of the recognition of the peoples of all the religions of the world. But the history and accomplishments of the Armenian people remain hidden because their attention is fixed solely upon the events of Ottoman Turkey; therefore, whenever an Armenian or Armenians are discussed in the media, the spotlight is on this past event, but never on any of their achievements and contributions to society, as an ethnic group.

Indeed, it appears that the totality of Armenian history revolves around the events of the 1915 period. It is not enough to profess "I am a Christian," if the teachings of Him who established the Christian faith are not practiced. We must not blame religion for the failures of people, and with the message of Judaism, Islam, and Christianity, universal peace and brotherhood will be our greatest gift to our children.

Therefore, you of Armenian ancestry, despite your pride in your ancient history and profound adherence to your Christian faith, have grievously negated the values which are the integral objectives of all peoples of good will. Specifically, the Armenian falsification of the historical events taking place in Ottoman Turkey, before and during the First World War, and the ceaseless infection of the minds and hearts of Armenian children with a bitter hatred for a people who had also suffered during the same war, remain contrary to the fundamental dogma of your holy church. You, the Armenians outside of Turkey, condemn this son of an Armenian mother because of my position, because of my work, and because I have embraced our Turkish brothers and sisters. It is beyond your comprehension as to how I could devote my life to the endeavors as revealed in this work, for two reasons: You have been taught to hate, because NO child is born with animosity in his heart, and as a result your life will remain imprisoned in the darkness of hatred. You are satisfied with your allegations against me, my motivations, and my sincerity, rather than accepting the facts of Turkish-Armenian history. It was the good fortune of my brother Terrence and me to be born to parents who taught us our history – totally void of animosity for the Turkish people and their beloved, former homeland.

The conclusion of my autobiography draws near, and as I have reviewed these many pages, I ponder my final statements and my final words. Certainly I must extend my sincere appreciation to the reader of this humble offering, while I recognize that these pages, by any stretch of the imagination, do not make an author. But the contents, events, major projects, opinions and the people we have met, as have been described here, are all based upon irrefutable facts. These pages will not merit the recognition of being considered as a literary work, and that it would interest people outside of the Turkish-American communities is questionable. *But hatred and brotherhood have no flag, no ethnicity,* and in a world where political strife and ethnic hostilities continue to bring Mankind closer to another world conflagration, then the message of this story is for *everyone.* The world will never come to know this writer, nor should it, but for the affection exchanged with thousands of people, and for the many honors presented to us (he said in all humility!), I feel my humble life has indeed served my God, my family, and people of good will. For those who harbor hatred toward other people because of their race, creed, ethnic origin or historical conflict, will only destroy themselves with the cancer of hate.

Among the many factors which, since my early youth, have developed my affinity with the Turkish people, is their inherent quality of being manifestly void of hate. Another feature of the Turkish character is their eternal "gűler yűzlű" (smiling face) offered to a friend or even a stranger. If I were to smile at a stranger in the streets of New York City, I could probably be considered as being mentally challenged, or cause anger, an expletive, followed by a shouted: "What the hell are you smiling at?!"

One of thousands of sayings or proverbs in Turkish reveals the generosity of the Turkish heart in this manner: *The stranger that comes to one's doorstep is considered a Guest from God and should be accommodated accordingly.* Have you ever been a guest in a Turkish home? If not, plan your next vacation to the homeland of Santa Claus, of Saint Paul, the Home of the Virgin Mary, and the early history of Christianity, Judaism, and Islam.

Of one thing I am certain: You will one day return to the Republic of Turkey.

We Christians talk about 'turning the other cheek,' but it has been the Muslim Turk who has followed this teaching of the Prince of Peace. Because of the relentless anti-Turkish posture of the wealthy Armenian and Greek communities in the United States and other 'friendly' countries, the blatant prejudice on the part of the news media and most politicians against Turkey continues as it has for generations. I have always found the Turkish response to be most ineffective. In my hundreds of letters to a 'prestigious' New York newspaper, in response to their anti-Turkish editorials or news reporters NOT ONE sentence of my correspondences has ever been printed. In the early 1970s an article in *The Reader's Digest* blamed Turkey for the heroin addiction of American youth. In my lengthy response to: "Let's Stop Heroin at its Source," I had stated in part: "We should examine WHY Americans are so consumed with drug addiction, rather than accuse the Turkish Government which institutes strict controls of the poppy seeds for the legitimate use for pharmaceutical production of heroin for medical purposes, It continues to be a part of the 'Let's Blame the Turks' syndrome which never ceases to preoccupy certain groups. To compound this outrage, when we observe the drug consumption in our country today, and coupled with the stench of the pornography merchants, I condemn our Congress which sits in judgment of the Turkish people with Armenian Resolutions!

Let my country consider its own history and have the American-Indian sit in judgment.

PROPOSALS FOR YOUR CONSIDERATION:

Keeping in mind the United States continues to endanger its friendly relations with a loyal ally, the Republic of Turkey, by appeasing illogical demands of a small but wealthy Armenian community, I therefore offer the following proposals for the reader's consideration:

1 – Among other claims made by Armenian 'leaders' against the Turks, is their demand that Turkey 'return' portions of its land to the Armenians. Of course the Greeks want 'their' piece of the Turkish homeland, and let us not forget the Kurds, the Russians, the Syrians, the Iraqis, the Iranians, and the rest of the 'give me' crowd. After all the claims are satisfied by the generous Turks and since there will be no land left for them, then we will have 65 MILLION TURKS come to the United States of America, and settle here. Here and now, I propose the Turkish Government implement my proposal based upon only ONE condition, and when that condition is fulfilled, the Turks will begin packing their luggage. The condition, to which I have given much thought, is as follows:

The United States should FIRST *return all* former territories to the American Indian people; *return* Puerto Rico, and the island nation of Guam to Spain; and the lands of now occupied by the States of Texas, New Mexico, Nevada, Utah, Arizona, Colorado, and of course California, to the sovereign nation of Mexico.

Such a proposal would be considered as ludicrous by Americans, but when the fanatical fringe with its own map has designs on Turkish soil, WHICH American politician would dare to say: "The Armenian demands are ludicrous!"?

2 – My second proposal is as serious as the first, and equally well thought out. For years my country has been exposed to an epidemic of Armenian resolutions and many state legislators have brought the falsification of Turkish history into the American class room. Well, why then can not the Turks reciprocate? If my country can commemorate the mythical 'Armenian Genocide,' then Turkey should commemorate the factual genocide of the American Indian people. I propose the Turkish Parliament declare July 4th of every year as a *Day of Remembrance of the American-Indian Genocide.*

The above proposals will not be taken seriously, but for the allegations against the people I am proud to serve, Turkey is found 'guilty,' by groups more concerned with their own agenda rather than historical accuracy.

WILL TURKISH STUDENTS BE ABLE TO CORRECT THEIR TEACHERS?

Have you ever heard of expressions such as: 'It must be true, I read it in the newspaper,' or 'The story is factual, it's printed in a book'? Well, the reader has read *this* book; does it mean that because my autobiography was published it automatically makes my offering totally factual? In all clear conscience, I proclaim not one word of this work is based upon deception, but the critique of this book depends upon the perspective of the reader. Because I say the contents here are factual, it obviously does not suggest that the Armenians will concur. Likewise, because books are written about the Armenian 'Genocide,' does it mean that the Armenian allegations are gospel? Of course not. And history concurs! Let us return to the American classrooms, where young students are taught about the suffering of the Armenians of Ottoman Turkey. With an ever-increasing Turkish-American community throughout our country, in countless schools children of Turkish ancestry will participate in our education system. When school text books refer to a historical tragedy, which never occurred, will our Turkish children be able to challenge their 'educators,' and hence the heading question of this section. In yet another effort, to make my point on the Armenian issue, the following which has *no* relation to Turkey, is presented as *nine* perfect examples of *falsehoods* taught in high-schools as factual information:

On September 6th, 1999, on the ABC TV network, '20/20,' the host of the broadcast and well known news commentator Mr. Sam Donaldson, presented numerous text books from which *incorrect* information had been used to teach high school students around our country. The following information is taken from my notes which had been written from memory during the live broadcast:

1 – A text book reveals the Statue of Liberty outer covering as made of bronze; the fact is the outer covering is made of copper!

2 – A text book 'teaches' students the first atom bomb had been dropped on Korea; the fact is, it was dropped *twice* on JAPAN – Hiroshima and Nagasaki.

3 – A text book states garlic and ginseng are very beneficial for good health; the fact is the assertion has never been scientifically proven.

4 – A photo in a text book, taken in 1915, shows numerous men with joined hands around the trunk of a tree, supposedly to prevent the cutting of the tree, conforming with today's environmentalists. The fact is, they showed the *width* of the tree!

5 – A text book for high school students *teaches* that Christopher Columbus had appealed to the king and queen of Spain for EIGHT years for the funds necessary for his expedition in 1492, A.D. Which means Columbus would have landed in the 'New World' in 1500, A.D.! Fact is he landed here in 1492!

6 – Prentice Hall, the respected publishers reveal the names of FOUR authors, one of them named Ms. Maton, as being contributors to a book on history (I did not record the book's title). Mr. Donaldson interviews Ms. Maton and she admits she knew NOTHING about the book! The other three 'authors' had NOTHING to do with the writing of the 'history book,' either. FOUR NAMES were used illegally.

7 – Another history text book offers our students the history of the father of our country, George Washington, encompassed in THREE pages, while in the same American 'history book,' SIX pages are devoted to *Marilyn Monroe!*

8 – A girl student DID NOT believe her high school text book and informed her teacher before the class, because during her visit to the Statue of Liberty, she had learned the outer covering was made of COPPER.

9 – The following is taken from an ABC TV news broadcast, on October 21st, 1999: In a Philadelphia high school, library books show that Nelson Mandela of South Africa had been killed, and that Man *had not* reached the surface of the Moon as of that date! It is inconceivable that the above blunders could have taken place!

The answer to the question of this section is found in the # 8 entry shown above. The young girl knew the information in her textbook was incorrect, and she informed her classmates of the facts. This is precisely what Turkish students *must* do, wherever there is any reference to the Armenian subject. Equipped with the facts of Turkish-Armenian history, our students will refute the false descriptions of the events in Ottoman Turkey. Presented in a calm, intelligent manner, our students can reveal historical facts which the textbooks will not mention, but in order to offer the Turkish perspective, our students must be knowledgeable of their own history. Among other irrefutable facts: The Andonian Forgeries; the Ramgavar, the Hunchak and Dashnaksagan Revolutionary parties and their TWENTY FIVE YEARS of rebellion against Turkey; the freedom enjoyed by the Armenians in Turkey; the highest positions of the Ottoman government held by countless Armenians; the Armenian support of Nazi Germany during the early 1940s, including TWELVE Armenian battalions that served the Nazi Army; if our Turkish students are aware of these facts their teachers and fellow students will learn the truth of Turkish history and finally recognize the deception and fraud of the Armenians!

* * *

IN FINAL RECOGNITION AND CONCLUDING PERSPECTIVES OF THIS AUTHOR:

Before my concluding statements which will bring my autobiography to a final ending, I felt the following two sections needed to be addressed. First, because numerous individuals have affected my life and work, I should at least repeat their names with my eternal debt and gratitude, without further description:

My beloved parents, Dr. Selahattin Büyűkünal, Dr. Oktay Akkent, Dr. Cenk Büyűkünal, Mr. Tarik Bulut, Mr. Ergün Kirlikovali, Mr. Egemen Bağiş, the late Armenian Patriarch His Eminence Şnork Kalutsyan, the clergy of the Syrian-Orthodox Church (in Turkey and here), Mrs. Sevinç Yaman, Dr. Ata Erim, for his patience and wisdom, and Mr. Ibrahim Kurtuluş, for all his work. I must recognize our countless friends within the Federation of Turkish-American Associations, Inc., and the Assembly of Turkish-American Associations (located in Washington, D.C. area). A new and most dedicated friend has requested to remain anonymous and therefore I shall refer to H.W. by extending my deep gratitude for his magnificent efforts as our Webmaster. His talents have not only served this writer, but also the Turkish people!

One more name remains to be mentioned and this person will be recognized as I bring this work to its conclusion.

The second final section here is my personal perspective of this writer: Dear Reader, much of my life's story is missing from this autobiography, such as a more elaborate narrative of my youth, and an informative description of my life-long poor health, and the difficulties of caring for my mother during the final years of her life. But these subjects are purely of a personal nature, which are similar to the experiences of many of our readers. These pages hope to reveal the inception and the passion of my life's work, my humble efforts, and before my life comes to an end, to offer this book as my legacy to ALL the peoples of our earth with particular attention and sincere dedication to Turkish and Armenian Youth. In all honesty, I must reveal to my reader, my conscience is clear and free of doubt. My humble efforts have never sought to convey a message of hate; in reality I have revealed the utter futility of hatred. My humble efforts have never sought material gain or the adulation of the people I have served, in reality I have attempted to reveal the unique compassion of my parents who had suffered and yet taught us to love. They deserve endless praise!

This has been the most arduous effort on my part, during a lifetime of work. My wife and I continue to be a living testimony to the inseparability of the Turkish and Armenian peoples! So it has been and so it will continue to be!

The following lines will bring this work to a conclusion:

You are my reason to live

These words are the beginning lyrics of the chorus of a beautiful song from the mid-1950s called: *Till.* Yes, one more is to be recognized in my most unique autobiography, but I am faced with an impossible task, namely, how will I be able to bring to paper my concluding statements which will refer to the most important person in my life? The one individual who has given me the most happiness, who has supported me in my work, who has displayed patience and self sacrifice, far beyond my ability to express, who to this day, refers to me as her "hero," all these and in spite of much more, she has been recognized the least in this book. Her name is Mary, and she is my beloved wife of forty-six glorious years of married life.

As revealed earlier, our families were friends before Mary and I were born; she, born in Watertown, Mass., and I, in Troy, New York. At the age of three, Mary lost her father, and her mother was left with five children, the oldest of which was eleven years old. To say she had a difficult childhood is an understatement. The circumstances which brought her to New York to become my wife, is the topic for another book. Our life together, has had its share of joy and sorrows, but our mutual happiness by the grace of God, far exceeds our periods of difficulty and grief. Romantic songs, poetry, words of art, and volumes of literature, worldwide, have expressed love and longing for our beloved mates, parents, and children, but I am convinced no poet, no lyricist, no artist, could hope to describe my supreme and eternal love for my beautiful wife, Mary. To describe even briefly, her qualities of perfection would require many pages and though the purpose of my autobiography has been the subject of Turkish-American relations, my Mary, has for years been and continues to be, an integral component of my work.

My endless memories, most of which can not be described here, begin the day when Mary becomes the major part of my life. It took place on May 4th, 1958, in our Syrian-Orthodox Church, in West New York, New Jersey, during our wedding ceremony. The clergy stood in front of the altar, the bridal party, flowers, family members and guests, were all in place, waiting for the entry of my Queen. Then the organist began to play the 'Wedding procession,' and everyone stood up and turned their attention to the back of our church. There she was, an image of indescribable beauty! My angelic wife-to be, escorted by her brother, Peter, stepped slowly toward the altar, where I stood, overwhelmed by the magnificence which approached closer and closer. I can not believe almost a half a century has passed; Mary has fulfilled my life with supreme joy.

It is an honor and a privilege for me to be in a supremely joyous position to at least attempt to reveal my pure love for my wife Mary, in these pages and before the world. The reasons for loving her are infinite; to define my love for her in verse or rhyme would be futile; to express my love for Mary would require an eloquence which is not consistent with my vocabulary. However, in spite of the infinite and the futility, I feel obliged to divulge a minimal compilation of some of her many sacrifices, her efforts, and devotion to and support of me in my defense of Turkey.

For years, *'kizim'* (my Turkish pet name for Mary, meaning: my girl/daughter), took care of my family and my elderly parents, especially my mother. My mother, who had labored all her life, became very ill and for many years could not be left alone; Mary would cook, bathe, dress, and prepare for sleep my mother, in a manner which many daughters would not do for their own parents. As a professional cosmetologist/beautician, she has performed works of art with the psychological and emotional transformations with the hair, make-up, and beautification of her clients. She has maintained our home impeccably clean and furnished with Turkish motifs *everywhere.*

Her cooking talents are equaled to her magic with a needle and thread. Her knowledge of fashion and medical subjects and so much more, have made my life the recipient of her kindness, her talents, her caring, and her eternal beautiful smile.

In the autumn of our lives, *'kizim'* is more beautiful than ever. Just as a pet puppy has no concept of time, in other words, when the owner leaves the room, the pet believes it is forever and becomes distraught, so it is with me! When Mary is out of my view, when I can not hear her voice, when I can not feel her close to me, I am distraught over her absence. But her return rejuvenates my spirit and comforts my soul. Beloved Mary, a very old Turkish song says: "If I did not know there was a God, YOU then would be my God!" Most precious wife, these words I speak to you, as I love you with every breath I take. For the goodness of your heart, for your comforting smile, for the perfection of your beautiful eyes, and for reminding me every day to take my medicine, and for so much more I cherish the ground you stand on!

Dear Reader, I conclude with the two most beautiful words in ANY language: I wish for my Mary, my family, and ALL peoples of good will, the supreme blessings of

GOD'S LOVE!

XIII - Epilogue: September 11, 2001

Those of us who are fortunate to have lived beyond the age of sixty years, will vividly recall a speech which President Franklin Roosevelt, had delivered to a joint session of the Congress of the United States, in which he had referred to the date of the December the 7th, 1941, as "... a day of infamy ..." America's entry into the Second World War, had been precipitated by the sneak attack of the Japanese Air Force upon our Military Naval Base in Pearl Harbor. Close to two thousand American Military Personnel were killed and the United States was hurled into a world conflagration which would eventually take the lives of many millions of people in the conflict of Europe, Africa, and Asia. At the conclusion of the war, the United States and her allies had defeated Nazi Germany, her puppet Italy, and Imperial Japan. But in spite of the scientific advancements of the modern and free world, Man's inability to live in peace with his fellow-human beings continued to manifest itself by wars of every measure in every region of our world.

Other than the attack on Pearl Harbor the many wars in which the United States had been involved, the singular aspect which had prevailed in all these wars, was the fact that the American Homeland had never been the field of battle. But America's destiny was changed forever during the morning of September the 11th, 2001, when hatred and fanaticism once again revealed its evil philosophy. The horrific end results of the terrorist attacks upon the World Trade Center in New York City and the Pentagon Building, in Washington, D.C., have no relation to this autobiography, nor to Turkish-American history. However, even though it was my intention to conclude this work with the word: LOVE, the savage assault upon my country – the United States of America – and the barbaric murder of close to three thousand innocent civilians, compels me to offer the reader my perspective on this horrible event, which will include a Turkish component. Once again, Turkey has not received the recognition she deserves.

The depraved and Godless regime of the Taliban 'Government' of the war-torn country of Afghanistan, came to power after years of war with the former Soviet Union. But the withdrawal of the Russians did not bring peace and freedom to the people of this devastated homeland.

The incarnate of evil named Osama bin Laden as leader of the Taliban and Al-Queda bands of terrorists, proclaim themselves as the 'Defenders of Islam,' and their worldwide web of deception and military aggression with the attack on the homeland of the United States. Their indoctrination of their followers and the mercenaries from Arab countries, produced an 'Army,' of suicidal fanatics. As a result terrorists flew two jet planes into the Twin Towers of the World Trade Center and another one into the Pentagon building. The terrible loss of thousands of lives, the countless thousands of injured, and those traumatized for life, the monumental destruction and the facts that of this writing, six months later, the recovery of hundreds of bodies still continues, has made this dastardly attack upon innocent civilians one of the worst events in the history of the civilized world!

The utter revulsion of the civilized peoples of the world brought an immediate military response from the United States and her allies against the Taliban and Al-Queda forces in Afghanistan. The struggle against these elements continues, but their cruel domination of the Afghan people has been crushed, and a semblance of democracy and democratic institutions have begun primarily due to American assistance. An interim leader, Hamid Karzai, has formed a new government and an effective military force, which will eliminate the remaining enemy from their mountainous cave. American and Allied Forces continue their search for Osama bin-Laden, who like a scorpion has dug a hole in the sand as he attempts to avoid capture. From its inception no one expected our military operation in Afghanistan would be short or without the loss of our brave fighting men. To confirm this, we have just learned that eight American soldiers have been killed during an encounter with the enemy. How many more of our young men will make the supreme sacrifice in eradicating these evil elements?

One potentially explosive tragedy of the war has been the negative attitude toward the Muslim communities by the news media and the general public in the United States. Believing the Afghan terrorists indeed represent and speak on behalf of the Muslim religion many educated Americans recognize ALL Muslim peoples as blood-thirsty killers, and consider the Holy Koran as the message of hatred of Jews, and Christians. This writer, by all means, is not an Islamic scholar but based upon my own research coupled with my close affiliation with the Christian and Muslim communities, I can state that Islam and her faithful do not harbor hatred towards ANYONE.

Negative attitudes soon became worse with the acts of violence against Muslim institutions and Muslim owned businesses throughout the United States. Women and children of Muslim families became fearful of being seen on our streets, even though they were loyal citizens of our country. Profiling of men with Middle Eastern backgrounds has caused many to be arrested without any charges.

This autobiography will not review the few Islamic states where the practice of non-Muslim religions is not permitted by Law (as in Saudi Arabia and the Sudan) because the scope of my work is the country of Turkey, and not the entire Muslim world.

After September 11, 2001, in the press and on the radio talk-shows, the allegations and stereotypical image of Muslim peoples has been seen on a daily basis. To associate all Muslims with terrorists or regimes, who in the 'Name of Islam,' perpetrate their evil deeds is a serious mistake. To consider the terrorist Osama bin-Laden as a Muslim religious leader is the embodiment of hypocrisy. Would the Christian world consider Jim Jones, David Koresh, Timothy McVey, Terry Nichols, James Baker, Jimmy Swaggart, or the devil incarnate Adolf Hitler, as representing and believing the teachings of Christianity?

The Republic of Turkey was the first predominantly Muslim nation to condemn the terrorist attacks upon the United States, and once again offered our country any assistance asked for by Washington. The Turkish response was also made in America in press releases, letters, and public statements, to which I shall refer to only one: On September the 12th, 2001, an open letter addressed 'to the American Public,' was sent to the media by the United American Muslim Association of New York, Inc. Above the signature of the Hon. Hilmi Akdağ, who serves as the Chief Imam and President of this Turkish mosque community, his message of condolences to America and his condemnation of the terrorists was well received in the community of Brooklyn, New York. The statement which had been prepared by Mr. Ibrahim Kurtuluş, who serves as a member of the Board of Directors of the mosque, as well as Vice President of the Turkish-American Federation, did not receive the coverage of the major media. The continuing anti-Islamic tirades repeat to this day: "Where is the condemnation of the Muslim community and its religious leaders?"

The Turkish-American community has publicly revealed its position emphatically and sincerely, but if the news media denies our voice, how can the American public be informed? Again, the Turks are not given the recognition they rightfully deserve.

While the religion of over 1,000,000,000 of the world's faithful was being described as 'wicked,' 'violent,' 'evil,' 'fanatical,' 'among other vile accusations, the Turkish Republic was the only predominantly Muslim nation which supported the United States in its decision to continue the bombing of the hidden bases of the Taliban and Al-Queda terrorist forces, during the month of Holy Ramadan (*Ramazan,* in Turkish). Indeed, the land of my ancestral, cultural, and historical beginnings, the Republic of Turkey, once again did not receive the recognition she deserves. The conflict in Afghanistan according to the military experts, will end in the near future. The coalition of nations which will reconstruct the devastated country, will include Turkish military forces to restore and maintain the peace and security of the people.

My humble effort in this autography draws to a close and as I now have come to recognize my own mortality, I pray God will allow my work to continue during this final phase of my life. My sincere hope has been that even in a small way, I have instilled in the hearts of ALL peoples the need for compassion and brotherhood. My affiliation with the Federation of Turkish-American Associations, Inc., will continue in close association with its incumbent President Egemen Bağiş, a young, brilliant, and tireless leader of the Turkish-American community. He has distinguished himself among many other accomplishments by serving as the interpreter for former President William J. Clinton, during his speech before the Turkish Parliament. In addition, this dynamic young man has also served as the simultaneous interpreter for the Secretary of State, Colin Powell. To Egemen, to Ibrahim, to Ergün, to Güler Kőknar, and the other countless young Turkish brothers and sisters, I leave my legacy of LOVE; to my many contemporaries, those ladies and gentlemen who have labored so much for their Turkish culture, I leave my legacy of LOVE. To my family and four nieces and their children, I leave my legacy of LOVE. To my parents, who gave their son to the Turkish people, I offer them (in heaven) my grateful

LOVE. And to her, my beloved wife, Mary, my source of peace and joy, I leave her my eternal memories of LOVE. In all the pages of this book, I leave you, the Reader, the most important word in any composition, in any language: GOD'S INFINITE LOVE.

The Ways of the Heart

A small selection from among a bevy of pictorial memories

Türkiye

HAUT COMMISSARIAT
DE LA
REPUBLIQUE FRANÇAISE
EN SYRIE & AU LIBAN

N° ~~5635~~ G.L. 7346

PASSEPORT A L'ETRANGER VALABLE POUR 1 AN

AU NOM DE LA REPUBLIQUE FRANÇAISE
MANDATÉE EN SYRIE ET AU LIBAN

Nous GENERAL GOURAUD Haut-Commissaire de la REPUBLIQUE FRANÇAISE requierons les Autorités Civiles et Militaires de la REPUBLIQUE FRANÇAISE de Syrie et du Liban et prions les Autorités Civiles et Militaires chargées de maintenir l'ordre public dans tous les pays Amis ou Alliés de la REPUBLIQUE FRANÇAISE de laisser passer librement

M Izabelle Nardikian

Originaire de Arménie
Né le 1896
à Balekesser
Demeurant à Beyrouth

et de lui donner aide et protection en cas de besoin pour se rendre à New-York U.S.A.
Motif Rejoindre son mari

Le présent passeport délivre à Beyrouth
Le 1 — 6 — mil neuf cent 21

Signalement
Age 25 ans
Taille 160 c.m.
Constitution Ordinaire
Cheveux Châtains
Sourcils "
Front Ordinaire
Yeux Châtains
Nez Moyen
Bouche "
Barbe —
Moustache —
Menton Rond
Visage "
Teint Brun clair
Sig. Portiliers ×
Signature du porteur

Prix du Passeport 50 P.S.

P. LE HAUT-COMMISSAIRE
DE LA
REPUBLIQUE FRANÇAISE
LE GOUVERNEUR DU GRAND LIBAN
et par délégation
Le Chef du Service Central des Passeports

Copy of Zabel Tashjian's (Edward's mother) passport

(The original of this document on permanent exhibit in Ankara, Turkey)

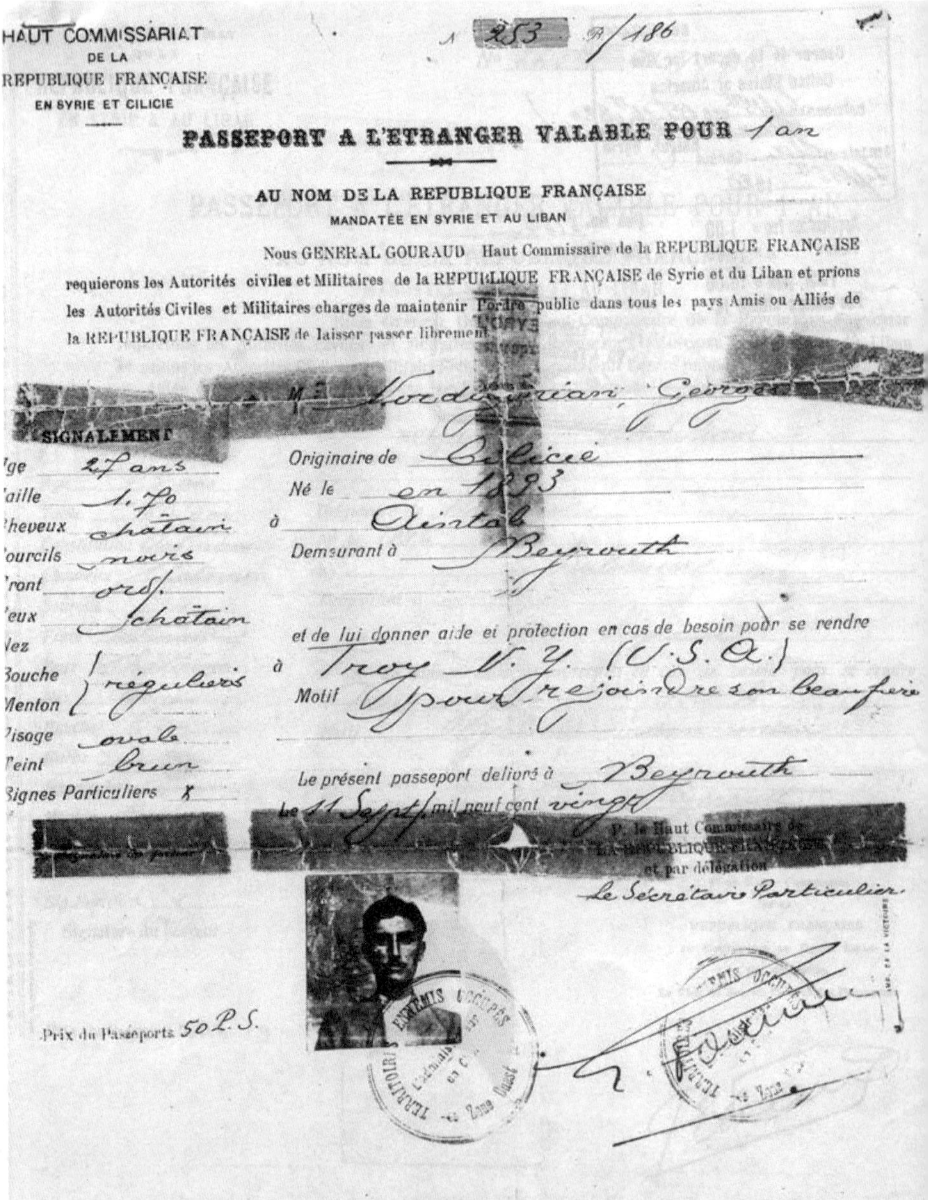

HAUT COMMISSARIAT
DE LA
REPUBLIQUE FRANÇAISE
EN SYRIE ET CILICIE

N° 253 R/186

PASSEPORT A L'ETRANGER VALABLE POUR 1 an

AU NOM DE LA REPUBLIQUE FRANÇAISE
MANDATÉE EN SYRIE ET AU LIBAN

Nous GENERAL GOURAUD Haut Commissaire de la REPUBLIQUE FRANÇAISE requierons les Autorités civiles et Militaires de la REPUBLIQUE FRANÇAISE de Syrie et du Liban et prions les Autorités Civiles et Militaires charges de maintenir l'ordre public dans tous les pays Amis ou Alliés de la REPUBLIQUE FRANÇAISE de laisser passer librement

M. Nordigian, George

SIGNALEMENT

Age 27 ans
Taille 1.70
Cheveux châtain
Sourcils noirs
Front ord.
Yeux châtain
Nez
Bouche } réguliers
Menton
Visage ovale
Teint brun
Signes Particuliers x

Originaire de Cilicie
Né le en 1893
à Aintab
Demeurant à Beyrouth

et de lui donner aide et protection en cas de besoin pour se rendre
à Troy N. Y. (U.S.A.)
Motif pour rejoindre son beau-frère

Le présent passeport delivré à Beyrouth
Le 11 Sept. mil neuf cent vingt

P. le Haut Commissaire de LA REPUBLIQUE FRANÇAISE et par délégation
Le Secrétaire Particulier

Prix du Passeport: 50 P.S.

Copy of Edward's father's passport as issued by the Ottoman Government

(The original of this document on permanent exhibit in Ankara, Turkey)

دولت علیهٔ عثمانیه تذکرهٔ سیدر

اسم و شهرتی	پدری اسمیله محل اقامتی	والده‌سی اسمیله محل اقامتی	تاریخ و محل ولادتی	ملتی	صنعت و صفت و خدمت وانتخاب صلاحیتی	متأهل وزوجه‌سی متعدد اولوب اولمدیغی	درجات و صنوف عسکریه‌سی

اشکالی				سجل نفوسه قید اولنان محلی						
بوی	کوز	سیما	علامت فارقهٔ ثابته	ولایتی		قضاسی	محله وقریه‌سی	زقاقی	مسکن نومروسی	نوع مسکن

بالاده اسم وشهرت وحال وصفتی محرر اولان ... دولت علیه‌نك تابعیتنی حائز اولوب
اول صورتله جریدهٔ نفوسده مقید اولدیغنی مشعر اشبو تذکره اعطا قلندی

مطبعهٔ عثمانیه

Copy of Edward's father's birth certificate

(The original of this document on permanent exhibit in Ankara, Turkey)

Edward's mother, Zabel Tashjian, born in Balikesir, Turkey; and Edward's father, Monofar Tashji (born in Urfa, Turkey).

The first time Zabel set her eyes upon her future husband, this is how he looked like: a dashing Ottoman officer.

Aznif Kayarian, mother of Mary (Mrs. Edward) Tashji,
Ottoman Turkey, ca. 1910

Zabel's brother (Edward's Uncle) Minas,
Balikesir, 1922

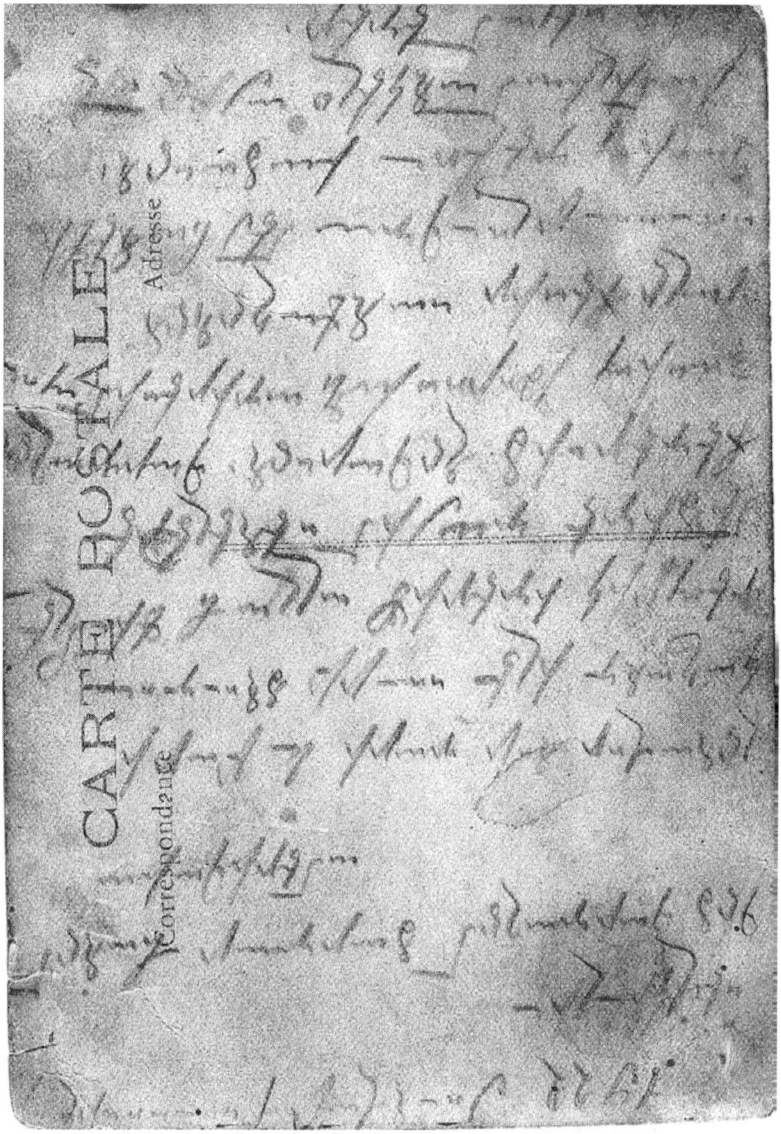

Note from Edward Tashji: This is the back of Uncle Minas' 1922 Photo - Written in Armenian! To this day, Armenians claim that it was "illegal" to speak and write in Armenian, during the days of the Ottoman Empire!

A close Armenian friend of Zabel Tashji; photo taken in 1921, Turkey

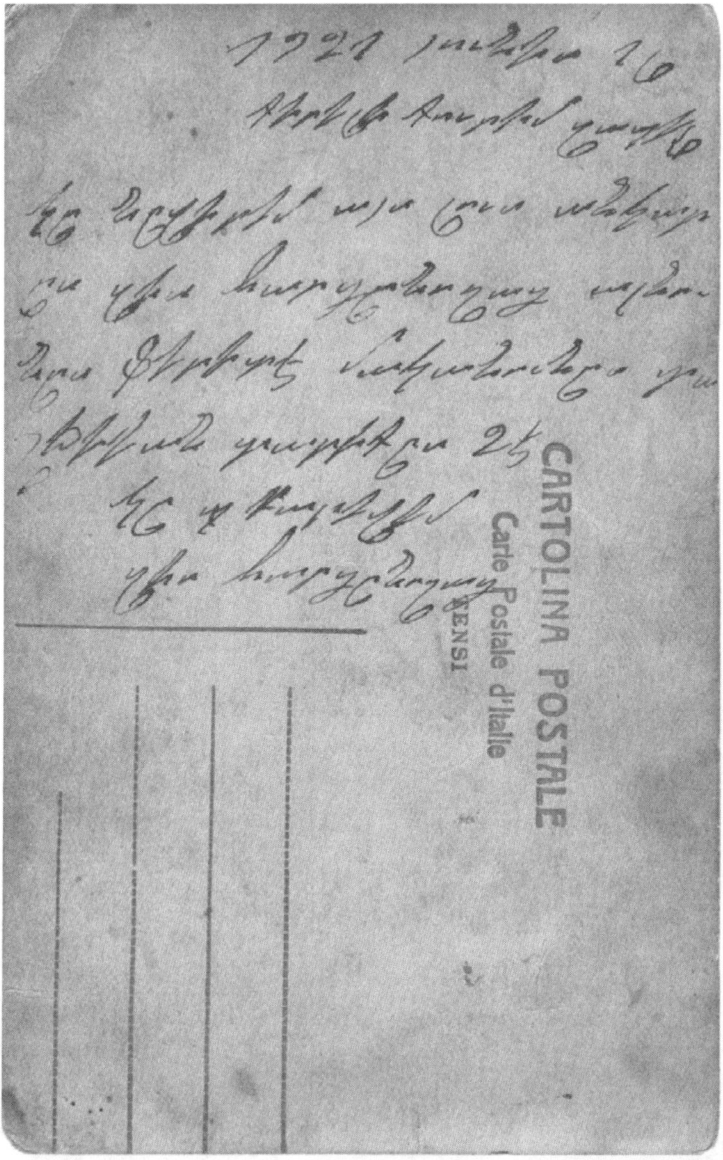

This is the back of the photo depicting Zabel Tashji's friend,in Turkey, 1921; the handwriting is in Armenian; consequently these two photos refute the allegations that speaking and writing in Armenian were illegal

Edward Tashji and the late John Cardinal O'Connor

Edward Tashji's entry in his Guest Book at http://www.edwardtashji.org :

Date:

3/21/2004

Time:

7:06:51 AM

Comments:

I am deeply grateful to those who have spent time to visit this and other of my websites. The events of a lifetime can not be described here. My interest in and love for ALL things Turkish begins with my beloved parents who had been witness to the horror of war in their former homeland, Ottoman Turkey. *The memories of war could not sever their affection for the land ravaged by war.* When my book is published, our historical bond with the Turkish people and the groundless allegations by the Armenian community against the Turkish Nation, will be defined in full detail. My book will respond to the false accusations by the Armenians and describe the blatant bias of the American news media. No book has ever been brought to print which reveals the Armenian allegations with the Turkish response. Till we meet again, our work continues.... Edward Tashji